D0278785

The Political Economy of Human Happiness
How Voters' Choices Determine the Quality of Life

This book is devoted to applying the data, methods, and theories of contemporary social science to the question of how political outcomes in democratic societies determine the quality of life that citizens experience. Benjamin Radcliff seeks to provide an objective answer to the perennial debate between Left and Right over what kind of public policies best contribute to human beings leading positive and rewarding lives. The book thus offers an empirical answer to this perpetual question, relying on the same canons of reason and evidence required of any other issue amenable to study through social-scientific means. The analysis focuses on the consequences for human well-being of three specific political issues: the generosity of the social safety net and the size of government more generally, the degree to which workers are organized, and the extent to which workers and consumers are protected by government regulation of the economy. The results indicate that in each instance, the program of the Left best contributes to citizens leading more satisfying lives – and that the benefits of greater happiness due to such policies accrue to everyone in society, rich and poor alike.

Benjamin Radcliff is a Professor in the Department of Political Science and is affiliated with the Rooney Center for the Study of American Democracy and the Higgins Labor Studies Program at the University of Notre Dame. He has also held academic positions at Rutgers University and Vanderbilt University. He has been a Fellow at the Merriam Lab for Analytic Political Research at the University of Illinois, the Robert Penn Warren Center for the Study of the Humanities, and the Netherlands Institute for Advanced Studies. Radcliff has published extensively in the leading peer-reviewed journals in political science, including the *American Political Science Review*, the *American Journal of Political Science*, the *Journal of Politics*, *Perspectives on Politics*, and the *British Journal of Political Science*, among others. His work has also appeared in prominent journals in sociology (including *Social Forces*), labor studies, and public policy.

The Political Economy of Human Happiness

How Voters' Choices Determine the Quality of Life

BENJAMIN RADCLIFF

University of Notre Dame

CAMBRIDGE
UNIVERSITY PRESS

CAMBRIDGE UNIVERSITY PRESS
Cambridge, New York, Melbourne, Madrid, Cape Town,
Singapore, São Paulo, Delhi, Mexico City

Cambridge University Press
32 Avenue of the Americas, New York, NY 10013-2473, USA

www.cambridge.org
Information on this title: www.cambridge.org/9781107644427

© Benjamin Radcliff 2013

First published 2013

Printed in the United States of America

A catalog record for this publication is available from the British Library.

Library of Congress Cataloging in Publication Data
Radcliff, Benjamin, 1963–
The political economy of human happiness: how voters' choices determine the quality of life /
Benjamin Radcliff, University of Notre Dame.
    pages cm
Includes bibliographical references and index.
ISBN 978-1-107-03084-8
1. Social choice.   2. Quality of life.   3. Right and left (Political science)   I. Title.
HB846.8.R33   2013
302′.13072–dc23   2012026683

ISBN 978-1-107-03084-8 Hardback
ISBN 978-1-107-64442-7 Paperback

Contents

Acknowledgments

I am grateful to the many people without whom this project would not have been possible. There is, first, the general community of scholars to whom I am especially beholden. In addition to those mentioned presently, I would like to thank, at the risk of omitting countless others equally worthy of note, David Blanchflower, Andrew Clark, Harold Clarke, Ed Diener, Rafael Di Tella, Richard Easterlin, Eric Foner, Robert Frank, Bruno Frey, Miriam Golden, Bruce Headey, John Helliwell, Evelyne Huber, Ronald Inglehart, Daniel Kahneman, Michael Krassa, James Kuklinski, Robert Lane, Richard Layard, Sonja Lyubomirsky, Robert McCullough, Darrin McMahon, Andrew Oswald, Robert Putnam, Bo Rothstein, Stephen Seitz, John Stephens, and Alois Stutzer. I owe them an intellectual debt beyond the cold academic citation of their work in the pages that follow. Special thanks to Ruut Veenhoven.

Among the friends and colleagues who read drafts of the manuscript or discussed with me ideas central to it are Peri Arnold, Robert Brathwaite, Robert Fishman, Patrick Flavin, Teresa Ghilarducci, Amy Gille, Carol Graham, Vincent Phillip Muñoz, Jan Ott, Tom Rice, John Roos, David Ruccio, Greg Shufeldt, Jennifer Smith, and Michael Zuckert. David Campbell, Michael Clark, and David Nickerson were generous with methodological advice. Christina Wolbrecht and Geoff Layman supplied important insights on the manuscript, as well as even more helpful moral support to its author. Amitava Dutt provided invaluable advice on any number of perplexing philosophical and theoretical issues, to say nothing of consistently thoughtful comments on innumerable drafts of Chapters 2 and 3. Above all, I am indebted to Michael Coppedge for both his careful reading of the manuscript and his exacting criticism of the wider intellectual project.

I am grateful to several graduate research assistants, all of whom deserve to be recognized for their contributions to the work: Ángel Álvarez-Díaz, Lauren Keane, Michael Keane, Annabella España-Nájera, Andrea Fernandez, Lucas González, Patrick Flavin, Richard Ledet, and Laura Philipp.

Lastly, I thank some dear friends and colleagues, who, while they escape specific mention above, have been people I have relied on for advice and support over the years in too many ways, and for too many things, to enumerate: John Patrick Aylward, Richard Braunstein, Suzanne Coshow, Robert Davidson, Patricia Davis, John Geer, Rodney Hero, Alexander Pacek, Greg Romano, Charles Taber, and Ed Wingenbach.

I dedicate this book to my wife Amy Radcliff and to my mother Linda Caise – the two people who have made the greatest contribution to my own happiness.

This project was supported by grants from the Higgins Labor Studies Program, the Institute for Scholarship in the Liberal Arts, and the Kellogg Institute for International Studies, all at the University of Notre Dame. Much of this work was completed while I was a Fellow-in-Residence at the Netherlands Institute for Advanced Study. I am extremely grateful to NIAS for that year of study and reflection (and also to the College of Arts and Letters at Notre Dame, which provided a portion of the funding that it made it possible).

A portion of Chapter 7 was previously published as "The Politics of Happiness: On the Political Determinant of Quality of Life in the American States," *Journal of Politics* 72(3): 894–905 (with Ángel Álvarez-Díaz and Lucas González). I hereby thankfully acknowledge the publisher's and my coauthors' permission to use a revised version of that material here.

Introduction

In 1949, Albert Einstein published an essay in which he asked "how the structure of society ... should be changed in order to make human life as satisfying
as possible?" This is, of course, *the* question that has always enlivened and
informed democratic politics: What should government do to best contribute
to a world in which citizens lead positive and rewarding lives? It is here that
we find the foundational issue over which candidates and political parties ultimately base their philosophical appeals to the public – what specific public
policies contribute to better lives? Of course, given that the structural conditions that promote happiness are political goods, there is naturally political
conflict – which is to say ideological conflict – over what policies we should
adopt in furthering the greatest happiness for the greatest number.

This ideological competition is inherent, as we will have ample occasion
to see in the pages that follow, because the production and distribution of
human well-being takes place within the context of a market economy. As the
most basic and important aspects of the "structure of society" are inevitably
economic, any approach to "making human life as satisfying as possible" will
itself of necessity depend upon the fundamental social choice between the two
approaches available for governing a market economy. The Right suggests
that we leave well-being to the individual choices of free citizens in a free
market, with politics largely limited to maintaining those liberties. The Left,
by contrast, maintains that happiness is best served by an activist state that
consciously seeks to improve the human lot by grafting principles of equity
and justice to market outcomes. For the Right, the economy should be self-
governing, and thus ultimately outside the purview of democracy. For the Left,
the economy is a center of public power, and thus must be considered as subject
to democratic principles, so that its power can be used in the public interest.
It is this core distinction that has been the most persistent and contested axis
of political debate from the birth of the modern liberal democratic state at the
close of the eighteenth century to the present.

I

The centrality of the market to politics is hardly surprising, given that social theorists widely agree that once introduced, the market touches all aspects of society. As Robert Heilbroner (1985: 79) succinctly puts it, the market has become society's "central organizing principle," in that it profoundly "influences all aspects of the social formation, whether these are concerned with material life, justice and the social order, or custom and belief." For this reason, any political program designed "to make human life as satisfying as possible" must of necessity embody some particular strategy for using the market as a means toward that goal. In the end, the two familiar options we label the Left and the Right always present themselves, however diluted or compromised, in two idealized forms. One suggests that we leave the market to itself (intervening only as necessary to protect it), the other that we attempt to manage the market for the public good.

We need only look around us to see that this discussion informs contemporary debate as much as it did in the time of Einstein. As the world remains mired in the worst economic crisis since the Great Depression, the choice between Left and Right could hardly be starker or more omnipresent. In the United States, the Republican Party stands increasingly in favor of a pre–New Deal public policy regime, arguing that the state should retreat from the minimal social safety net the country now provides. This is evidenced most clearly in their basic economic blueprint, the Federal budget plan prepared by the House Budget Committee Chair and, 2012 Republican vice presidential candidate, Paul Ryan. The core elements of the Republican agenda are thus the elimination of Medicare as a program entitling seniors to medical care by reducing it to a voucher program, draconian cuts to the companion Medicaid program that provides medical assistance to low-income citizens, repeal of the Affordable Care Act ("Obamacare") that promises universal access to health care, and changes in the tax code that would make it drastically more regressive by lowering taxes on the wealthy (e.g., by eliminating outright the estate tax and taxes on dividends) while increasing them on the poor (e.g., by cutting or eliminating the Earned Income Tax Credit). In addition, a myriad of other programs would also be severely cut, beginning with conventional "welfare" programs, such as Food Stamps (currently used by one in seven Americans), and extending across the full spectrum of government responsibilities, such as student aid, pursuant with the goal of "shrinking the size of government."

While all Republicans wish to minimize the scope of government, and to minimize the burden economic regulations place on business, elements of its ultra-right Tea Party faction goes so far as to suggest repealing long standing Federal labor laws, such as the minimum wage or even prohibitions on child labor, on the logic that such matters are best determined by the market itself. This drive for what proponents call "market-friendly" policies coincide with entirely mainstream and powerfully coordinated new attacks on the right of workers to organize labor unions, most famously those orchestrated (successfully) by Republican Governor Scott Walker of Wisconsin (who survived a recall election) and (unsuccessfully) by Governor John Kasich of Ohio (who had his legislative efforts reversed by a ballot initiative). Together, debate over the issues discussed above are precisely those which have, in all times and places, in different forms and manifestations, always embodied the conflict between the Left and Right: the size and scope of the state, the nature and extent of economic regulation, and the power of organized labor.

The same conflict manifests across the Western world. Everywhere there is pressure to shrink the welfare state and otherwise institute austerity measures that reduce the state's commitment to help those in need, to weaken labor market protections for workers, and to emasculate unions – as the former French president Nicolas Sarkozy put it, to make Europe "more like the United States." That his own attempts at domestic reforms devoted to that end invoked the same fervent public protests as his predecessor Jacques Chirac's had, and that he would lose his 2012 bid for reelection to a Socialist candidate promising to increase taxes on the wealthy, cancel an increase in the retirement age, have the government regulate rents, provide more public housing, and restore tens of thousands of lost public sector jobs only illustrates the passion and durability of this inherent ideological divide.

This basic tension, always present as a principal axis of political competition, is now indisputably the central issue facing all liberal democratic countries today. Everywhere, the political choices are the same as at the time Einstein posed the question about how to improve the quality of human life: Do we prefer a government that is actively concerned with the well-being of its citizens through the provision of a generous social safety net, or do we prefer one that leaves the aged, the sick, and the unemployed to whatever fate the "spontaneous order" of the market allots them? Do we want the state to use its power to protect workers in the labor market, or should we leave employees and employers to work out their own arrangements, free of such political interference? Do we wish to live in a world in which workers are able to organize in defense of their interests, or do we think that society as a whole is better off if labor unions are discouraged and their political power minimized?

If the essential question of whether the political program of the Left or the Right best contributes to people leading satisfying lives has not fundamentally changed since Einstein, the tools available for answering it have. We are no longer limited to the ideological, philosophical, or speculative methods that have limited inquiry in the past. We are now in a position to discover the empirical answer to the question of how to structure society so as to best serve the goal of human happiness, in that we possess what prior generations conspicuously lacked: the data and tools necessary to apply rigorous social-scientific methods to the subject. With the advent of sophisticated modern survey research methods, we have learned to measure and study happiness in the same way we measure and study other human attributes. So armed, we can apply to life satisfaction the same statistical methods that have allowed us to study so many other human attitudes, beliefs, and behaviors.

Studying happiness in this way naturally invites skepticism. We might doubt, for instance, that people actually know how happy they are, such that their answers to questions about it would be meaningless. We might wonder if happiness is too transient or complex a thing to capture with an instrument as blunt as a survey question, such that people's answers might reflect only passing moods, rather than their deeper emotional life. We might fear that findings based on surveys would be highly fragile, being a product of question wording or other technical aspects of the survey instrument. We might further speculate that people may feel social pressures to "over-report" how happy they are, in that admitting to unhappiness might be tantamount to admitting to a personal failing in some cultures – while in others, just the opposite tendency might prevail, so that people might feel social pressure to demur from declaring themselves to be more happy than modesty suggests. We might think too that linguistic or cultural differences create barriers to cross-national or cross-cultural comparisons, so that it might be impossible to say that people in this or that country are really happier than those in another. Finally, we might be apprehensive about our ability to separate the effects of the causal factors we are examining – the political programs of the Left and the Right – from all the other myriad individual-, cultural-, and national-level factors that might also influence happiness.

Social scientists have long understood that merely because one can ask someone a question on a survey does not guarantee that the answers will be intelligible. Before we can take the leap of accepting these measures for what they appear at face value, we have to consider objections such as those just noted. This was the first objective of the scholars who pioneered this field, and it is only after decades of research that we have wide agreement that these issues are not disabling. I consider these and similar concerns later in this book as part of a general introduction to the empirical study of happiness. For the moment, we need merely note that these objections do not seriously inhibit our ability to use survey research to measure subjective well-being. We have, then, the "intellectual infrastructure" required for studying happiness in a rigorous way.

This book is thus devoted to applying the data, methods, and theories of contemporary social science to the question of how political outcomes in democratic societies determine the quality of life that citizens experience. As we have already had occasion to see, the issue at hand is nothing less than this: which political program, that of the Left or the Right, best contributes to human beings leading positive and rewarding lives? I immodestly aspire to provide an objective, empirical answer to this question, relying upon the same canons of reason and evidence required of any other empirical question amenable to study through social scientific means.

THE PLAN OF THE BOOK

Chapter One examines the historical and philosophical origins of the enduring conflict between the competing ideological prescriptions for improving the quality of human life that have existed since the birth of modern representative democracy. Drawing upon the experience of the American and French Revolutions, I trace the embryonic development of the politics of Left and Right as a natural and inevitable reaction to two closely related historical phenomena. One is the emergence of the market economy, with the resulting division of society into classes with opposing material and political interests. The other is the advent of liberal democracy as the arena in which that political conflict takes place. The nature and origin of the debate between the Left and the Right on both sides of the Atlantic is illustrated through an examination and critique of the scathingly analytical and unsentimental interpretation of politics and economy offered in Madison's *Federalist 10*, which remains arguably the most influential document in modern democratic thought. Through this discussion, I hope to demonstrate how our contemporary understanding of happiness and the role of the state in fostering it can only be understood in the context of what today we conventionally understand as market democracy.

Chapter Two develops a conceptual model of that system. It examines more closely the nature of the market and its relationship to democracy, attempting to clarify what markets are and how they necessitate the kind of class conflict that Madison viewed as the origin of politics. In this way, the chapter develops a theoretical account of how the capitalist economy affects, and is affected by, democratic norms and practices, leading in turn to an understanding of "market democracy" as a coherent, unified phenomenon. Within this system, political conflict is structured around three issues that reflect the values of the Left and the Right: the welfare state and the size of government in general (which, whether for good or ill, limits the power of the market over individuals by making them less dependent on market outcomes), the organization of workers into labor unions (which changes not only the immediate bargaining power of workers versus employers, but, more critically, strengthens the working and middle classes in the "democratic class struggle" that is the second order class conflict in market democracies), and the general pattern of economic regulation (which determines the degree to which workers and consumers are protected against the natural indifference of impersonal market forces, though at potentially high costs in terms of economic efficiency).

While Chapter Two focuses on the immediate divergence of interests between market participants based upon their class position that is an inevitable and natural aspect of a market system, Chapter Three examines the abstract intellectual and theoretical disputes between the Left and the Right about which type of policies best contribute to human happiness. That employers and employees, for instance, have (or believe they have) orthogonal short-term interests over spending, taxing, and labor market policies is obvious, as evidenced by the divergent positions on these issues taken by the interest groups (such as the U.S. Chamber of Commerce and the AFL-CIO) that represent them. Whether the ideological position of one or the other proves to be more consistent with general human well-being is the empirical question this book attempts to answer. Chapter Three further contributes to the framing of that assessment through an analytical summary and an appraisal of the specific arguments for small government and the general sovereignty of the market associated with Ronald Reagan, Margaret Thatcher, and neoliberal economists before similarly dissecting the arguments for supplementing market outcomes with principles of justice and equity that are conventionally associated with New Deal liberalism and West European social democracy.

Chapter Four provides an introduction to the scientific study of happiness. It has three principal aims. The chapter first addresses possible philosophical and practical misgivings about applying scientific methodology to the study of happiness. It then reviews and critically evaluates the main theoretical approaches to understanding how economic, social, and political factors may affect happiness across persons and across countries. I contend that the best approach to understanding such differences is that which stresses the extent to which our needs as human animals are fulfilled, which in turn suggests that happiness may be highly sensitive to the public policy regimes that directly touch people's lives. The chapter concludes with the important practical task of reviewing the existing empirical research on the causes and correlates of happiness. Beyond the general goal of familiarizing the reader with the literature, my purpose is to specify the other known predictors of happiness, so as to be able to account for them – to control for them – in the statistical analyses that follow.

The next two chapters test hypotheses about the effects on human well-being of the political programs of the Left and Right using real world data on the industrial democracies of Western Europe, North America, and the Pacific. Chapter Five considers the fundamental issue of whether "big government" contributes to, or detracts from, the quality of human life. Using the pooled World Values Surveys (1981–2007) for the OECD countries, I provide an analysis of how the level of happiness of the overall population, as well as the happiness of particular subgroups in society (such as rich and poor), are affected by the generosity and universalism of the welfare state, the overall size of the state sector (reflecting the degree of government involvement in providing public services), and the total share of the economy that is politically (which is to say, democratically) controlled or allocated by the state through taxation.

Chapter Six extends the analysis to consider two other crucial aspects of market-state relations: (1) the degree of governmental regulation of the economy, principally labor market regulations that are designed to protect the interests of employees, and, more importantly, (2) the degree to which workers are organized into labor unions, which serve to provide representation – and thus power – to working- and middle-class citizens in both the workplace and in politics.

Chapter Seven completes the empirical analysis of the political determinants of life satisfaction by shifting the geographical focus from the universe of industrial democracies to a case study of the United States. I here consider the same basic questions about the politics of Left and Right when considering variation across the states of the U.S. federal system. This chapter not only considers the potential for "American Exceptionalism" in the factors that determine quality of life, but also extends the analysis by applying it to the experience of the fifty states as "laboratories of democracy." By considering such "laboratory evidence," we can determine if state policies are causally connected to greater levels of subjective well-being. By illustrating that the decisions of subnational governments do have powerful impacts on quality of life despite the modest discretion over policy choices that states possess, coupled with the fact that the variation in their policies is both modest and skewed toward the Right compared to that across nations, this analysis further demonstrates that the extent to which human beings find their lives to be positive and rewarding is in large measure the result of the political choices made by the parties that voters elect.

Chapter Eight concludes the book with an appraisal of the implications of the empirical findings for both our theoretical understanding of subjective well-being and the perennial debate between Left and Right. Regarding the former, I argue that subjective well-being should be explicitly conceived of as a political good – that is, one whose level is determined by the political choices of governments that citizens elect. Turning to the basic question animating the project – how should society be structured to make human life as satisfying as possible – I provide a summary judgment on whether the politics of the Left or the Right are most consistent with the goal of making human life as gratifying as it can be. In light of that discussion, I offer practical suggestions for public policy, concluding that if we really wish to improve the quality of human life, the democratic process offers a clear road to that end.

A PREVIEW OF FINDINGS AND CONCLUSIONS

In the argument between Left and Right over the size of the state, I demonstrate that "big government" is more conducive to human well-being, controlling for other factors. Indeed, the single most powerful individual- or national-level determinant of the degree to which people positively evaluate the quality of their lives is the extent to which they live in a generous and universalistic welfare state. Put differently, the greater the "social wage" that society pays its members, the happier people tend to be. Similarly, people find life more rewarding when a larger share of the economy is "consumed" by government through the "taxing and spending" that allows for the maximum provision of public services, such as education or healthcare. Overall, it is clear that the quality of human life improves as more of the productive capacity of society comes under political – which is to say, again, democratic – control. The subordination of the market to democracy thus appears to promote human happiness in precisely the way progressives and social democrats have always argued.

Similar conclusions emerge when considering political regulation of the economy. Labor market regulations that establish relatively strong protections for wage and salary workers appear to achieve their end of making life a more agreeable experience. They do so because they offer protections against market forces that most working people do indeed need to be protected from: full-time work that does not provide a living wage, unsafe working conditions, fear of arbitrary dismissal, inadequate paid leave time, and so on. More generally, a legal structure that limits the authority and discretion of business, both as it affects the amount of job security workers enjoy, and as it relates to how workers are treated on the job, fosters norms of human dignity and respect for the working person, whereas the absence of a worker-friendly structure may tend to promote the alienation and anomie that is the logical consequence of "flexible" labor markets in which workers are treated just like any other commodity. The empirical evidence is unambiguous: the more we rely on the law to protect employees, the more satisfied with life people tend to be.

The effect of applying democratic principles to the economy is also evident when considering the consequences of labor organization. For the Right, unions merely exploit workers and distort the otherwise efficient operations of the market; for the Left, the union is a democratic entity that represents employees against their employer in the same way that representative institutions protect the individual against a potentially arbitrary government. Simply stated, the data suggest that being represented by a labor union makes people happier, other things being equal. Further, and more momentously, the evidence clearly indicates that a strong labor movement – in the sense of a larger share of workers who are organized – has strongly positive effects for society in general, not merely for organized workers per se.

It is equally important to note that all of the factors discussed above also contribute to greater well-being without particular regard to socioeconomic status. While some of the relationships are indeed stronger for working- and middle-class citizens, in every case, higher-status persons also benefit. Thus, everyone profits from a more generous welfare state, from labor laws that protect workers, and from strong labor unions, whatever their income. The welfare state, labor unions, and political regulation of the economy thus contribute to creating a world that offers the promise of a satisfying life to all citizens, rich and poor alike.

This cross-national pattern obtains equally across the American states: big government, a more generous safety net, more economic regulation, and stronger labor unions create greater levels of well-being. The evidence is perhaps most readily summarized in one result: people are happier in states whose government has in recent decades tended be to be controlled by the Democratic Party, in that such control has allowed for the establishment of the progressive public policy regimes that are the most consistent with human flourishing.

Collectively, these empirical results have important theoretical implications for the academic study of subjective well-being. Two are of particular moment. One is that the extent to which individuals find life rewarding is largely the result of the political factors discussed above, given that the impact of these factors on subjective well-being dwarfs conventional individual-level indicators such as income, social connectedness (e.g., marriage or cohabitation), and even unemployment. As the most powerful causes of happiness are things that governments are entirely capable of controlling, we can follow Thomas

Jefferson and Jeremy Bentham in believing that happiness is something that is politically produced and distributed. Happiness, then, is a function of public policy – and thus a result of our collective choices as citizens in electing the governments that make policy.

Second, in documenting the existence of a powerful relationship between political interventions in the market and human happiness, the empirical results naturally focus our attention on the market itself. However much there is to be said in favor of the market – and I would argue that whatever its failings, it remains one of humanity's signature achievements, something to be criticized in the spirit of improvement precisely because it commends itself in so many other ways – it also has costs. These manifest themselves in a currency more valuable than money: in the degree to which people actually enjoy being alive. It is thus in the internal dynamics of the market that we find the keys to understanding how human happiness is produced and distributed. We should thus surely look to the market, and our political efforts to control it, as the arena in which to understand human happiness.

cause-effect evidence?

I

The Democratic Pursuit of Happiness

In some of the most familiar and inspiring sentences in the English language, the American Declaration of Independence expresses the spirit of a new political age:

We hold these truths to be self-evident, that all men are created equal, that they are endowed by their Creator with certain unalienable Rights, that among these are Life, Liberty and the pursuit of Happiness. That to secure these rights, Governments are instituted among Men, deriving their just powers from the consent of the governed, that whenever any Form of Government becomes destructive of these ends, it is the Right of the People to alter or to abolish it, and to institute new Government, laying its foundation on such principles and organizing its powers in such form, as to them shall seem most likely to effect their Safety and Happiness.

However vital the first two elements in this trilogy of "unalienable Rights," it is the last that strikes the most evocative chord in the human imagination. The idea that individuals have a natural right to "the pursuit of Happiness" has proven inspirational across centuries and cultures for an obvious reason: it suggests that the happiness of the ordinary person can be the foundation of a political order. Indeed, as Jefferson explicitly proclaims, the very reason that "Governments are instituted" is precisely to "secure" this right. Thus, the state exists not to serve the interests of a divinely appointed sovereign or a privileged commercial class, but to guarantee the right of all people to lead free and satisfying lives.

The new political order the Declaration proclaimed was thus to be, at least in aspiration, not merely a context in which people would be safe in their lives and liberty from an arbitrary government. The state was to be not merely something that citizens need not fear, but rather a positive resource that they might collectively use in furtherance of their right to pursue rewarding lives. It is in this spirit that Jefferson suggests that the people may choose the "principles" by which the state makes policy "in such form, as to them shall seem most likely" to provide for their "Safety and Happiness." What makes the Declaration so radically democratic, as opposed to merely republican or liberal, is that by explicitly recognizing a right to the pursuit of happiness (that governments are in turn argued to be created specifically to guarantee), it consciously recognizes the further right of citizens to use *their* government as an instrument for creating the conditions they collectively believe most conducive to the betterment of human life. The Declaration thus offers nothing less than the promise that "popular government" would offer citizens the opportunity, as citizens, to participate in politics so as to determine what path toward human betterment the state, constituted for just this purpose, would pursue.

In its stress on the idea of happiness, the Declaration is offering a break with the past that is historically rather more revolutionary than the assertion of popular sovereignty that is its immediate purpose. In arguing that we have a natural right to search for happiness, Jefferson is proposing what was at the time a far more radical proposition than the familiar social contract arguments about the origins of legitimate government that date back to before Locke that inform the rest of the Declaration. To suggest that ordinary people might realistically hope for a life they found satisfying, whole, and meaningful – and that this hope might form part of the foundation for the political order of society – is what the makes Jefferson's words ring down the centuries with such force. The world he was envisioning was thus not merely one free of the petty tyrannies of despotic governments, but also one that enshrined happiness as a legitimate and valued end for both individual citizens and the governments they instituted.

This may seem unremarkable to the twenty-first-century reader, but it is, as Darrin McMahon (2006) has meticulously documented in his history of happiness, a monumental break with the past: "It is really only in the eighteenth century that considerable numbers of people began to think of happiness as a this-worldly possibility." In the past, happiness had always been conceived of as either something that only a tiny handful of exceptional people might obtain through long application or something to be found only in the next world. The former tradition is of course associated with Aristotle, who, as McMahon notes, conceived of happiness as a "prize" to be won only "by the virtuous – the happy few – those whose excellence of conduct and character allowed them to rise above normal human conditions, to live what Aristotle describes . . . as a 'god-like' life. To be happy might be within human power, but it was a power that would only be realized by a very small percentage of the human population." In the other traditional interpretation, happiness might be accessible to the ordinary person, but it was not to be found in life-as-lived, but only in some promised and distant future (e.g., the arrival or return of a prophet) or in the after-life (our "heavenly reward"). As McMahon summarizes, "happiness in the here and now – in the normal conditions of life – wasn't considered an earthly prospect."

It was in exactly this sense that Tom Paine would say, "we have it in our power to begin the world over again," in that he saw in the American Revolution the prospect for a reorientation of society around a more humane set of organizing principles that might in turn offer the ordinary person – the laborer, the small farmer, the shopkeeper – a chance for happiness. In much the same way, the French Revolutionary Louis de Saint-Just would report with pleasure that "happiness is a new idea in Europe," to which he believed the new republican order should devote itself. This same impulse led the French to adopt their new calendar in which 1792, the year the French First Republic was proclaimed, became the Year One. We have to understand the Declaration, which preceded and to some degree precipitated these later visionary gestures, as representing precisely this kind of dramatic break with the past.

It would, of course, be wrong to attribute the values expressed in the Declaration solely to its principal author. Such ideas were already common, if disapproved of by the state, on both sides of the Atlantic. Jefferson emerged as their leading publicist in much the same way Voltaire came to be the public face of the less explicitly political side of the Enlightenment, but both men were synthesizing ideas already enjoying wide intellectual currency. Thus, we find that the entry on happiness in the *Encyclopédie*, the quintessential expression of Enlightenment ideas, proclaims "Does not every man have a right to happiness?" From there, it is a small step toward suggesting that government be looked to as an agent to defend that right, as it is presumed to defend others. Thus, the English scientist and political theorist Joseph Priestley (1768) proposed in *The First Principles of Government and Liberty*: "The good and happiness of the members, that is the majority of the members of the state, is the great standard by which every thing relating to that state must finally be determined." There are similar incarnations of the same ideas, most famously in Tom Paine's *Common Sense* (1776) and in John Adams's *Thoughts on Government* (1776). The latter, published a few months before the Declaration, anticipates that document's emphasis on happiness:

Upon this point all speculative politicians will agree, that the happiness of society is the end of government . . . [just as] all agree that the happiness of the individual is the end of Man. From this principle it will follow, that the form of government which communicates ease, comfort, security, or, in a word, happiness to the greatest number of people, and in the greatest degree, is the best.

The lasting influence of such ideas is everywhere to be seen in politics and philosophy. The connection between politics and happiness that we see in Adams and Jefferson anticipates the hugely significant project of Utilitarianism, founded as it is on Bentham's and Mill's contention that politics and economy should be based on the principle that "the greatest happiness of the greatest number is the foundation of morals and legislation." Jefferson himself was the obvious inspiration for much of the language of the landmark French Declaration of the Rights of Man and of the Citizen of 1789, wherein in the National Assembly offered its "solemn declaration" of "the natural, inalienable,

1 Hutcheson ? !

and sacred rights of man" because the establishment of such rights would "redound [i.e., contribute to] to the happiness of all." Through these vessels, and many others beyond the need to review here, the happiness of the ordinary person, living in the here and now, became the nominal basis for politics in the modern world.

THE BIRTH OF MODERN IDEOLOGIES

To fully appreciate both the full significance of the ideas of the Declaration in its own time as well as their continued relevance to the contemporary world, we must look more closely at the immediate political context in which they emerged. The reason, as we shall see, is that this context helped define the fundamental question facing a democratic government: how to best use the power of the state to protect and nurture natural rights, including that to seek happiness. In formulating the question, of course, the context also contributed to defining the possible answers.

We can conceive of that context as having two aspects. The first is the ideational legacy of the Enlightenment, in its presumption that human beings are rational and moral actors, who can aspire to lead lives of their own choosing with the hope and expectation of happiness. The second is the hardly coincidental advent of the market economy as society's central organizing principle, and with it, the system of representative government that emerged as its natural and necessary complement. What we today call democracy – and the accompanying regime of civil rights and liberties we associate with it – had its origin in the triumph of the same market principles that have also come to permeate popular conceptions of the nature and the centrality of the individual, the purpose and origin of political power, and the methods by which we attempt to study, understand, and manipulate the world.

All of these elements come to synergistic fruition in the second half of the eighteenth century, nowhere more famously and transparently, as we have seen, than in the founding of the American republic. This process is best conceived as a single event that takes place in two phases. The first was the War of Independence, which was fought to establish the abstract principles so vividly expressed in the Declaration of Independence. The other was the subsequent, and arguably still extant, struggle over the nature of the resulting constitutional regime. The latter, then as now, pits a conservative element, as suspicious as Socrates of the political instincts of the ordinary citizens that form the *demos*, and even more devoted to maintaining the privileges of the propertied against their leveling tendencies, against a more progressive movement that puts greater faith in the capacity of people to govern themselves, and is thus sympathetic to the idea that the reduction of poverty, inequality, and privilege is a legitimate and necessary task for government.

These conflicting ideologies find compelling expression in two of the greatest works of political argument in the revolutionary period: James Madison's contributions to *The Federalist Papers* and Tom Paine's *The Rights of Man*. Thus, we find Jefferson in the Declaration providing the landmark intellectual argument for the now-universal notion that the purpose of government is to help citizens in their collective pursuit of happiness, while the subsequent debate over means to that end, between what today we would call the Right and the Left, are to be found in Madison and Paine. As these competing ideological perspectives arise naturally as the two possible solutions to the inherent tension between the principles of market and democracy, they form convenient historical guideposts for the options that remain available in the modern world, to borrow Einstein's phrase, in choosing how best "to structure society so as to make human life as satisfying as possible."

As already noted, any ideas capable of contributing to or actively inhibiting social change do not emerge out of political and economic vacuums, but rather express changing political and economic conditions. The values and logics we associate with the Enlightenment were thus not merely a set of abstract principles that gained currency through their intellectual superiority in the "marketplace of ideas." The emergence to prominence of such ideals cannot be attributed to the admitted eloquence of their intellectual champions. Could we transport Hume, Locke, or Voltaire backward in time – to, say, the coronation of Charlemagne in the year 800, much less to the court of Constantine in 330 or to Alexander's of 330 BCE – and somehow grant them the ability to express and publicize their ideas to a wide audience, it is inconceivable that they could make any material impact on the structure of dynastic feudalism, the Roman Imperium, or the Greek city-states. In the same way, Voltaire and the Encylopédistes did not invent the Enlightenment the way Edison invented the light bulb, any more than Hobbes and Locke invented the notion of a social contract. In each instance, the contribution of the philosopher was principally to give voice to new trends in society and economy that were in need of being rationalized and systematized.[1]

By far the most profound of these trends was the emergent market economy, which, as we discuss in more detail in Chapter 2, required for its success an approach to understanding the world predicated upon the primacy of the individual and the centrality of individual choice – liberty – in a "free" market, coupled with a government that could be held accountable, as the arbitrary rule of divinely sanctioned kings could not, for protecting and maintaining market relations. Thus, as market forces gained prominence, market ideas about human nature and the structure of human society followed. This formed what proponents of the new thinking, such as Adam Smith, viewed as a virtuous

---

[1] Of course, the very metaphor of a "marketplace of ideas" is intelligible to us only because we live in the age of the market economy. Such a notion would have been unimaginable not merely to men of action like Charlemagne or Constantine but also to such passionate devotees of reason as Plato or an Aristotle, all of whom had, in their own fashions, entirely different conceptions about the truth or validity of ideas, united only by the conviction that such things were not governed by the same motives or decided by the same evidence as the ones that determine at what price we buy wine or grain.

circle, wherein material change produced ideational change, which made further material change easier, and so on.

To focus specifically on the American case, it was questions of taxation and the regulation of commerce that were the most proximate causes of the Revolution, as summarized by Jefferson in his list of grievances against the king: "For imposing Taxes on us without our Consent," and "For cutting off our Trade with all parts of the world." Among the former, the Stamp Act was only the most onerous of the means by which the British imposed "taxation without representation" on the Colonies. This burden fell most grievously, of course, on the commercial, industrial, professional, and mercantile segments of society – i.e., on precisely those associated with the emerging market economy. Taxation without representation is of course a convenient, popularized slogan for the more profound notion that the productive (i.e., profit-making or non-subsistence portion of the economy) should not be subject to a political authority over which it has no influence. Further, the absence of representation had greater economic implications than those associated with taxes. The commercial classes in the colonies wanted more than just to be left unmolested by the British: then, as today, they wanted to harness the power of the state for their own purposes. They desired, for instance, that the state organize and fund public works that would facilitate commerce, such as the building of roads, bridges, harbors, and other infrastructure beyond their means, as well as the development and enforcement of a legal system consistent with their interests (e.g., one recognizing corporations and protecting creditors or slave owners against their natural adversaries).

Equally offensive to the colonists were the Townshend Acts, which imposed tariffs and otherwise severely limited trade, so as to reduce the colonies to captive markets for English goods. They did so by awarding trading monopolies to English companies for many imported commodities, of which tea became the most famous. The effect was to inhibit the development of both American trade and industry (as people such as Alexander Hamilton rightly argued), and with it not only the national interest but, of more immediate political import, the financial prospects of the class that hoped to profit by trade and industry as well.

We see, then, that intellectually the Revolutionaries, whatever their subsequent disagreements on the shape of the post-colonial regime that we shall presently examine, are united on a set of core principles. The first is that the purpose of government is the social good, defined in terms of the happiness of the population, which can be obtained only through a representative government answerable to the population. The second is their implicit commitment to a market economy as another necessary condition for the maintenance of "liberty" as much as the successful "pursuit of happiness." It was thus agreed that liberty required what today we call a "free market," meaning one free of the exploitative inhibitions of an arbitrary monarchial government (such as those of George III discussed earlier) or even, especially in Continental Europe, the remnants of feudalism that still grossly restricted trade and production (e.g., tithes, guilds, and forced labor).

Where the different revolutionary factions fell out was in dealing with the contradiction that inevitably emerges between the inequalities of wealth and privilege that a market economy implies and the principle of equality that democracy demands. If we grant that individuals have a right to pursue happiness, and that such happiness is the correct end of government, then it is certain that rational agents who do less well vis-à-vis market outcomes will attempt to utilize the ballot box to affect redistribution, given that the distribution of wealth will largely determine the distribution of happiness. Political equality, then, creates natural pressures for economic equality in the form of redistribution, which is certainly contrary to the interests of the dominant class that benefits from the "natural" outcomes of the market. It must be added that such redistribution might, abstractly or theoretically, produce a situation in which everyone is made worse off, if redistribution were to have the negative economic consequences frequently argued to accompany it, but this is another issue entirely. The immediate conflict is not over philosophy or who benefits in the fictional "long run," but over who benefits tangibly, in the here and now. In any event, if the market is, as we have seen, thought to be essential to liberty, there must be a tension between the legitimate desire of one class for a more equal (and in their eyes, more just) distribution and the equally legitimate demand by the other to maintain their wealth (and, in their view, therefore, their liberty).

Another way of conceiving of the same clash of interests can be found in the theory of democracy itself. At the time of the Founding, "democracy" was not the term of universal approbation that it is today. Many of the Founders, and the Federalists most of all, viewed democracy with hostility and so conceived of themselves as "republicans" rather than as democrats. They would champion the Constitution of 1787 on the grounds that it created a republic, not a democracy. Their animosity to democratic principles is easier for the modern reader to understand if we recall that at this time, democracy was not thought of as merely a *method* for choosing a government but rather also as a specific political *outcome*: that of a more egalitarian society in which distinctions based on wealth or status were to be absent or muted. Thus, as C.B. Macpherson (1977) prudently reminds us, democracy has always been "very much a class thing," wherein the democratic project generally has been – and was certainly in the eighteenth and nineteenth centuries understood to be – the movement for building either a classless society or, equivalently, a society comprised of only one class of citizens.

It is in the equation of egalitarianism with democracy that one sees most plainly the logic of the historical opposition to democracy by the propertied classes as well as the inherent contradiction between democracy and the market as abstract principles. This tension is clearly evident at the Founding, where it finds expression in the period of consolidation after the War of Independence in the conflict between what we would now label as conservative and progressive factions. Should market outcomes, reflecting as they do the "natural right" to be secure in one's "property" (i.e., wealth or "capital"), be equated with the natural order, such that attempts to redistribute wealth or otherwise interfere with the market to protect those who prosper less from its "free" operation are to be seen, in James Madison's words "as wicked and improper?" Or, while admitting the moral claims of property, should we also consider other moral claims on the products of wealth, particularly if, as Paine would presciently argue, we grant that society, being integral to the creation of property or wealth, also has a legitimate claim to a portion of the wealth it is instrumental in creating?

As this debate continues to be the principle axis of ideological conflict in industrial societies, it is worth considering its original form. As we shall see, such a discussion not only illuminates the nature, and the long historical pedigree, of the Left and Right as ideological poles but also illustrates the hugely influential role, then as now, of class conflict to politics.

JAMES MADISON AND THE CONSERVATIVE IMPULSE

The *Federalist Papers* are, of course, the name commonly given to the set of essays that articulated the ideology of what would emerge as the victorious side in the struggle to define the American constitutional order. The most famous and studied is Madison's *Federalist 10*, one of the most influential and extraordinary documents in the history of democratic thought. In it, Madison boldly lays out the set of assumptions about the nature of society and the purpose of politics typical of the educated elites of the time, and then goes on to deduce the appropriate form of government implied by such assumptions. In a few hundred words, he effectively lays the foundation for what has become the modern understanding of, and argument for, what he called "popular government." It is worth examining in detail.

Madison's view of "democracy" reflected the conventional understanding of the times in two respects: democracy was equated, first, with the Athenian assembly of all citizens, and thus with the disorder and injustice of the "mob rule" believed to be inherent in the Athenian model. According to Madison, "democracies have ever been spectacles of turbulence and contention [and] have ever been found incompatible with personal security or the rights of property." The danger posed by a democratic system was that it would empower the majority of ordinary, relatively poor citizens who would naturally form a dangerous "faction" – meaning a group "united and actuated by some common impulse of passion, or of interest, adverse to the rights of other citizens or to the permanent and aggregate interests of the community." Given that the basic divide in society was universally agreed to be one of social class, the majority faction (composed of what today we could call the working and middle classes) would naturally be at odds with the privileged orders, whose wealth (and privileges) they would seek to expropriate. Says Madison, "the most common and durable source of factions has been the various and unequal distribution of property. Those who hold, and those who are without property, have ever formed distinct interests in society."

Madison, thus, clearly conceives of society as naturally and inevitably divided into two classes, based on ownership of property – meaning, again, what we today would conceive of as wealth. By extension, this division is predicated on the relative positions of each class in the economic system of production and exchange, so that their interests diverge based upon whether the system of privileges favors or disfavors them. Thus, Madison believes that their interests are naturally opposed, rather than being complementary. These conflicting interests become the basis of political conflict whenever there is liberty – they arise spontaneously when not artificially suppressed by authoritarian structures. In sum, society is divided into two classes, one relatively rich and small in number, one comparatively poor and large in number, and it is the political conflict between them – class struggle – that animates the politics of free peoples. The class, or faction, comprising those "who are without property" have always been the majority, as Madison recognizes, and it is precisely this "majority faction" that so troubles him.

The majority faction was, of course, what the Greeks called the *demos*, meaning the most populous, and thus less economically privileged, class. Rule by this faction (democracy) was anathema to Madison and the Federalists because the demos would be naturally inclined (given Madison's Hobbesian assumptions about human nature) to use the governing power to expropriate the property of the privileged. Such expropriation was surely "adverse to the rights" of the propertied, and doubtless, because of its injustice, to the "interests of the community." This problem is inherent in the form of "popular government" because it "enables" the majority faction "to sacrifice to its ruling passion or interest both the public good and the rights of other citizens." Consider, for instance, the question of (progressive) taxation:

The apportionment of taxes ... is an act which seems to require the most exact impartiality; yet there is, perhaps, no legislative act, in which greater opportunity and temptation are given to a predominant party to trample on the rules of justice. Every shilling with which they over burden the inferior number is a shilling saved to their own pockets.

The example is telling. Taxes and other economic issues (e.g., laws "concerning private debts" or the prospect that the government might succumb to the popular "rage for paper money") dominate Madison's discussion, as they should, given his emphasis on the importance of class interests in politics. The presumption is that the demos ("the predominant party") will use the legislative process to invoke ruinous taxes on the rich (or manipulate the supply of money to benefit creditors at the expense of debtors to similar effect), which is, self-evidently, to "trample on the rules of justice." Madison's goal in *Federalist 10* is thus to provide a mechanism for having the popular sovereignty that he and other conservatives sincerely believed in (rather than monarchy or dictatorship) while protecting society against the unjust "leveling tendencies" of the demos:

The friend of popular governments never finds himself so much alarmed for their character and fate, as when he contemplates their propensity to this dangerous vice.

This vice takes shape in the "wicked and improper" projects of the majority for the redistribution of wealth through taxation (or outright seizure), monetary policy (such as favoring growth and thus employment and wages at the expense of inflation), or other interference with the market. Madison's prescriptions for leaving the demos "unable to concert and carry into effect their schemes of oppression" are less interesting, and certainly less relevant to present purposes, than his analysis of the problem. The economy – the market – divides citizens into opposing classes, based upon their position in the market. The wealthy minority, whose fortunes are not only a product of the market but, of course, a resource that generates yet more wealth, benefit from the system, and thus look to the state to protect and nurture it. The less-affluent majority, who have little or no property and who instead rely upon their ability to sell their labor in the unstable and frequently unrewarding market for that commodity, are likely to believe (rightly or wrongly) that they are the victims of the system, and thus naturally to look to the state to redistribute the wealth that the market creates, or even to alter market principles themselves.

Madison argues that "the principle of government" is to ensure that the property-owning class is protected against redistributive policies, which he, of course, conceives of as a "schemes for oppression."[2] The Constitution of 1787 is recommended both because its structural features should inhibit the emergence of the demos as a coherent "faction" (principally via the hope that a large republic and a system of representation will "refine and enlarge public views"), and because of specific clauses (such as prohibitions against progressive taxation, to say nothing of the recognition of slavery) that also limit the power of the demos. As many scholars of the Founding, such as Jennifer

---

[2] It must be admitted, as some interpretations of Madison stress, that his arguments about the "tyranny of the majority" are meant to apply to minority rights abstractly, rather than being limited narrowly and exclusively to class interests. Some point in particular toward passages in his collected papers (particularly *Papers* 14: 266–8) that extend the idea of "property" to include "everything to which a man may attach a value and have a right," the most important of which are his "opinions and the free communication of them," especially his "religious opinions." Although it is doubtlessly the case that Madison did put great value on freedom of expression and religious liberty (as evidenced, for instance, by his opposition to the Alien and Sedition Acts, and his successful efforts with Jefferson at de-establishing religion in Virginia), it equally cannot be denied that Madison's principal, even obsessive, concern in *Federalist 10* is with property in the conventional sense of property as wealth. It is impossible to make sense of *Federalist 10* (much less Madison's own notes on the Constitutional Convention of 1787, wherein he portrays himself as perpetually anxious about protecting "the minority of the opulent against the majority") if we stretch property in this way. If we wish to think of Madison's legacy as being that of institutionalizing the idea of limited government – a noble enough legacy – we must also grant that his limits include protecting the privileged from the demos (for incisive discussions for this perspective, see Nedelsky, 1990; Matthews, 1995; for general reviews, including criticism of this perspective and alternative accounts, see Gibson, 2006, 2010; Zuckert, 2003).

Nedelsky (1990) and Richard Matthews (1995), have argued, Madison thus stands as a convenient and historically compelling symbol of one method of accommodating "popular government" with the market by favoring the latter at the expense of the former. Thus, a central goal of Madison's project was indeed precisely "to withdraw the rules of the market from political debate" (Nedelsky, 1990: 180), thus ensuring that politics would be subordinated to and limited by the market. The modern incarnation of Madison's attitude toward the state and the economy is readily apparent in Friedrich von Hayek, Milton Friedman, and Margaret Thatcher, the chief intellectual reference points for the ideological right, who argue for a state whose function is limited to maintaining a minimalist legal order appropriate for free individuals in a free market, in that redistribution would be contrary to the *morally* superior "spontaneous order" established by the market.[3]

JEFFERSON, PAINE, AND THE DAWN OF THE LEFT

As we have seen, Madison clearly believed that society was divided into social classes vis-à-vis their relationship to wealth. He thought that the axis of political conflict in a class society would inevitably be over not merely the unequal distribution of wealth, but the *system* that produced such inequality by privileging one class over another. The relatively poor – the demos – comprising as they did the vast majority of the population would naturally resent both the wealth of the minority, and the socio-economic practices that appeared, in their eyes, to arbitrarily supply wealth to some and poverty to others. The demos, if allowed to, would therefore use the vote to express their class interest, that is, to change the system that appeared to favor people other than themselves.[4] An essential purpose of government, then, was to protect the natural right of the privileged against such redistribution. In a word, Madison and the Federalists viewed society as inevitably being divided into classes with conflicting material interests, and placed themselves squarely upon the side of the privileged.

This should not surprise us. That society was, and is, divided by class is obvious. Once we grant that society is composed of different classes, it follows

---

[3] It is perhaps worth observing that Adam Smith, as we shall have occasion to see in subsequent chapters, does not fit comfortably with such company. His views of capitalism and the role of the state within that system are hardly as simplistic as sometimes portrayed by those who find it convenient to cite him as an authority. One can scarcely find a more straightforward condemnation of Madison's view of the state as a protector of property than Smith's in *The Wealth of Nations* (2007: 556): "government, so far as it is instituted for the security of property, is in reality instituted for the defense of the rich against the poor."

[4] As Matthews (1995: 198) observes, for Madison "the *demos* were to be feared; their participation in politics had to be limited as far as politically feasible [through, among other methods, the institution of representation, which helped to remove them from access to power, and property qualifications on the right to vote itself]; and they were to be granted full membership in the political system [only] when there appeared to be no other option available." The essential goal, as Nedelsky neatly summarizes it, was to limit the influence of the demos enough to ensure that "the propertied would do the ruling" (1990: 181).

by definition that these classes often have opposing interests, for if the two were not in adversarial positions, they would not form different classes. Further, given that the basis of class conflict is over distribution, in which one class wishes to keep what another would prefer to appropriate, conflict is unavoidable. To be sure, classes may often have a commonality of interest, either when the immediate issue at hand is not one of distribution, or when questions of distribution may be avoided by increasing the overall level of consumption. As Madison argued, the natural "faction" of the demos can also be dissolved by the increasing relevance of other interests beyond class, such as that of one region or sector of the economy against another, a function served in the contemporary era more by religious and cultural issues. Partisans on either side of the class divide may also develop perfectly sincere theoretical prescriptions which similarly endeavor to avoid the basic divide by maintaining that policies favoring the immediate interests of their class will in the long run improve conditions for all.

In the end, though, the existence of class forces political actors to choose sides, in two respects. The first is, of course, that of which class to favor over the other when interests do diverge. The second is whether to favor the maintenance of the class system or to work for its diminution. Madison (to say nothing of people like Hamilton or Washington) naturally genuflected both toward the propertied, commercial class and to the acceptance of an enduring class division as a natural aspect of society. As we have already seen, Madison's primary goal, like that of most of the Framers, was to protect liberty, in the classical liberal sense that equated liberty with the unequal distribution of wealth, and the consequent unequal distribution of political power, as a market economy implied. Madison's vision of the world the market would foster was thus that of "a permanent division between *dependent* laborers and *independent* employers" (Appleby, 1986: 33, emphasis added). This situation was not something to be overcome, but precisely what was to be protected by the constitutional order he advocated. As Nedelsky aptly puts it, "The Constitution was designed to make republican government work and the market secure *given* that division" between classes (1990: 181, emphasis in original). In this sense, we see an essential element in Madisonian thought that still animates contemporary conservative politics: that the political system must be resistant to attempts to alter the class inequality that flows from, and is essential for the maintenance of, the market society.

In Thomas Jefferson, we find the door opening to a different course: a politics devoted to the material interests of the demos, and, more generally, to reducing or leveling class distinctions. Of course, we must be careful not to exaggerate the differences between Madison and Jefferson[5]. Despite Madison's legacy as the "father" of the Constitution, and his consequent deep intellectual

[5] For an analysis of Jefferson's political thought at the time of the American Revolution and its evolution in the decades that followed, see Zuckert (1996: 13–89, 202–43) and (forthcoming), respectively.

association with the Federalists who were its political champion during the battle for ratification, he was a life-long political ally of Jefferson. Madison joined Jefferson in forming the Democratic-Republican Party (in opposition to Federalist policies in the Washington and Adams administrations), served as Jefferson's secretary of state when Jefferson became president in 1801 and succeeded him to the presidency with Jefferson's support in 1809. While the closeness of their political alliance thus suggests no small degree of shared values on matters both political and, more abstractly intellectual (both, for instance, were especially proud of their role in drafting the Virginia Statute for Religious Freedom, nearly as radical in its own way as the Declaration of Independence), they differed profoundly over issues of inequality, property, and redistribution.

In a now-famous letter written to Madison in 1785 (Hutchinson and Rachal, 1973: 385–7), Jefferson argued for a far different interpretation of property rights than Madison held. While Jefferson certainly believed in the right to property, he held that such a right was contingent upon, or derived from its contribution to, the public good. Jefferson similarly maintained the right to property must be made consistent with man's natural right to work, i.e., with a right to an independent livelihood, rather than being merely a "dependent laborer." As he told Madison,

Whenever there is in any country uncultivated lands and unemployed poor, it is clear that the laws of property have been so far extended as to violate natural right. The earth is given as a common stock for man to labour and live on. If, for encouragement of industry we allow it to be appropriated, we must take care that other employment be furnished to those excluded from the appropriation. If we do not the fundamental right to labor the earth returns to the unemployed.

In language that is clearly reminiscent of Locke, and thus expressed squarely within the liberal tradition that all the Founders shared, Jefferson was actually proposing an idea that remains an axis of intense political conflict even today: that one has a natural right to employment – or, equivalently, a moral claim, as a member of society, for society's help when work is not available. He was thus proposing that people possessed the "social rights" that animate so much contemporary progressive and social democratic political thought. Not merely that, but Jefferson also goes on in the same letter to suggest precisely the kind of redistribution that so alarmed Madison by noting that "the consequences of this enormous inequality producing so much misery to the bulk of mankind [is that] legislators cannot invent too many devices for subdividing [i.e., redistributing] property." Redistribution, he concludes, "is a political measure, and a practicable one."

Jefferson, limited as he was by his essentially agrarian vision of America, naturally thought of redistribution primarily as an issue of land reform. While he favored progressive taxation and state-provided primary education to all as means toward alleviating inequality, he looked above all to extending the independence that came with land ownership as the real solution. The cure for inequality would thus be to give everyone who wished it access to an independent livelihood by having the state guarantee them land, as he proposed as early as 1776 in his draft of Virginia's state constitution. This grant would not only ensure a living, but in so doing would politically empower the recipients, consistent with his strong belief that only the economically independent could possibly "enjoy the personal independence required to exercise the rights of citizenship" (Rakove, 2010: 305). In this fashion, the basic class division in society – between those who do and do not own property – would evaporate, leaving an egalitarian, and even democratic, society.

We may leave Jefferson with two closely related observations stressed most famously by Gary Wills (1978). First, Jefferson consciously and purposely neglected to include the right to property in his list of inalienable rights. The substitution of "the pursuit of happiness" for "estates" in Locke's enumeration of our fundamental rights reflected the fact that Jefferson understood the right to property, as I have suggested previously, as contingent, given that it was predicated upon the social good and was thus only a form of social convention. Property for Jefferson was thus not a foundational or "inalienable" right worthy of the special protections accorded it by Madison and the Federalists. Further, Wills vigorously maintains – as had Arthur Schlesinger (1964) – that the emphasis sometimes placed on the word *pursuit* in the language of the Declaration is a modern ideological construction which obscures Jefferson's meaning. Gibson (2006: 125–6) nicely summarizes the argument: "Jefferson was arguing not merely that Americans have the natural right to strive for happiness. Instead he was emphatically maintaining that Americans had a natural right to the practice of happiness and that it was the government's duty to provide it." Although happiness is not, of course, literally a commodity that the state can provide by the post, government can see to the material and social conditions that promote happiness, such that it remains possible for Jefferson to conceive of happiness, as Wills notes (1978: 148), as something "susceptible of numbered measurement and distribution."

Turning from Jefferson to Paine, we find not only a more dramatic break with conventional thought about property rights within the Lockean social contract theory tradition (for an insightful discussion, see Zuckert, forthcoming), but also a more informed and prescient understanding of economics. Indeed, Paine provides what is the first major, realistic vision for how the state could provide and distribute happiness in the way Jefferson imagined. His basic proposal is both simple and sublime: that we accept a mercantile and industrial market economy – the free market and free trade – as the basis of economic life, but we view it to be the responsibility of the state, as an agent of the citizens it purports to represent, to use its power to tax, spend, and regulate so as to supplement, manage, and otherwise improve market outcomes in ways that provide citizens with greater health, happiness, and human dignity. We thus see in Paine the first systematically articulated and widely read defense of the perspective that would culminate in the idea of the welfare state, and thus by extension, social democracy.

It is difficult to overstate either the importance or the popularity of Paine's work. His *Common Sense*, *The Rights of Man*, and *The Age of Reason* are the three best-selling books of the eighteenth century. As the title of *Common Sense* suggests, it was an effort at persuasion aimed at the ordinary person through the appeal of what Paine maintained was nothing more than mere common sense. It did indeed reflect the shared, or common, view of the Founders regardless of faction. Even Adams would commend it, though in his typical curmudgeonly fashion, he felt obliged to complain that Paine was not only too "democratical" in tone, but was also in the end merely repeating the same arguments he, Adams, had long been making, to far less acclaim. It is the former shortcoming, though, that eventually would cause Adams and other Federalists (including Washington) to denounce Paine as too radical. The reason is easy to see: in all his work, and in *The Rights of Man* in particular, Paine provides a truly revolutionary vision of politics in which securing the interests of the demos emerges as the signature purpose of the state.

The contrasts to Madison are obvious. While Madison and the Federalists were adamantly opposed to the idea of democracy, understood as an egalitarian society in which the demos ruled, Paine was its ardent proponent. He agreed with Madison that the Athenian model was infeasible because of questions of scale, but he viewed this as only a practical problem, an "inconvenience." As Paine put it, we should look to the "original simple democracy" of Athens as our source for "the true data" about how government should be constituted, and thus be able to "ingraft" representation upon democratic principles, so as to produce a feasible, modern incarnation of the spirit of Athens. Madison, by contrast, viewed this kind of democracy as a positive evil to be avoided, and looked to representation (to say nothing of limiting the franchise as much as possible to property owners) as a means toward its subversion. More fundamentally, Madison has as a first principle the notion that the state must respect the right of the wealthy to be secure in their property, whereas Paine believes that this right must be interpreted in light of its effects on those who lack property. Thus, says Paine, government "ought to have no other object than to protect the *general* happiness" (emphasis in original). This is the heart of their disagreement, and the ultimate basis for the differences between the Right and the Left that exist today: Do we view the state as having an obligation more to protect private wealth (or, in the lexicon of the Right, "liberty") or to provide for the "general happiness"? As there are principled reasons for honorable and sincere men and women to disagree on that question, they do today as much as they did in 1787.

As an ideological partisan, Paine provided the structure of what would evolve over time into the modern program of social democracy. Thus, in the *Rights of Man* and later in *Agrarian Justice*, he argues for what subsequent scholars would call a "social wage," meaning a basic level of income (or similar benefits, such as housing or health care) provided by society (through the apparatus of the state) for those who are incapable of providing for themselves through no fault of their own. Thus, those either unable to work, because of illness, injury, or age, or unable to find employment simply because of the absence of jobs in hard times, are to have their welfare ensured by the government that they have themselves "instituted" to protect them via policies that look to their "Safety and Happiness."

In making this argument, Paine was merely extending the logic of the social contract tradition, as Foner (1976: 250) makes clear: having surrendered a portion of their natural rights for the sake of a social compact that allows the accumulation of wealth through social relationships rather than labor, the ordinary citizen may morally demand that the economy so formed be regulated in the public good, with a portion of the wealth it generates redistributed according to human needs.

With this foundation, Paine explicitly calls for the establishment of what we today label the welfare state:

There should be "annuities" (i.e., pensions) "for all poor persons over fifty years of age," anticipating the idea of social security benefits for retirees. Similarly, "widows" faced with the prospect of caring for themselves and their children alone would also receive such payments, pursuant with what would become survivor benefits.

The state should provide "donations" of money at the birth of every child, the equivalent of the contemporary "family allowances" common in Western Europe that are devoted to preventing childhood poverty and otherwise strengthening families from economic stress.

The government should provide free education to all.

The state should pursue a policy of full employment (being required to ensure "employment at all times") through macroeconomic management and, when necessary, the direct provision of jobs through public works. In this way, Paine was calling for the recognition of a de facto right to employment – and, thus, presumably compensation in the form of unemployment benefits should employment not be available. We have thus the proposition that one has a right to a livelihood, i.e., a job, and when jobs are not available, a guaranteed minimum income. This is equivalent to what contemporary scholars of the welfare state conceive of as "decommodification," an idea that will receive much attention in the chapters that follow.

All the aforementioned governmental activities should be funded through "a progressive tax."

In sum, Paine argues for charging the state with providing for the aged, the sick, and the unemployed; for subsidizing the cost of raising children through both cash payments to parents and the provision of free education; for managing and regulating the economy so as to maximize employment (and thus, in theory, driving up average wages and living standards to the maximum the economy can support); and for providing the funding for all these exceedingly costly endeavors by taxing the affluent. As is apparent, these proposals are all violations of market principles, attempting as they do to substitute human need, fairness, and the collective good for the "natural" outcomes that the market is argued to produce. Put in the terms of the debate as articulated in *Federalist 10*, we have nothing less than exactly the attack on the sanctity of wealth that Madison feared – the very epitome of the "wicked and improper" scheming of the demos to redistribute the wealth of others that so animated his prose.

Before concluding our discussion of Paine, it is worth observing that he was hardly indifferent to the rights of property, agreeing with Madison and Locke that one did have a right to security in one's property. Indeed, Paine's general view of the market economy was much like that of Adam Smith, whom Paine admired. Like Smith, he was a strong advocate of the market, precisely because he believed in its potential to improve the human condition. In the *Rights of Man*, Paine observes, amid long passages extolling the virtues of free trade, that "In all my publications . . . I have been an advocate of commerce, because I am a friend to its effects." His program is thus not one of destroying either the market or the wealth that it creates. He does not dispute the necessity and even the justice of a certain level of inequality, and he certainly does not begrudge the wealthy for being so, in the way some of his more radical contemporaries (such as the French proto-communist Babeuf) did. Paine wishes instead only to recognize that there are other rights in addition to property, ones that a representative government must also recognize and support. His agenda then is not to destroy the market system, or to ruthlessly appropriate the wealth of others, but only to intervene in it at the margins, to reduce the poverty and human suffering that make a rewarding or satisfying life impossible.

Thus, Paine, unlike Madison or contemporary conservatives, would anticipate modern progressives like Franklin Delano Roosevelt in believing that government has an inherent responsibility for providing "freedom from want." As Paine puts it, the mere existence of poverty suggests that "something must be wrong in the system of government." This perspective, readily apparent in the *Rights of Man*, is elaborated in his *Agrarian Justice*. He argues that holding private property, even the ownership of land, is both natural and just. At the same time, he maintains it is equally natural and just that those possessing property must assist in providing for those without it. He thus suggests a basic social compact in which society recognizes and protects the right to own and accumulate, and expects in return that those profiting from this arrangement share some portion of their gains with those who might be argued to lose by it. In simple class terms, the wealthy offer compensation to those their possession of wealth disadvantages. Owners, whether of land or of more portable forms of capital, thus pay a de facto tax to those they are denying ownership rights to by the very fact of owning themselves.

Paine thus can be interpreted as favoring the position, associated with Rawls (1970), that inequality is ethically acceptable and often commendable, but only when its existence contributes to the greater good. The mechanism by which the social agreement to inequality is to be accomplished is, of course, redistribution of some of the gains of inequality, so to speak, to those who otherwise suffer. This could be accomplished through what today we would call transfer payments, paid for via progressive taxation. In this way, the wealthy would subsidize the less affluent in return for the latter's acquiescence in a system – capitalism – that *otherwise* would be contrary to their interests. Put differently, a capital owning class would (happily) pay for the maintenance of the system of capitalism, and with it their individual fortunes, by providing a modest portion of the income they realize on their fortunes to the less privileged. Property and thus inequality are to be secured by guaranteeing a minimum income to those who inequality may harm.

Paine also makes the argument, which Madison did not feel obliged to entertain, that this approach would prove advantageous to the rich as well as the poor. This is, again, in part because he proposes only to limit the privileges of the wealthy, not to confiscate their fortunes or to inhibit the institutions of business that allow them to use that wealth to create more wealth, but even more so because he believes that curing poverty will allow for greater commonality of interests between classes. The "discontent" of the poor, he believed, "will be taken away" through these means, with two profound results. First, the social pathologies that result from mass poverty and privation, such as crime, will be dramatically lessened, which not only benefits everyone directly (all have an interest in public safety), but also because social resources used to combat crime and to imprison (or execute) its perpetrators can be shifted to more productive uses or returned to the population through lower taxes. Second, reminiscent of the view more cynically associated with Bismarck, is the contention, noted earlier, that some redistribution will in fact make the wealthy more rather than less secure in their wealth, given that the welfare state Paine proposes will reduce hostility and anger toward the affluent – "all riots and tumults will cease" – as will demands for a fundamental change in capitalism itself.

Paine, then, is proposing for virtually the first time in history a hypothesis that will occupy us throughout the rest of this study, just as it has occupied political thought and action over centuries: the proposition that the welfare state, and by implication the entire left-liberal approach to government that hopes to improve the human lot through government intervention in the market, is, contra Madison, neither "wicked" nor "improper," but instead is the only way to build a just and equitable society that best allows individuals to pursue happiness. Critically, this is not merely the belief that redistribution will benefit the have-nots with only marginal cost to the better-off but the hope that political interventions in defense of individuals against the market will improve the lives of everyone, rich and poor alike. In the end, it is this question more than any other that animates political conflict in the modern world: whether to protect the market against politics or to make the market subject to politics – which is to say, subject to democracy.

A REVOLUTION DEFERRED

The year 1776 saw not only *Common Sense* and the Declaration of Independence, each devoted to establishing the principle of popular sovereignty as the basis of political life, but also the publication of Smith's watershed

The Wealth of Nations, which strove to institutionalize the practices and ideals of the market as the foundation of economic life and thought. Each would become a sacred text, appealed to and mythologized to the present day. Paine's *The Rights of Man* represents another and still bitterly contested intellectual revolution in its suggestion that the new democratic principles be extended to the emergent market system itself. It so alarmed the establishment in Britain that the book was banned and its author indicted (and convicted in absentia) for sedition merely for expressing such ideas. Political parties of the Left and the Right carry on the debate over democratic intrusion into the market to this day.

It is all the more remarkable that although Paine and his contemporaries lived and wrote during the early adolescence of capitalism, their political differences set the stage for the contemporary politics of Left and Right – terms which themselves famously derive from the seating of the different factions on the floor of the French National Assembly of 1789. We see thus that the basic fault line in the system of capitalist democracy was present from its birth in the form of an inescapable contradiction between the idea of a free market, composed of free individuals making free decisions about their own private lives without oppressive governmental intrusion, and the idea of "popular government" in which one of the explicit purposes of the state is to protect the right to "pursue happiness" and thus to further "the greatest good for the greatest number." It is to a closer examination of this inherent tension in market democracy that we now turn.

2

Market Democracy

The prior chapter traced the historical evolution of the idea that the ordinary person has a political right to the "pursuit of happiness," such that representative governments, which are instituted precisely to protect that right, are inevitably charged with the task of seeing to "the greatest happiness for the greatest number," even by those who believe that this charge is best served by leaving the task to the market. This basic understanding of happiness and of the role of the state in fostering the conditions necessary for it was seen to be the product of a particular sociopolitical context that is conventionally understood, in today's lexicon, as market democracy. Having provided the structural conditions under which the question of how to maximize human happiness emerges as the central question of politics – that is, having defined the problem – market democracy also supplies the two strategies available for solving it: either (a) resisting popular demands for redistributive and regulatory policies on the hope that a relatively unrestrained market will actually best promote happiness or (b) consciously attempting to use the power of the state to improve human well-being by infusing principles of equity and justice into market outcomes through political means.

As students rather than practitioners of politics, we have the liberty of approaching this situation from an abstract and purely theoretical point of view. The present chapter thus develops a model of capitalist democracy, to illustrate the nature and logic of political competition over the production and distribution of human well-being within the context of the market society. I begin by considering how the essential feature of the market system – the commodification of labor – naturally produces, first, an inevitable division of society into social classes that the institution logically requires, followed by a liberal democratic political order that emerges to protect commodification (and resulting class division) as the market requires, and, subsequently, a pattern of political competition based upon class interests. As we shall see, normal politics within market societies naturally comes to be patterned upon the traditional Left versus Right dimension that was already apparent at the time of the

American Founding and the French Revolution. At its core, this debate is over commodification itself, but finds tangible expression in three particular domains: the ability of workers to organize labor unions (and, ultimately, political parties), the size or generosity of the welfare state, and the degree of political control or regulation of the economy in general and the labor market in particular.

CIVILIZATION, SURPLUS, AND SOCIAL CLASS

Anthropologists generally conceive of all civilizations, from the first incarnations in Mesopotamia, the Indus Valley, and Egypt to the present, as having among their defining characteristics a mechanism that allows an elite segment of society to expropriate from the productive majority a portion of the surplus wealth created by that group's labor, with surplus conceived of simply as the difference between the actual level of economic production and the amount required for the subsistence of the workforce. Thus, in Pharaohic Egypt, as much as the feudal society of Western Europe, a main function of the state was the collection of surplus, in the form of rents or taxes from agriculturists and artisans. The wealth so extracted from the population provided for the pharaoh or king, along with his or her expanding circles of subordinate nobles, households, attendants, bureaucrats, and soldiers. The ability of a pharaoh or king to appropriate the goods produced by the population was made possible by the establishment of a monopoly of force, itself paid for by extraction, which made resistance irrational and ineffective.

The process was made more efficient still, as in these examples, by supplementing coercion with a religion or an equivalent mass ideology that justified and rationalized the collection of surplus, to manufacture something approaching consent to the established order. We thus see the pharaoh claiming to be a god and the medieval king maintaining that he is God's earthly lieutenant. Each was, in turn, served by a subsidiary clerical class, itself provided for by surplus (as in obligatory tithes to the church), courtesy of the political authority. From a political perspective, the official clergy functioned to maintain and enforce the spiritual or intellectual legitimacy of the system by enforcing and maintaining the patterns of thought and belief consistent with the system of exploitation. This can be most readily seen in the familiar structure of the *ancien regime* in France, wherein the population was divided into three "estates": the clergy, who were responsible for inculcating values consistent with obedience to authority in general (and acquiescence to the appropriation of surplus in particular) in the name of a divine order; the nobility, who provided the monopoly of force that made extraction possible; and a "third estate" of ordinary persons actually laboring.[1]

---

[1] Nobility and clergy might sometimes find themselves in conflict, but they must also recognize their shared interest in maintaining the system of privilege that sustained them. One of capitalism's more interesting features is the rise of a single dominant commercial class that not only indirectly

It is in this sense that Jared Diamond summarizes accepted anthropological theory in his Pulitzer Prize–winning *Guns, Germs, and Steel* (1999) by labeling all known human civilizations throughout history as "kleptocracies" – literally, rule by thieves. The rationale for the term is readily apparent: the great mass of ordinary citizens labor and produce, while a minority lives off that labor. The dominant classes use their position of authority to appropriate, i.e., to purloin, a portion of what commoners produce. To be sure, this extraction of surplus may often have decidedly positive social consequences. One need think only of the enormous physical infrastructure of roads, bridges, aqueducts, granaries, and other public works created by the Roman Empire, to say nothing of the establishment of peace and something at least approaching the rule of law within its borders, to see the indisputable good to which surplus extracted by a central authority can be put. For this reason, civilization itself is frequently defined in terms of the very existence of a system of authority capable of efficiently and regularly collecting surplus. It is only through authoritatively extracting surplus, which we can conceive of as a kind of enforced saving (though, of course, of the value created by other people's labor), that makes it possible for the owners of the surplus to "spend" it on projects, ranging from roads to the Pyramids, that tillers of the soil or urban artisans could never have conceived or produced. Appropriately spent, surplus also gives rise to the complex social orders that produce medicine, science, art, and engineering, as the privileged classes find themselves capable of employing individuals (who would otherwise devote their lives to subsistence labor) to provide these luxuries.

Capitalist democracy represents the dominant variant of kleptocracy in the contemporary Western world. As we shall see, part of its genius is fostering a ruling ideology that deflects attention away from its basic organizing principle, such that the extraction of surplus is less immediately visible than in past kleptocracies. This is a functional aspect of the system, compensating for other features, such as the necessity of a literate and broadly educated workforce, which foster a rational-skeptical approach to human knowledge that might otherwise draw attention to the exploitative nature of the system. We thus begin our appraisal of capitalist democracy with an assessment of the method by which surplus is created and extracted within it.

For the sake of analytical clarity, let us assume that there are two classes of people, which for convenience we classify as owners (of capital) and workers. Owners possess the productive resources of society – land, factories, banks,

controls the state (because it maintains control over surplus extraction), but which also disposes of the church as a competitor, first by destroying its ability to gather surplus through obligatory tithing and then by absorbing the traditional social-control functions of the clergy either directly (e.g., by "manufacturing consent" via its ownership of the media) or indirectly (e.g., by absorbing into the state, which the capital owning class again dominates by virtue of its ownership and control of the economy, other traditional functions of the church, such as education, regulation of marriage/divorce, and the provision of help to the needy). Capital, then, emerges as a more hegemonic force than nobility or clergy ever achieved.

money, etc. – and thus are able to live off the income that ownership of these assets provide, while workers must earn a living by obtaining employment from the owners. Owners hire workers to extract surplus from them, that is, to profit from their labor. They do so, of course, through the manner suggested by both Adam Smith and David Ricardo: by systematically paying a wage that is less than the true value of the work performed, wherein the difference between value created and wage paid is surplus extracted (or, if one prefers, retained) by the employer.

It is telling to note that while Smith sometimes uses the word *surplus* as the anthropologist does, meaning production beyond the subsistence level of the workforce, he more commonly applies the label "surplus" to a more specific notion: the value that human labor creates when added to raw materials (or other means of production) after paying the laborer's wages. It is this surplus that the employer hires the worker to create: it provides the profits that motivate employment. To quote Smith (2007: 42), "The value which the workmen add to the material . . . resolves itself into two parts, of which the one pays their wages, the other the profits to the employer." Put starkly, but entirely consistently with Smith's (to say nothing of Marx's) understanding of capitalism, one class of persons lives on the labor of others by hiring them to produce goods and services for which they are paid less than the value they create.[2]

This is in no way an indictment of the market system, for it would be entirely irrational to employ people to work if one did not gain more from their work than the value of the wages one paid them. Owners offer workers a wage labor contract only with terms that require those employed to surrender a portion of the value their labor creates to the employer, since no rational agent would otherwise offer employment. Workers, who must find employment in order to provide a livelihood for themselves and their families, must accept such a contract. Although workers are at liberty to pick and choose among wage offers, and may find some more agreeable than others, all wage labor contracts are of necessity exploitative, for the reason noted. To be sure, the system may leave both worker and capitalist better off than they were – such, indeed, is presumed by the fact that both enter the wager labor contract freely – but this does not alter the fact that the contract must be exploitative.

This system is naturally a conflictive one, given that workers and owners are competing over the amount of surplus extracted by the employer versus that retained by the worker. Workers wish to minimize the amount going to the employer, thus maximizing their wages; owners naturally prefer the reverse. We see thus that class conflict is inherent and unavoidable, given the diametrically opposed interests of owners and workers over the distribution of surplus. Adam Smith (2007: 56) recognized this irreconcilable difference: "What are

---

[2] For an analysis of the shared understanding of the nature of the extraction of surplus in both the classical economic tradition, best represented by Smith and Ricardo, and in the critical Marxian tradition, see Garegnani (1984).

the common wages of labour, depends everywhere upon the contract usually made between those two parties, whose interests are by no means the same. The workmen desire to get as much, the masters to give as little, as possible."

It is, again, true that workers and owners need each other for employment and profit, respectively, but the asymmetry could not be greater. The worker needs employment, having no other resource to earn his or her living. The owner is by definition already wealthy, and is merely seeking to employ others so as to use his or her wealth to generate yet more wealth. The owner can agreeably pass a year, or perhaps a lifetime, without "hazarding" his or her capital by devoting it to the production of goods and services, whereas the worker depends for his or her survival on the *owner's* decision to dissolve capital into production. It is the worker, clearly, who depends on the employer.[3]

The naturally exploitative nature of wage or salary labor in capitalism is partially obscured by two important distinctions between it and precapitalist modes of production. In the latter, most persons, as peasants, serfs, or slaves, worked under compulsion to a single lord, so that they were neither free to seek "employment" elsewhere (and thus to negotiate wages and working conditions) nor free to refuse work. By contrast, wage labor is at least nominally a choice. One is never compelled by coercion to work for anyone she does not chose to, under terms and conditions freely agreed on. Similarly, the worker does not face the lash or the gallows as discipline for inadequate industriousness, and has recourse to law to ensure that all aspects of the wage-labor contract are honored. These are not small points, as they surely represent an enormous advance in the liberty and well-being of the modern worker. Although that point cannot be emphasized too strongly, it is equally necessary to stress that the conflictual nature of the process remains: surplus continues to be extracted from the labor of others just as under a pharaoh, an emperor, or a king.

It is similarly true that under capitalism, the wage laborer almost certainly has a higher standard of living than his equivalent in prior epochs, reflecting the fact that both the absolute level of the retained wages, and, perhaps, the relative portion of the surplus they keep vis-à-vis their employer, are both higher than the feudal serfs or the eighteenth-century peasants would have received. In this sense, capitalism, as even Marx was frequently at pains to observe, is certainly an advance relative to prior modes of production. One need not deny these (and many other) commendable features of capitalism to note that wage labor remains a method of extracting surplus, in which workers create wealth of which they receive only a portion, just as has been the case in all prior economic systems. The market economy remains a kleptocracy.

What is unique to capitalism is that wage labor becomes for the first time in history the principal means of gathering surplus (for a discussion, see Heilbroner, 1985). This in turn became possible only when the bulk of the

---

[3] In Adam Smith's summary (2007: 57) "Many workman could not subsist a week, few could subsist a month, and scarce any a year without employment. In the long run the workman may be as necessary to his master as his master is to him, but the necessity is not so immediate."

population found themselves dependent upon others to provide them employment. Put another way, the general nonslave population, for the first time, does not have access to a kind of independent livelihood – as even serfs and peasants traditionally did through their right to work the land, however extortionate their landlords rents might be – but instead must depend on another class, which owns "the means of production" (land, factories, capital more generally), to offer employment. This, in turn, was accomplished by two basic processes, one purposely calculated to "reduce" citizens to the status of wage laborers, the other a consequence of economic development. The first is the familiar history of the elimination of the collective right to work land, most readily seen in the Enclosure Movement in Great Britain, which drove armies of dispossessed agriculturalists into cities seeking industrial employment.[4] The other is the ever-increasing technological innovations and economies of scale that make the option of self-employment (as in the traditional artisan who owns his or her own shop) effectively impossible for all but the tiniest portion of the population.[5] These developments are elements of what Polanyi (1944) aptly calls *The Great Transformation* in which the "market society" emerges as a "specific [kind of] civilization."

It is conventional to think of such a world, in which the labor force consists almost entirely of wage and salary workers dependent upon others for the employment that is their livelihood, as one characterized by the "commodification of labor." The phrase is designed to illustrate the fact that people's ability to work – which is to say, their human capacity for intelligence, creativity, imagination, and judgment that separates them from the machines they manipulate – is something that is bought and sold in the market like any other commodity. Implicit in this idea is the notion that individuals must, of necessity, sell their capacity to work, referred to by economists as their "labor power," in order to survive. Given the intimate connection always assumed between one's self and the work that one does, hour upon hour, day after day, coupled with the fact that what is at stake is one's ability to provide for oneself and one's family, it is typical to take the further step and simply think in terms of people themselves being "commodified," i.e., being themselves turned into commodities. This tradition, rather than being an invention of Marx or other critics of markets, originates in Adam Smith, who, in a typical passage

---

4 Enclosure is the historical label given to the process by which land that had been traditionally open to the community was converted to private ownership and use. Under enclosure, communal land is fenced (*enclosed*) or otherwise deeded to private owners to the exclusion of all others. Effectively, enclosure deprived families of the right to raise crops or graze animals, and thus earn their living, so that they were compelled into wage labor in the nascent industrial economy. It also, of course, served as a means by which landlords accumulated capital.

5 When even doctors, lawyers, accountants, and other professionals generally find it necessary, as they do, to work in firms in which they are employees rather than partners, it takes no great insight to see that the practical barriers to self-employment for artisans and the unskilled are sufficiently prohibitive to make this option infeasible for more than a trivial portion of the population in any industrialized nation.

from *The Wealth of Nations*, reminds the reader that "the demand for men" is precisely "like that for any other commodity" (2007: 67).[6] Indeed, this idea remains conventional in neo-classical economics.[7]

Although there are certainly advantages to the working class that result from the institution of free wage labor, it also cannot be denied that reducing people to commodities also imposes costs on them. This is apparent in two obvious fashions. The first is that people's incomes, and indeed their life chances more generally, become subject to market forces that are beyond their control. Individuals face not only hardship when the market for the sale of their labor power is weak, manifesting itself in the form of unemployment or reduced wages and hours, but they are also subject to the persistent insecurity that comes with being at the mercy of the market. In Charles Lindblom's (1977: 82) words "a pertinent objection to markets is that they foist insecurities upon the population" that become "all the more a problem when one's livelihood is what is at stake." So long as individuals depend for their financial survival on the sale of their labor power as a commodity, they are subject to the range of market forces that may cause disruptions in the market for any other commodity, such as business cycles, technological innovations, and, increasingly, the pressures of globalization. In countries such as the United States, where health care and pensions are tied to employment, the prospect of losing those benefits is added to the insecurity over losing one's income.[8] It is for this reason that many analysts of capitalism, while granting its commendable qualities, nonetheless liken the position of wage and salary earners to that of being imprisoned by the market. As Gøsta Esping-Andersen (1990: 36) memorably puts it, consciously echoing the similar usage by (among many others) Polanyi (1944) and Lindblom (1977), "the market becomes to the worker a prison in which it is imperative to behave as a commodity in order to survive."[9]

---

[6] Marx's point (his famous "commodity fetishism") is that under capitalism it only *appears* (i.e., we are ideologically encouraged to believe) that the market for labor is like that for other commodities when in fact it is not (which serves to "mask" the existence of the conditions by which the extraction of surplus are made possible).

[7] That the individual worker is an ordinary commodity is even more transparently and enthusiastically embraced by contemporary business culture, as witnessed by an entire industry of career coaching predicated upon precisely this idea. Entirely typical of the hundreds of popular and business-professional books devoted to this theme is the popular volume tellingly titled *You, Inc.: The Art of Selling Yourself* (Beckwith and Beckwith, 2007), which repeatedly reminds the reader that "the most critical thing you sell is literally yourself."

[8] These concerns are, of course, most painfully felt toward the bottom and middle of the income distribution, but they hardly disappear as one enters the upper-middle class. As Barbara Ehrenreich (1990) reminds us, a higher income and greater social status may, if anything, contribute to yet greater anxiety, because the precariousness of that status is more keenly felt, as is the realization that one has farther to fall.

[9] That the individual, to be a free citizen rather than a subject, must not be in the position in which wage labor is the only recourse for survival is a common theme in democratic thought. Rousseau, for instance, famously denounces the prospect of so much inequality in society that wage labor could become the only feasible option, suggesting the importance of ensuring that "none [be] poor enough to be forced to sell himself" (*The Social Contract*, Book II, chap. 11).

Like all prisons, this one is characterized by conflict, wherein the buyer and the seller of labor power have the same divergence of interests as the buyers and the sellers of any commodity do: one's gain is the other's loss. Continuing the analogy of buyers and sellers, both may benefit in the long run from a more vibrant economy in which, say, buyers pay less and thus buy more, leaving both better off than they might have been before, but on any given transaction in the market (such as an exchange of labor for wages), buyers retain an interest in paying a price lower than sellers would prefer. Thus, even granting that the market may very well benefit all *in the long run*, the employer and the employed are by logical necessity in a perpetual struggle in the here and now over wages – or, more precisely, over the distribution of the surplus the worker creates. Given that we live only in the here and now, rational actors faced with trade-offs between a tangible present and near future and some undefined "long term" that may span many generations are likely to follow John Maynard Keynes's judgment that "in the long run, we are all dead," and thus maintain the focus on short-term gain that is indeed typical of market participants. To the extent the two classes do have a commonality of interest that is more immediate, it is typically one in which the workers find it in their interest that the corporation that employs them prospers, in that continued employment depends on it.[10]

LIBERAL DEMOCRACY AND THE MARKET SOCIETY

If the market can be fairly compared to a prison in one sense, it may just as easily be conceived of as an emancipator in another, in that the emergence of

As Macpherson (1977: 17) notes, this is transparently "not a reference to slavery" but rather a call for "a prohibition of the purchase and sale of free wage labour." The phrasing is a deliberate attempt to equate one's labor with oneself, such that when one sells their labor they are themselves the commodity being sold. Both Thomas Jefferson and Abraham Lincoln expressed the same disquiet with wage labor, because they too equated it with lack of independence: those who must of necessity work *for others* (meaning, for the profit and gain of others) have been reduced to the means to other people's ends.

[10] It may be worth observing that up to this point, Smith and Marx share a very similar view of the logic, advantages, and costs of capitalism. Where they finally diverge it is over a theoretical point that, happily, is beyond our concerns, and thus, one we need neither adjudicate nor examine in detail. This is over the structural difference between the market for labor and the market for everything else. Smith clearly recognizes that employers utilize their superior position to extract surplus from workers who agree to such terms only out of necessity, and thus recognizes, as Marx does, that profits originate in appropriating a share of the value created by workers. For Smith, the issue is only whether, as he acknowledged was frequently the case, the share appropriated is unfairly high, a situation he believed could be cured by destroying artificial restraints on the labor market that tended to benefit employers; eliminating such would create a genuine free market in labor power, which would ensure that its price would be fairly set, like any other commodity. Marx argues instead that the market for labor power is fundamentally different, reflecting as it does the structurally dominant position of capital, which manifests itself in a difference which exists only for labor power and no other commodity: that its use-value (to capitalists purchasing it) is of necessity greater than its exchange-value (the wages paid to workers). Its price could thus never be "fairly" set.

capitalism is widely agreed to be the central motivating force in the political institutionalization of the idea of natural rights of the sort enumerated in the Declaration of Independence, and the notion that representative governments exist to protect such rights. Indeed, the intimate connections among capitalism, representative government, and classical liberalism are not accidental, as conservative defenders of capitalism are right to stress. Market mechanisms, once established as the basis of the economic production on which everything else in society ultimately depends, eventually extend their internal logic to the foundations of politics, creating both a type of state and an accompanying protective public ideology consistent with market imperatives.

Under the feudal system that capitalism replaced, the functionally equivalent ideology was one predicated upon the existence of officially recognized hierarchical social relationships, the revealed truth of the church, and the maintenance of a traditional, group-focused form of social organization. These elements were all incompatible with the market, which required instead a vision of society focused on individuals, who in turn pursue a rational self-interest of private material gain in their capacity as market participants. The new protective ideology of liberalism thus presumes society to be a collection of autonomous individuals who makes free choices, predicated on individual monetary profit and loss, and who are liberated from outdated religious or philosophical scruples that might interfere with the otherwise profitable transactions rationality might imply. In the phrase popularized by the English historian E. P. Thompson (1971), the precapitalist world contained elements of a "moral economy" in which economic activity was regulated by custom (and sometimes law) for what was believed to be the collective good, rather than personal gain. The most common example was the regulation of food prices, especially bread, such that the price could not fluctuate during shortages in response to supply and demand as other commodities might, on the presumption that to profit from human misfortune in such a fashion was immoral. These restrictions reflected traditional apprehensions about treating other people as the means to one's ends (e.g., usury), which were thought to have both deleterious consequences to one's self and to the community. The market society thus required a transformation of thought, converting what was for centuries thought of as the "deadly sin" of avarice into the virtues of prudence and good judgment that we associate with the rational pursuit of self-interest.

No one less than Adam Smith himself suggested that a market economy promotes this tendency, which he judged in his *Theory of Moral Sentiments* (2006: 164), to be "in the highest degree contemptible." Of course, Smith thought, on balance, as we in the modern world at least hope to be the case, that the costs of this transformation, as great as they might be, would be outweighed by the benefits, that is, the material advancement in the human condition that capitalism made possible would more than compensate for what he clearly recognized as its moral costs. Thus, a free market in bread might indeed involve moral costs for society, but in the end, he thought, market incentives would provide a more consistently supplied, and fairly priced, product, which would serve both producer and consumer better than well-intentioned but foolish efforts at price-fixing.

An archetype of this New Market Man, to take a familiar literary example, is the cold and miserly Ebenezer Scrooge, whose obsession with the calculus of gain and loss at the expense of all human feeling is only an exaggerated, cartoonish version of the real patterns of thought that capitalism tends not only to engender but to glorify. Of course, the incentives to accept market values apply equally to worker and employer, in that both are market participants, despite their divergent interests. If Scrooge's unfortunate clerk Bob Cratchit is a more likeable character, he just as transparently and necessarily measures out his life in the same calculating, self-interested response to the market as his employer. As a pair, they exemplify, at the characteristically insightful level of caricature, a microcosm of market forces, as well as market relations.[11]

The modes of thought and behavior consistent with the new market principles, as against the traditional "moral economy," are of course associated with Smith and the French Physiocrats, who, among many others, successfully promulgated the ideologically convenient (if, nonetheless, possibly quite true) view that the world as a whole is actually better served by individuals pursuing their own self interest. This is of course most readily seen in Smith's "invisible hand," which suggested not merely that individuals pursuing their own self-interest are also serving the interest of the community, but that the community's interest is *best* served in this way: "by pursuing his own interest, he frequently promotes that of the society more effectually than when he intends to promote it" (2007: 349). As Robert Heilbroner (1985: 114–15) nicely summarizes, "Now any last lingering doubts about greed and rapacity . . . are removed by the demonstration that the happiness of all can be achieved – in fact, can *only* be achieved – by the self-regarding pursuit of happiness of each" (emphasis in original).

This, then, is the new ideology – liberalism – at its maturity: society is composed of nominally equal individuals, who enjoy the right to pursue in easy conscience their own material self-interest, which they do with dispassionate rationality. Thus, rather than "a society based on custom, on status, and on authoritarian allocation of work and rewards [as in feudalism]," we find instead "a [market] society based on individual mobility, on contract, and on impersonal market allocation of work and rewards in response to individual choices" (Macpherson, 1966: 7).

This world clearly requires a different type of government than the arbitrary rule of a feudal nobility. Nobles were answerable to no one but the king,

---

[11] To press this analogy farther than perhaps it should go, the question for social theorists is whether the amicable reconciliation between them by the book's end might be attainable by a method more feasible than visitations from the other world, and whether, in any event, a kinder, gentler Scrooge truly would be any less of a class antagonist to Cratchit. One can only presume that their relationship remains adversarial, given that Cratchit is employed by Scrooge entirely because Scrooge is able to turn a profit for himself from the work performed by Cratchit, and thus must rationally act to suppress Cratchit's wages and benefits.

who in turn answered only to God. Both would naturally be inclined, given the assumption of self-interest, to rule for themselves and, above all, in the maintenance of their economic and political privileges. They were consequently obstacles to both liberalism and the market. As power in society shifted toward the new class that controlled and owned the emerging capitalist economy, this group required a state that was responsible to them, not to God. They needed, in sum, a government whose function was to facilitate and protect the market – and thus their own private material and political interests.

The obvious solution was an elected government, or parliament, in which political power was held by individuals elected to limited terms and subject to removal at periodic intervals in which there was a choice between competing individuals or parties. This competition between elites would ensure their good behavior, in that those guilty of malfeasance or mismanagement could be readily, and efficiently, replaced through the electoral process. Of course, for such a system of responsible government to flourish, other ancillary liberties must also be established. Chief among these would be freedom of speech, and of the press, as these would be necessary to hold government accountable. Similarly, freedom of association is equally implied, as individuals would need to be free to form the political parties that would contest elections, as well as the interest groups and popular societies that would organize to give expression to their legitimate interests. The free competition for political power would thus depend upon individuals being at liberty to say what they like and to associate with whom they pleased, because they were secure in their person against arbitrary arrest (suggesting the principle of habeas corpus) and in their property against arbitrary seizure. So is born the liberal polity consisting of an elected government, subject to constitutional constraints that limit its power over the liberties of those who are now citizens, rather than subjects.

At its inception, this system was scarcely democratic, given that the status of citizenship was limited to the propertied, which was of course the class which the new system was designed to protect. Thus, in post-Revolutionary America, and even more so in the Britain of that time, the franchise was highly limited, and would remain so in both countries well into the twentieth century. Nonetheless, there was a logic to the market principles of equality and the legitimacy of pursuing one's self-interest that fostered democratic aspirations. The right to vote, and with it the more general rights of citizenship, became the immediate demand of those excluded. Thus, rather than attempt to radically alter or abolish the liberal order, outsiders agitated instead for inclusion, using the system's own internal values, including the right to organize and to speak, as their weapons. Although this battle was long fought, it did succeed because it was in the logic of the liberal order that it should. Thus, as groups organized for inclusion, there was, as Macpherson laconically comments (1966: 9) "no defensible ground for withholding the vote from them . . . So [thus] democracy came as a late addition to the competitive market society and the liberal state."

Once the structure of modern liberal democracy was established, it became another locus of the class conflict that is inherent in a capitalist economy.

This is inevitable in two respects. First, the state maintains a monopoly on the use of force, and otherwise provides the legal shell that surrounds society and the economy. It thus remains the ultimate authority, one above and beyond the employers to whom workers are mere commodities, and thus one that workers may hope to influence. Second, liberal ideology legitimates the worker's desire to receive better terms from employers, as this is merely the rational pursuit of self-interest. By legitimating this interest, the system also legitimates the organization of interest groups to press such demands collectively, beginning with labor unions and culminating in the organization of political parties that directly contest elections. We thus find what both mainstream (e.g., Lipset, 1960) and social democratic (e.g., Korpi, 1983) theorists conceive of modern democratic politics as a "democratic class struggle" in which workers and business, the rich and the poor, compete in the "marketplace" of politics.

But what, precisely, is the basis of such class conflict? As I discuss presently, the democratic class struggle is a second-order conflict over the institutional context in which the more immediate and fundamental struggle between classes over the distribution of surplus takes place. To simplify to the most elemental level, the democratic class struggle is over the nature, extent, and consequences of what we have seen to be the fundamental characteristic of capitalism itself: the commodification of labor. This manifests itself in three specific axes of conflict in which success is valued both as an end in itself and also as a means toward furthering class interests in the struggle for power. The remainder of the chapter is devoted to understanding these three areas of conflict over the permanent interests of labor and capital: the organization of workers into labor unions; the development of an expansive welfare state; and the creation of a public policy regime that recognizes the need to regulate economic activity in defense of the interests of workers, consumers, and citizens in general.

THE DEMOCRATIC CLASS STRUGGLE

The centrality of organized labor in capitalist democracies is easily understood, as it is the most immediate and obvious avenue by which the inherent economic conflict between classes is extended into democratic politics. To see how, let us return to the obvious fact that the great majority of the population in any industrial country are wage and salary workers, i.e., individuals who depend primarily on work (rather than on investments or other assets) for their livelihood and who are dependent upon others (by definition, the capital-owning class) to provide employment. This group, or class, includes anyone who, again, depends on earning an income through employment (rather than living off interest, dividends, rents, and so on). It thus includes not only the working and middle classes, but also many upper-middle-class professionals. We can thus conceive of the class of "wage and salary earners" or "workers" as including the vast majority of the population in all industrialized countries.

The business, or capital-owning class, representing the balance of the population, quite rationally offers the employment workers require only when it is to their advantage as investors to do so, such that workers face the perpetual uncertainty that comes with the knowledge that transient economic conditions can reduce the demand for their ability to labor, whose sale they depend upon for their economic survival. Even during times of relative prosperity, investors understandably seek to minimize the portion of the value created by workers actually paid to them, for the obvious reasons already discussed. Class struggle is, thus, first and foremost, over this fundamental divergence of interests.

Further, owners, by virtue of their ownership of the capital that allows and organizes the workplace, are used to setting not only wages, but equally, the conditions of work. The resulting situation, which economists dispassionately describe as the "command workplace," is, of course, one designed to maximize worker productivity, rather than to make work pleasant, enriching, or even safe, with concessions toward those goals made only when they foster productivity or are necessary inducements for attracting labor because of competition between owners in attracting quality workers. Again, an inescapable conflict of interest manifests itself between the investor, who wishes to use workers as a means to his or her own profits, and the workers themselves, who understandably are inclined to focus on their own well-being.

Both workers and employers wish to make an ally of the state in the immediate conflicts just described. Just as owners are clearly in a dominant position in their struggle with workers – the capitalist system as we have seen can exist precisely and only because of that power asymmetry – they also enjoy structural advantages in the struggle to control government. One is merely their wealth itself, which allows them to finance generously candidates and parties espousing ideologies friendly to their interests. Another, and vastly important, advantage flows from their very ownership of the economy, providing as it does the ability of capital to discipline government when it acts contrary to the interest of business. Lindblom (1977) characterizes this situation as the "privileged position of business," while other scholars describe it more transparently as the "structural dependency" of the state on capital. In simple terms, it means just this: a change in governmental policy toward the interests of workers will result in a worsening of the ability of business to make profits (i.e., to extract surplus from workers), such that individual investors, making perfectly reasonable calculations about their individual self-interest, remove capital from the economy, which precipitates recession, which in turn inflicts costs on the workers that reform was intended to protect, in the form of unemployment, reduced working hours, and lower wages. Given that citizens (being unable to hold investors accountable) naturally tend to hold the government, as the one authority that is accountable to them, to be responsible for the state of the economy, they react to faltering economic performance by withdrawing political support from the government, which must then either retreat from the public policies that troubled investors (so as to "restore confidence") or face the wrath of voters in the next election. Because this happens without any coordinated strategy, or even conscious intent, by the investment community, Lindblom refers to the phenomenon as the "automatic punishing mechanism," through which the owners of the market economy protect themselves. Having already witnessed how the market "becomes to the worker a prison in which it is necessary to behave as a commodity in order to survive" (Esping-Andersen 1990: 36), we find that, as Lindblom notes, the market also tends to "imprison public policy" through this automatic punishing mechanism.

Still, the fact that the position of business is "privileged" does not imply that it is unassailable or that it always prevails. Although capital must always remain dominant, because otherwise capitalism would by definition cease to exist, there are still a range of possible outcomes in the extent to which the interests of business subordinate those of workers, as Lindblom himself is quick to concede. This is also the conclusion, supported by much theoretical as well as empirical evidence, of the class mobilization (or "power resource") approach to theories of the state (e.g., Korpi, 1983). Without digressing into the details that make this model rather more theoretically intricate than Lindblom's intuitive "capital strike," this interpretation stresses the ability of the working class, broadly construed, to partially overcome the inherent privileges enjoyed by capital in the parliamentary process when workers mobilize *as a class*. In effect, the structural advantage of business vis-à-vis workers can be limited by the degree to which workers as a class successfully organize in that by organizing they increase their bargaining power in politics in much the way that organization into a union increases the position of a particular set of workers in their particular struggle with their employers (for an appealing summary, see Huber and Stephens, 2001: 337–45).

Labor organization affects the power relationship between workers and employers at both the level of the workplace and that of politics. The advantages of organization in the first are not difficult to discern. By forming unions that bargain collectively, workers change the entire dynamic of work. Through organization, they are typically able to negotiate higher wages and benefits; that is, they increase their share of surplus. Moreover, they modify the "command" nature of the workplace, in that their union contract provides both a guarantee against arbitrary dismissal (or other forms of discipline) and at least some say in the manner in which work is organized, pursuant with their interests in safety and relative enjoyment. Unions thus reduce some of the immediate deleterious consequences of commodification by providing workers greater material rewards and greater security, to say nothing of what they are likely to interpret as greater respect, in that their contracts recognize that they possess a right to a voice in the enterprise, not merely a right to a wage.

Organization also provides the basis for mobilization in the electoral and policy-making processes. Unions collect dues from their members, a portion of which is devoted to political action. These small contributions, when aggregated over large number of members, can amount to a substantial monetary resource, which acts as a counterweight to the money that business and the wealthy "invest" in the system. Unions are thus able to offer generous contributions to progressive candidates and parties, or, as in some of the social democratic and labor parties, to form a de facto party of their own. In either case, their husbanding of financial resources must unavoidably increase their political influence. This in turn may set in motion a virtuous circle: once enough workers are organized to guarantee their incorporation into a governing coalition, they may use their political power to alter the legal structures that govern organizing, to make organization easier, further increasing their numbers and, thus, their power. That is doubly so given that large labor movements may also be able to provide additional resources beyond money that are less readily provided by their ideological opponents.

One is a large potential "army" of voters, who can be relied on to support the party associated with the interests of workers at the ballot box. A closely related second is a large base of dedicated activists, who provide an ideal pool of campaign volunteers. In each case, an organized labor movement provides "power in numbers" as a balance to the financial power of business and the wealthy. Finally, and most importantly, a strong labor movement may provide an ideological or an intellectual alternative to the seemingly "natural" rules of the market and the relationship between worker and employer a pure market implies. Thus, in all these ways, organized labor has always been seen by its advocates as embodying "a broad moral authority as the advocate of society's non-rich" (Kuttner, 1986), standing not merely for the interests of particular workers organized in particular industries, but (at least when the labor movement is strong and encompassing) for the general interests of the ordinary worker or citizen. By representing "society's non-rich" whether organized or not (or, as in the case of the Nordic countries, actually organizing virtually the entire class of wage-salary earners from service workers to college professors), unions can be conceived of as nothing less than the political manifestation of the demos itself. Thus, as Margaret Levi (2003: 45) nicely summarizes it, organized labor is viewed by class theorists "as the most effective popular vehicle for achieving a democratic and equitable society."

For this reason, of course, following the conservative intellectual tradition given such articulate expression by Madison, organized workers – like organized citizens of any kind when they form or represent a majority – are castigated by their detractors with vitriol. The labor union is anathema to a Madisonian approach to politics precisely because the institution has the potential to become the most basic, fundamental, and potentially transformative of all possible "factions": that of the majority of relatively modest means, organized against the minority of the affluent. Like all factions, and especially all majority factions, organized labor is in this interpretation a palpable danger to the "permanent interests of the community" and thus a form of "tyranny." For the same reasons, contemporary progressives and leftists, following as they do in the tradition of Paine rather than Madison, view the labor union as a decidedly positive force with much potential to change the world in ways that might contribute to the goal "of making human life as satisfying as possible."

It is easy to see why. Unionized workers in the United States earn dramatically more than the nonorganized: 15 to 28 percent more than their nonunionized equivalents, depending on the employment sector (Kaplan, 2009), a range not atypical of other industrial economies. Economists also understand that higher wages and more generous benefits for the organized eventually translate into higher wages for other, nonorganized workers, given that once union density reaches a certain level (typically, 25 percent to 30 percent), wages and benefits in nonunion shops tend to raise toward the higher standard, because nonorganized and organized enterprises have to compete for the same workers. Unions thus contribute to a higher wage floor in the same way that minimum wage laws do. Strong unions, then, mean higher wages and benefits, not only for the organized but also for everyone.

Further, in the United States, as in the United Kingdom and much of Western Europe, the union movement was instrumental in the creation of many contextual features of the working world that we take for granted, such as the forty-hour week, prohibitions against child labor, the adoption of the aforementioned minimum wage, the creation of state agencies responsible for establishing and enforcing workplace safety rules – to say nothing of such staples of the welfare state as unemployment benefits, compensatory insurance for those injured or killed on the job, and (among many other things) old-age pensions. Collectively, these laws amount to a kind of general employment contract, in which everyone comes to be represented by the equivalent of a union contract via the law rather than by negotiation with employers.

Economist James Galbraith (quoted in Kaplan, 2009: 14) nicely summarizes the effects of unionization:

Historically, unionization basically created the middle class. First, by its direct effects on wages and benefits for unionized workers; second, by its indirect effects on the wages of workers who weren't unionized; and third, by the impact unions had on the creation of the social institutions that underpin the middle class, such as Social Security, Medicare, and Medicaid – the very structures of the New Deal and the Great Society.

The centrality of labor unions in capitalist democracy is clearly exemplified in the debate over the proposed Employee Free Choice Act in the United States. The central provision of the bill is to bring the laws covering organization in the United States closer to those that exist in Western Europe or even Canada, by allowing workers to gain union certification just by succeeding in obtaining a majority who formally express support for creating a bargaining unit. The expected result of the proposal, if enacted, is universally agreed to be a dramatic and rapid increase in the proportion of U.S. workers belonging to unions. When the prospects for passage early in the first years of the Obama administration seemed good, business groups led one of the most vociferous and aggressive lobbying campaigns of the last thirty years to stop it. As a representative of the American Chamber of Commerce explained, passage of the bill would be "Armageddon" for business.[12]

The stakes are threefold, following the pattern previously elucidated. First, the surge in organization would produce a substantial increase (at the expense of corporate profits) in wages, salaries, and benefits to workers, organized and otherwise, throughout the U.S. economy. Second, there would be a political shift, wherein the increased membership of organized labor would mean yet more political resources for unions to distribute, which would translate into greater financial (and activist) support for progressive candidates, and thus, greater systematic pressure on the Democratic Party to move toward the left. The combination of greater resources (and thus greater electoral prospects) for Democrats, coupled with a movement of the party farther away still from the preferences of Republicans, would be disaster for the GOP and the interests it represents, as Republican leaders have not been shy about noting. Finally, and perhaps most tellingly, at stake more than anything else is the relative power of workers vis-à-vis business in the rules and conditions of work, above and beyond concerns over salaries and benefits. Organized workers can force employers to make the workplace more accommodating (and thus certainly a less authoritarian, if also less purely "efficient" place) – and can then attempt to extend those standards to the economy in general by lobbying to incorporate such protections into laws covering all workers, as they have done so often in the past on other issues. It is this question of power that prompted the CEO of Walmart, the United States' (and, indeed, the world's) largest private employer, to tell financial analysts that his corporation would aggressively fight the Employee Free Choice Act because "We like driving the car, and we are not going to give the steering wheel to anyone but us" (quoted in Kaplan, 2009).

What unions do, in sum, is limit the extent to which humans are commodified. They do so directly, as we have seen, but they also influence the social order in ways that produce still greater decommodification through their influence on the two other fundamental arenas of political conflict in capitalist democracies: the generosity or size of the welfare state and the extent to which the state creates legal rules that limit the authority and discretion of business, to both protect the health and safety of workers and to foster, more generally, norms and practices consistent with human dignity and respect for the working person. I examine each presently.

---

[12] This is of course the same logic motivating recent assaults on the right to organize by Republican governors in Wisconsin, Indiana, Ohio, and other states. In the most dramatic of these efforts, Republicans in Wisconsin continually stress that their plan to eviscerate public sector unions would leave some residual right to bargain over wages alone, as if that were the main or only issue at stake. As the unions and their defenders are quick to point out, the right to organize is not only about wages – it is about the power that comes from organization for influencing the day-to-day operation of the workplace, to say nothing of the ability of workers to continue to act collectively within the political arena. The argument is thus over denying workers a power resource that affects both their immediate livelihoods and their ability to act politically.

THE WELFARE STATE

Aside from the right to organize itself, no issue separates the interests of capital and labor, employers and workers, as absolutely as does the existence and generosity of the welfare state. Conflict over a guaranteed minimum income for the aged, the sick, and those unable to find work is fundamental not only because the existence of such an institution profoundly affects the prospects of workers in their ambition to lead more secure lives, but also because it alters the balance of power between workers and owners in the conflict over the distribution of surplus (i.e., in the setting of wages and benefits), as well as in their second-order conflict over control of the state.

To understand why, we need merely return to the reality of commodification, such that in order to survive workers must of necessity sell their labor power to those who, through their control over the productive means of society, control access to a livelihood. Because of this dependency, workers agree to work, as we have seen, for wages or salaries that are systematically less than the value of the work they perform, with the difference retained by their employer in the form of profits. It is, of course, this very difference that makes employment rational, for a profit-making business could hardly be expected to employ workers out of charity. Adam Smith himself stresses this commonsensical proposition when he notes that a business hires workers only "in order to make a profit by their work" and that "he would have no interest to employ him, unless he was to share in the produce of his labour" (2007: 56).

It is equally apparent that rational workers agree to this transaction only because they must. To again quote Smith, who can hardly be accused of being hostile to the logic of capitalism (2007: 56):

> ... the greater part of the workmen stand in need of a master, to advance them the materials of their work, and their wages and maintenance, till it be completed. He [i.e., the "master" or employer] shares in the produce of their labour, or in the value which it adds to the materials upon which it is bestowed; and in this share consists his profit.

Thus, the worker depends upon the capitalist, who provides employment in return for a share of the value created by the worker. That the worker consents to having the value of his labor "shared" with the capitalist because he must (lacking as he does access to capital, or "stock") is obvious, since otherwise he could retain the full value of his work (2007: 56):

> It sometimes happens, indeed, that a single independent workman has stock sufficient both to purchase the materials of his work, and to maintain himself till it be completed. He is both master and workman, and enjoys the whole produce of his own labour, or the whole value which it adds to the materials upon which it is bestowed. It includes what are usually two distinct revenues, belonging to two distinct persons, the profits of stock [i.e. to capital], and the wages of labour.

This, then, is how capitalism thrives: workers would maintain the full value of their work if they had independent means of earning a livelihood, but given the absence of such access, they are compelled to accept a lesser reward. This is the source of power by which "in disputes with their workmen, masters must generally have the advantage" (Smith, 2007: 57). If workers were to possess either of the two advantages enjoyed by the owners of capital – direct access to the means of production or the independence that comes with the accumulated wealth that such ownership provides – the basis of power between employer and worker, and thus by definition the nature of capitalism itself, would be fundamentally altered.

The welfare state provides this change in dynamic by providing a semblance of independence to the worker. Suppose that the unemployed enjoy, as they generally do in even the minimalist U.S. welfare state, a guaranteed income for at least some months after being made redundant. Suppose, further, as is the case in virtually all other industrial democracies, that one has medical insurance not strictly tied to employment, so that job loss does not imply the loss of medical care. Such a worker is suddenly less dependent upon capital for employment, in that his or her immediate financial (or even physical) survival is not at stake. The worker has the liberty of declining employment at rates below what he or she deems fair, at least for some time. Through the welfare state, then, he or she is less commodified, which is to say, less dependent on persons and forces beyond his or her control.

This represents a seismic shift in the relative balance of power between labor and capital. The strength of capital, the ability to refuse would-be workers employment, has become of less immediate social consequence. In losing (some of) this power, capital in turn loses (some of) its ability to discipline and control the labor force. Consider, for instance, the consequences of unemployment insurance. First, our hypothetical worker need not accept just any job at any salary, with the probable consequence that he or she will eventually earn a salary higher than he or she otherwise might. This supports the general level of wages, to the benefit of all workers, and to the detriment of capital. Second, the tangible benefits the system provides to workers tend to draw them closer to the unions and political parties that champion such programs, increasing the electoral power base of labor. Finally, because workers are relatively secure in the face of unemployment – or, equally, the fear of such – there are fewer incentives for them to behave in competitive rather than cooperative ways with other workers. Labor unions thus become easier to form in the first place, and once created, have more solidarity; for example, workers are less compelled to abandon a strike out of financial duress, and are equally less driven by the need to accept the jobs offered by other companies attempting to break other striking workers.

In this way, the welfare state is not only a source of security for individual workers and their families, but once established is a source of power that labor can rely upon in its political struggle with capital. As Esping-Andersen (1990: 11) puts it, once the welfare state is introduced, "the balance of power [between classes] is fundamentally altered" given that a regime of social rights (such as unemployment insurance) "lessens the worker's dependence on the market and the employers, and thus turns into a potential power resource." This is because the welfare state "is a Trojan horse that can penetrate the frontier between capitalism and socialism." In this way, "de-commodification strengthens the worker and weakens the absolute authority of the employer. It is for exactly this reason that employers have always opposed de-commodification" (1990: 22).[13]

The arguments for and against decommodification as an agent of human happiness are discussed in detail in Chapter 3. The outline of the argument in favor should, though, already be readily apparent. Decommodification lessens the dependence of the wage or salary earners (who constitute a large superma-jority of citizens) on a capital-owning class that offers, and sets the terms of, employment. It thus increases the relative bargaining power of the individual worker (especially those represented by labor unions) over wages and working conditions. It provides security against the reality, or the fear, of unemploy-ment, and the potentially devastating consequences of that event on one's (and one's family's) well-being. The welfare state also has the potential for affect-ing social values and norms, as Rothstein (1998) reminds us, encouraging as it does greater interpersonal trust, solidarity, and social capital by removing some of the competitive pressures of the market. Finally, it provides a powerful resource for wage and salary earners, as a class, to use in their political struggle with capital, opening the prospect of enacting other public policies that may, in the view of the Left, further improve the quality of human life for the ordi-nary person. Chief among such policies are the expansion of political rights to include social rights, which ultimately involve the attempt to impose polit-ical, which is to say, democratic, regulation of economic activity in the public interest.

---

[13] It is worth noting that although capital certainly shares in the tax cost of social insurance programs, it should be apparent that it is not chiefly the tax burden that animates their hostility to the welfare state. In the United States, as in most countries, the bulk of the costs of such programs are actually paid for by workers themselves through payroll deductions and income taxes, and their elimination would not provide the enormous financial windfall to corporations that anti-tax advocates sometimes suggest. Rather, it is the loss of power that motivates capital's opposition to the welfare state, evidenced most graphically by their sometimes violent hostility to completely privately funded worker self-help organizations, cooperatives, and collectives in the developing world (particularly in Latin America). This is also the primary motive behind business hostility toward unions, whose existence (as we have seen) similarly threatens the power of business to discipline workers not merely as individuals, but also as a class. That said, capital may sometimes acquiesce to the creation of welfare state programs, especially when (as is increasingly agreed to be true in the United States in the case of providing medical insurance) the creation of national, tax-funded programs might be in their interests (i.e., be less costly to them than providing health benefits as part of employee compensation). Similarly, capital may, under some circumstances, agree to welfare state provisions when their bargaining position with organized labor requires it, or when compelled (as in Bismarck's Germany) by an authoritarian state not (yet) entirely answerable to market imperatives.

SOCIAL RIGHTS AND MARKET REGULATION

The advent of the market economy is undeniably one of the most emancipatory events in human history. Adam Smith, of course, was the first major apostle of market, and we find in his list of the commendatory aspects of this institution the fact that it had the potential to be truly revolutionary, not only because it would create unprecedented wealth per se but also because it would free individuals from the chains of social class. For Smith, the market would not only help to eradicate poverty, but would even more so contribute to genuine human liberty. By eradicating mercantilist and feudal restraints on both labor and exchange, which only served in his view to maintain class privileges, the market would create a more equal society. Similarly, the intellectual foundations upon which markets are built – which depend, as we have seen, on the idea of autonomous individuals making free choices predicated upon their own interests – would create just such individuals: autonomous citizens capable of pursuing *their* own interests, rather than being just pawns of either the privileged orders or a corrupt and authoritarian state.

This is also the view of Marx, who shares the view that capitalism has made vital contributions to precisely the kind of progress imagined by Smith. "The bourgeoisie" or capital owning class, says the *Communist Manifesto* (Marx and Engels, 2005: 5), "has played a most revolutionary part... [it] has put an end to all feudal, patriarchal, idyllic relations. It has pitilessly torn asunder the motley feudal ties that bound man to his 'natural superiors.'" Further, capitalism is also to be celebrated, in words again reminiscent of Smith, for ending the "slothful indolence" of feudalism:

It [capitalism] has been the first to show what man's activity can bring about. It has accomplished wonders far surpassing Egyptian pyramids, Roman aqueducts, and Gothic cathedrals; it has conducted expeditions that put in the shade all former Exoduses of nations and crusades... It has created enormous cities, has greatly increased the urban population as compared with the rural, and has thus rescued a considerable part of the population from the idiocy of rural life... [It] has created more massive and more colossal productive forces than have all preceding generations together.

Where Smith and Marx, and contemporary social theorists of the Right and the Left, part company is thus not about the positive aspects of the market, since all agree that it represents an advance in human development, but rather on the question of whether the advance in liberty, equality, and standard of living that the market society created should be viewed as an end-state or merely as a stepping-stone toward further advancement. For the modern conservative defenders of the market, its ascendancy represents "the end of history" (Fukuyama, 1992). For its left-liberal critics, the market certainly did end a certain kind of class privilege, but at the cost of creating another. The program of social democracy that we have been examining, founded as it is on the mobilization of workers and the creation of the welfare state, is viewed by its defenders as mitigating the negative effects of the market by providing individuals in the class that is relatively disadvantaged within the market further gains in liberty, equality, and standard of living. In sum, what is at stake is the question of whether the regime of rights associated with liberalism is sufficient or whether the frontier of rights should be extended to what are called "citizenship" or "social" rights. In subsequent chapters, I examine empirically the question of which approach appears to contribute better to the "greatest happiness of the greatest number." For the present, our task is limited to explicating what the extension of such rights might entail.

As formulated by Marshall (1950), the idea of social rights is predicated upon the notion that individuals may have rights to society's protection because they are members of that society – because they are citizens – rather than because they are capable of purchasing protection as a commodity. Thus, for instance, no one disputes that everyone has a right to "life and liberty" without regard to ability to pay for such. The police, thus, do not ask for a credit card number before they agree to protect someone, for the same reason that public schools provide education as an equally free and universal service. It is from there only a small step to suggest that individuals may have rights to other services, such as medical care, housing, or an income sufficient for sustenance when one is unable through no fault of one's own to find work. The social democrat wishes to extend our conception of rights to include such items, whereas the classical liberal or the modern conservative does not.

For our purposes, the question might be put in this way: if we accept that we have "unalienable rights" that include not merely life and liberty but also the "pursuit of happiness," might we not conclude that the last includes the right to medical care, education, housing, and so on, providing that society has the resources to make such available to all, in, again, the same way that society attempts to provide for the safety of all by the provision of a police force that does not limit services to those capable of paying for them? This is the spirit of Paine's call in *The Rights of Man* for a state that takes as one of its purposes the well-being of its citizens, and is the antithesis of Madison's vision of a government as limited in its scope as possible. This difference in the interpretation of rights provides a convenient, if overly simplified, summary of the difference between contemporary Left and Right.

The idea of social rights takes us squarely to an even more basic difference between modern conservative and leftist or progressive approaches to government. At its base, the issue is whether the state has a role in *actively* promoting the values of social justice and human dignity or whether such attempts, however well intentioned, produce results opposite of those intended. In other words, we may confidently presume that all persons of good faith, whether ideologically disposed toward Left or Right, take the dignity of the individual as a valued goal, and believe that the state should act to defend it. Where they differ is in the means to that end. For the Right, human dignity is best served by a limited government that leaves the provision of incomes and other social needs to an efficient private economy (and to ancillary nonstate actors, such as churches and charitable organizations). In this view, government intrusion hinders rather than promotes human dignity. For the Left, by contrast, society has a responsibility, to the extent it possesses the latent resources necessary, to ensure human dignity through the obvious means of intervening in the market precisely because the market, whatever its otherwise laudable features, cannot logically have any interest in promoting dignity or well-being. Given, as Robert Lane (1978) observes, that "markets are indifferent to the fate of individuals," it inevitably falls – in the view of the Left – upon human agency, not blind and uncontrolled market forces, to ensure that the interests of citizens are served.

How does the Left propose to do this? The answer, beyond championing labor organization and the welfare state as discussed earlier, is to regulate labor markets in particular, and the economy in general. From this ideological vantage point, human well-being is best served by an explicit social commitment to the well-being of persons, which is to say, by the conscious elevation of the individual's inherent worth to a value that society recognizes. It is thus necessary to have something more than the "efficiency" of the market as a compass for social policy. In novelist Wendell Berry's formulation, "Rats and roaches live by competition under the laws of supply and demand; it is the privilege of human beings to live under the laws of justice and mercy." Thus, for the Left, the redundant middle-aged worker, as much as the underprivileged, futureless teenager, needs more from society than the dubious consolation that their unenviable circumstances and marginal life chances are allotted to them "efficiently." They require, in the view of the social democrat, not only material help to improve their circumstances and chances, but also society's moral assurance that they are not disposable or undeserving of respect. Regulation of the economic arena in which people live and work is thus the most obvious path to ensuring that people are treated as people, that is, with "justice and mercy," rather than as mere anonymous, abstract "market participants" without moral claims on society. It is from this perspective that the goal of the Left becomes that of controlling the market for the benefit of society, rather than of leaving the market in control of society.

The Right is generally unwilling to concede this moral high ground, and indeed, it is capable of offering a theoretically consistent argument, typically drawing upon Smith's "invisible hand" or von Hayek's "spontaneous order," in which goals such as justice and mercy are indeed best served by "freeing" rather than regulating markets.[14] They do so by reversing the equation, arguing that society is best served by leaving the market free, in that by doing so one leaves individuals themselves free. Economic regulation and management, which the Left sees as collectively empowering citizens by allowing them to "tame" the market, is opposed by the Right because "taming" or,

---

[14] That said, prominent leaders of the Right do sometimes take a more extreme view, exemplified by Margaret Thatcher's much-quoted contention that there is in fact "no such thing as society," which seems to deny the validity of the very idea of the *public* good, and to mock the Left as "naive" in attempting to pursue it. As her critics have not been shy in observing, it is but a small step from here to Social Darwinism.

"subjugating," the market means subjugating the individuals who would otherwise make free choices in the free market. In subsequent chapters, I attempt
to provide empirical answers to these seemingly irresolvable philosophical disputes in interpretation, but before doing so it is necessary to briefly review the
nature of the type of market regulations in question.

To workers, the most immediately important involve the labor market. An
excellent empirical summary of labor's concerns can be found in the work of
conservative think tanks, such as the Heritage Foundation or the Fraser Institute, in their attempt to measure the amount of "economic freedom" across the
world. They are, of course, defining "freedom" from the ideological vantage
point of capital, whose agenda is the absence of regulation. As one economist
observes, what is being measured by such indices is how much "private businesses and investors are relatively unfettered by government policies, rules, or
practices" (Stanford, 1999). It is thus illuminating to consider the agenda of
business in labor market regulation, which illustrates is polarity to the interests
of workers.

In the Heritage Foundation's *Index of Economic Freedom* (2008, chap.
4:53–5), they suggest four key components in a country's system of regulation:
(a) the level of a country's minimum wage, presuming it has one, (b) "the
rigidity" of the rules regulating the number of hours employees can be required
to work, (c) the "difficulty of firing redundant employees," and (d) the "cost of
firing redundant employees." These are the central issues about which workers
and employers differ in their interests, and in that sense the index provides
an ideal example of how the class struggle is played out, and of the radically
different policy options available to political parties in deciding whether, and
how, to regulate.[15]

Considering each of the elements sequentially, labor unions have always
favored higher minimum wages, just as business has consistently opposed
them. The same clash of interest is even more apparent in the other domains of
the Heritage index. In considering the "rigidity" of work hours, for instance,
the authors of the index consider (as examples of infringements on freedom) whether there are legal restraints on night and weekend work, whether
the workweek can extend beyond forty hours per week, and, most tellingly,
whether workers are entitled by law to twenty-one days or more of paid vacation per year. Need one look further for differences between Left and Right
in their approach to the rights of workers? The skeptic wishing to do so may
find satisfaction in the remaining items. Thus, in considering "the difficulty of
firing" we come to the question of "whether employers have the legal authority to lay off workers efficiently, or whether that act has to be justified to

---

[15] Conspicuously absent from the list are workplace regulations of particular relevance to women
(e.g., family leave, sexual harassment, legally mandated equal pay), which are generally (though
it must be admitted, not consistently) advocated by labor unions and left/liberal political parties
and (with more consistency) opposed by business and conservatives.

the government or third parties [e.g., labor unions]." On what level could the interests of workers versus employers be more at odds than over the existence of laws that protect workers from arbitrary dismissal? Having examined the degree to which employers are unfettered by such rules, the Heritage report turns to the cost of firing workers, considering "the legally mandated notice period, mandatory severance pay, and a penalty the employer must pay when dismissing a worker." Here, again, it takes no special insight to understand what workers prefer and why these are the polar opposite of the preference of business.

It is equally apparent which types of rules are most likely to contribute, in the immediate sense at least, to the dignity of the individual. Workers are more likely to feel that the society they live and work in respects them when they are protected by law from employers that wish to pay them unconscionably low wages, make them work excessively long hours, deny them paid vacation time, or dismiss them without reason, notice, or compensation. These rules also imply an equality of persons, from the waiter and the janitor to the manager and executive, especially when the benefit of regulation is high (e.g., when all are entitled to three or four weeks of paid vacation by law). Of course, it is entirely possible that in the longer term, such rules actually have more negative than positive consequences, either by stifling economic growth or even by unintentionally reducing the liberty of individuals by making them subject to state rules and bureaucracy. This is an empirical proposition we consider in subsequent chapters.

The other side of the regulatory coin involves the protection of consumers. Business naturally prefers not to be regulated for the sake of consumers for the same reason it prefers not to be regulated in defense of workers: because it limits discretion and imposes costs. Business thus naturally, and understandably, is opposed to the existence (or, more realistically, the extension or aggressive enforcement) of the usual panoply of consumer protection protocols that limit the ability of profit-motivated enterprises to impose costs on society through externalities, such as pollution. It is similarly hostile to laws that seek to ensure that the public receives safe and quality-controlled goods and services, which are in turn produced in workplaces that are safe for the individuals laboring in them. We might also include under the rubric of consumer protection governmental regulation of a country's banking and financial system. The Heritage Foundation again provides us a convenient summary of what is involved, in their assessment that there is less "economic freedom" in reverse proportion to "the extent of government regulation of financial services; the extent of state intervention in banks and other financial services; the difficulty of opening and operating financial services firms; and government influence on the allocation of credit." That the global economic crisis that began in 2008 was at the very least facilitated by insufficient regulations of these sorts, especially in the United States, highlights the relevance of such issues to the lives of ordinary people

CONCLUSION

The market economy is among humanity's greatest achievements. At the same time, and through precisely the same mechanisms, it imposes a multitude of material and psychological costs on society, which are – like the market's benefits – distributed inequitably. As we have seen, a market society is also a class society in which the economic system privileges one class of citizens by reducing the other to a commodity. The conflict between classes, which in turn motivates conventional political conflict within a system of representative democracy is at its base about the question of whether, or to what degree, to limit commodification, and, thus, the power of the market in determining people's life chances.

The organization of workers into unions, the creation of the welfare state, and the establishment of a regulatory public-policy regime designed to ensure the health, safety, and dignity of the ordinary person: these are the mechanisms by which citizens can limit the power of the market over their lives. Whether such interventions actually contribute to the general welfare, or simply interfere with the efficiency of the market to the detriment of all, is the empirical question to which this book is devoted.

3

Citizens or Market Participants?

Before proceeding to examine empirically the consequences for human happiness of Left versus Right economic and social policies, it is necessary to first clarify what, precisely, the argument between these ideological poles is about. This requires in turn an appraisal of the arguments that the Right and Left make about the wisdom of attempting to manage or displace the market through political means. As will become apparent, the underlying axis of conflict ultimately concerns where sovereignty should be presumed to reside: in a self-regulating market of free individuals making free choices or in a democratic process of authoritative allocation through free political competition.

IN DEFENSE OF THE MARKET

The Grand Argument for the Market Economy

The market economy is a fact. The dominance of market ideas in the economic realm inevitably encourages citizens to interpret the wider world in ways that are consistent with market principles. There is thus a tendency for the market outcomes that surround us to appear as part of the natural order, and as such, deserving of respect and, perhaps, even reverence. Socially, we become accustomed to conceiving of the free market as the normal state of affairs, such that the burden of proof appears to be on those who advocate changing or "intervening" in the natural order it seemingly provides. Arguments in favor of markets, then, generally adopt a strategy of discrediting the arguments made against it, resting in effect upon the presumption of innocence that the market has come to enjoy. I examine a variety of such claims presently. In the interim, it may be instructive to actually consider the intellectual case *for* the market.

The basis of the Grand Argument is the idea of economic "efficiency." This term is somewhat elastic, having different meanings in different contexts, but at its base, it is merely the idea that a process or a method of production is efficient if no other method or process allows more to be produced with the same amount of resources. Market economies are widely argued to be the most efficient in the sense that they produce the greatest possible economic output with the human and material resources that are available. This, then, is the main argument in favor of the market: it maximizes efficiency in the sense that society produces more than it otherwise might, to the presumed benefit of all.

A more specific meaning of efficiency, more generally invoked in academic discussion of the market as a general method of economic organization, is Pareto efficiency or Pareto optimality. Thus, when considering how society might distribute "goods" – meaning anything that might provide utility, such as incomes or access to medical care – imagine a series of possible allocations across individuals. This distribution would include "a complete specification of who produces what and who consumes what" (for an accessible but more technical discussion, see Dasgupta, 1997: 82). We label as a Pareto improvement any change that makes at least one person better off while making no one else worse off (in terms of their own preferences), and an overall allocation as Pareto efficient when no additional improvements of this sort are possible. Everyone, then, is as well-off as he or she can be, without making anyone else worse off.

In what economists denote as the First Fundamental Theorem of Welfare Economics (or First Welfare Theorem), it can be proved mathematically that, given a host of very restrictive theoretical assumptions, a competitive ("free") market produces a Pareto efficient outcome (Lange, 1942). This in turn is generally conceived of as a more theoretically rigorous proof of Adam Smith's invisible hand: leave the market alone and it will produce Pareto efficiency. Market interventions, however well intentioned, will simply cause market "distortions" that take society away from its efficient equilibrium. So, again, the market is to be commended because it makes people as well-off as they possibly can be, subject to the condition that, in so doing, we do not make anyone else worse off. One normative difficulty with this approach is that it says nothing about distributional fairness. As we shall see as we proceed, an efficient outcome is by no means necessarily one that most people would find equitable or just.

The economist most publically associated with protecting the efficient world against attempts to "socially engineer" outcomes that also consider fairness or equity is Friedrich von Hayek. He emerged as the poster child for market fundamentalists when Margaret Thatcher, in a now mythicized incident, angrily waved his *The Constitution of Liberty* (1960) at a political event, saying, "This is what we believe." At the level of economic theory, von Hayek maintains that attempts at redistribution though economic planning are doomed because we cannot obtain the information necessary for success. Without digressing into the details of what is an arcane theoretical issue ("the economic calculation problem"), von Hayek insists that only a decentralized market, aggregating the millions upon millions of decisions made daily by market participants themselves, can provide the information necessary for an efficient allocation of resources. Any attempt to control the market, as through the heavy taxation required to fund the welfare state, would prove to be *The Road to Serfdom* (1944), in that it will only empower the state to utilize these resources to control society, rather than to serve it. Attempts to impose political control over the market will thus produce at best an inefficient outcome, because the authority figures entrusted with that control lack the information to pursue their goals, even when they act in good faith, and at worst a "totalitarian" one when those same holders of authority employ it to subjugate society. Our only hope then is to avoid the *Fatal Conceit* (1988) that we as citizens can successfully impose a collective will on the economy (and thus the world) through "social engineering," given the enormous costs to humanity that such schemes entail. This can be achieved only by relying on the "spontaneous order" that the market mercifully supplies.

We thus see in von Hayek the central threads of the standard arguments for the market and against the welfare state and other social democratic institutions. Interventions in the market inevitably move society away from efficiency in the widest sense, i.e., they reduce the amount that society produces given its resources. Economic growth is thereby inhibited, to the presumed detriment of society. These same "anti-market" interventions also prohibit the development of efficiency in the more narrow sense of Pareto optimality. The redistribution that the Left seeks to induce, in these terms, can by definition be achieved only by taking from some for the sake of others. Although von Hayek would resist the comparison, this might be argued to be the equivalent of the extraction of surplus we have already encountered – the forcible confiscation of the wealth of others – though now the victim of confiscation is the capital-owning class that the market otherwise privileges. The welfare state itself could then be dismissed as just another manifestation of a kleptocracy.

In this view, the program of the Left aggrandizes the power of a state that cannot possibly possess the knowledge to use such power (and could not be trusted to use such knowledge in any case), such that there are "unintended consequences" of regulation that are difficult to foresee or control (e.g., inflation and unemployment), whose negative effects on well-being would outweigh whatever positive benefits to workers they might provide. Further, as the size or power of government increases, more and more of society's activities come under government purview, so that people's lives become increasingly captive to an intrusive state bureaucracy that manages an ever-larger part of our daily lives. Liberty is also threatened by governmental regulation of what should be the private decisions of entrepreneurs in how they run their enterprises and compensate their workers. More threatening still are the labor unions that the Left encourages, in that these organizations are inherently coercive both to the workers they allegedly represent as well as to the employers ("entrepreneurs") that they seek to extort through collective bargaining (i.e., "price-fixing").

Arguments Against the Welfare State

The remaining arguments typically made in favor of the market take the more familiar form of castigating challenges to it, with the welfare state the most frequent target. We begin with a closer look at the notion of the "unintended consequences" on the economy alluded to earlier.

The welfare state, as with any public policy that requires extensive public spending, is detrimental to economic growth. For neoliberal economists, and the public intellectuals who take them as a compass, it is a matter of faith that high levels of public expenditures are inimical to economic growth, with negative consequences on well-being for all, because government does not spend money as efficiently as markets do. The difficulty with this argument is that it is not supported by the empirical research, which on whole finds little evidence for such fears (for extensive reviews and discussion, see Atkinson, 1999; Lindert, 2004). In an influential recent book, Nobel Laureate Douglass North (with his collaborators John Wallis and Barry Weingast) demonstrates that high levels of taxing and spending do not in general serve to depress economic performance (North, Wallis, and Weingast, 2009). A principal reason is that public spending provides public goods, that is, things that the market cannot produce itself but that are nonetheless conducive to the effective operations of a market economy. As North et al. note, this category includes not merely things like infrastructure, but, even more importantly, social insurance programs and similar public services that contribute to a population of healthy, productive, and happy workers and consumers as well. Indeed, there are reasons to believe that the social democratic model is more rather than less supportive of economic prosperity, given that by reducing inequality it also reduces the social pathologies that accompany inequality (e.g., Pontusson, 2005). All of this is reflected in the simple fact, as Rothstein (2010) wryly points out, that "when the World Economic Forum (the main international business organization) ranks economic competitiveness, the [high spending] Nordic countries come out at the very top." This demonstrates with absolute conclusiveness that, at the very least, the generous, universalistic welfare state is not incompatible with a thriving and dynamic market economy.

The welfare state directly harms those it seeks to help. This line of reasoning, popularized by Charles Murray in the book that serves as the ultimate artifact of Reaganism, *Losing Ground* (1984), and analyzed as a more generalized "ideational" phenomenon dating from the nineteenth century by Albert Hirschman in his *The Rhetoric of Reaction* (1991), is what has become known as the "perversity thesis": in attempting to ameliorate problems created by the market, the welfare state creates "perverse incentives" for individuals to behave in self-destructive and immoral ways. Thus, Murray maintained that the U.S. welfare state, minimalist to the point of anemia compared to most industrial democracies, nonetheless created a powerful system of disincentives for people to work to better their own lives, and to otherwise behave responsibly, at tremendous cost to themselves, their families, and society. It also discouraged marriage among the poor, who might otherwise lose benefits, while simultaneously encouraging "unwed mothers" to have yet more children merely to qualify for larger welfare payments. Income maintenance programs, he argued, were themselves actually an important *cause* of poverty because they destroyed the ethic of work and self-reliance, thus making people indolent and feckless. These programs, he argued, were not only too generous, but they also did not provide sufficient "shame" to clients of the welfare state, who were encouraged by "the system" to think of themselves as blameless victims, and powerless ones at that, who must resign themselves to their unhappy fate. This situation he described as the "culture of dependency," which was not only costly but, worse, was also morally corrupting to the individuals trapped within it. The welfare state was thus poisonous, not merely for the working middle class that had to bear the tax burden it required, but for both the poor and unemployed themselves.[1]

Somers and Block (2005) document the long pedigree of such arguments in debates over social policy, noting their centrality in the two most successful attacks on the public provision of welfare in the history of the Anglo-American world: the 1996 Personal Responsibility and Work Opportunity Reconciliation Act (PRWORA) in the United States, which realized Murray's dream of destroying what was then the country's major anti-poverty program (Aid to Families with Dependent Children [AFDC]), and the passage in England of the infamous The New Poor Law of 1834, which similarly "demolished" the (relatively) generous existing system in favor of a vastly more punitive one. In both of these model cases, the dynamic identified by Hirschman, and exemplified by Murray, was utilized. As Somers and Block (2005: 260) put it, the conventional structural explanations for poverty and unemployment as by-products of the market system are rhetorically discredited, while "the real problem is attributed to the corrosive effects of welfare's perverse incentives on poor people themselves – they become sexually promiscuous, thrust aside personal responsibility, and develop long-term dependency." Thus, we see the now-standard triad of ills alleged to be perpetrated on society by the welfare state: "laziness, illegitimacy, and degradation." Public welfare programs are thus to be opposed not only because of their adverse effects on the macro-economy, or because of the intrusiveness of the bureaucracy necessary to implement them, but because they ultimately harm the very people they are designed to help.[2]

---

[1] A more sophisticated version of this argument, rooted more strongly in economic theory, focuses specifically on unemployment benefits, maintaining that their existence (at least in their most generous form) provides "perverse incentives" for job seekers to avoid employment, which only serves to maintain high levels of unemployment in the aggregate; for a balanced review of this issue, see Pollmann-Schult and Büchel (2005).

[2] The empirical veracity of these arguments is difficult to evaluate, in that some of their claims, such as the idea that the welfare state causes "degradation" are too vague to be actually falsifiable. However, the peer-reviewed literature devoted to appraising Murray's (1984) particular claims is nearly unanimous in finding them vacuous (see, for example, Blank 1997). More generally,

The welfare state delegitimizes other institutions essential to human well-being. All the arguments directed against the traditional political program of the Left that we have examined thus far depend on the rejection of the core concept of decommodification – making people less dependent on the market – because of its negative consequences for either the economy or human liberty, or because of the immorality that it is alleged to promote. There is another critique of the welfare state that is more interesting, and more theoretically challenging, precisely because it avoids taking issue with the inherent value and justice of limiting how purely commodified human labor (and thus human beings) can be. It is possible to avoid the simplistic and logically tortuous arguments of the sort offered by Charles Murray or Margaret Thatcher by refusing to take issue with the very idea that there is something to be said for limiting the harm done to the aged, the sick, and the unemployed by providing them with some minimal income. In this line of argument, we take issue not with the desirability of decommodification, but only with making the state its major provider. Further, this preference for nonstate providers does not depend on attributing to the state any ulterior motives or on claiming that society cannot afford to assist those in need. Instead, it is maintained that the social welfare programs administered and fostered by the state tend to diminish the role and importance of the traditional nonstate sources of decommodification: the family and the church.

Prior to the advent of the modern welfare state, decommodification was left to these institutions, who endeavored as best they could, given their limited resources, to provide for those in need. These institutions, of course, provided an inconsistent and generally very low level of social support, but they had the signal advantage of providing emotional and spiritual support rather than merely subsistence. This was because providing for social needs was not the conscious object of such institutions: we presumably do not have families, or churches, specifically to take care of those who cannot take care of themselves. They took this role upon themselves, out of a sense of charity. However noble that motive, its inadequacy for actually providing for human needs prompted the development of an institution that was consciously devised to help those who cannot help themselves, and not as a matter of charity but rather of social right: the welfare state. As the welfare state developed, it replaced church and family as the central provider of decommodification, which, as a consequence, left those institutions less socially relevant. This decline in relevance to people's lives, it can be maintained, has had negative effects on

the contention that social welfare programs either increase poverty (per the perversity thesis) or just fail (for whatever reason) to reduce it is similarly not supported by the literature, which generally confirms the commonsense conclusion that welfare programs reduce levels of poverty (measured, importantly, relative to either an absolute, internationally comparable standard of what constitutes poverty, or to a relative standard tied to the consumption norm of a given country); for a general discussion and review, see Kenworthy (1999).

society, precipitating a decline in the extent to which people tend to find life rewarding.

The logic is not complicated, but it may be most readily seen by noting that both the family and the church are institutions of social control. The family patriarch taking in a poor relation reinforces his role as patriarch in so doing, in that those living under his tutelage could be expected not only to be grateful, but also to accept his authority. The same incentives made it entirely rational for the church to consolidate or expand its position in society by offering care to those in need. In each case, while the motives for charity may be mixed, combining both a sincere desire to help the less fortunate with an equally honorable desire to further worldly motives, it is not entirely fatuous to conceive of the welfare benefits so provided to be infused with a quality missing from the cold-cash payments provided by cold and emotionally indifferent state bureaucrats. Thus, the argument goes, the welfare state doubtless provides a greater level of economic support to the needy, which is also distributed in a more equitable, consistent, and predictable fashion, but the *quality* of that support is of a different and lesser kind than that which emanated from the more traditional sources. As Ruut Veenhoven (2000) characterizes the issue, the net effects of the welfare state might cancel one another out, such that the greater the quantity of decommodification made available might have to be discounted by a decline in the quality of what it provides.

In this simple form, the argument is not especially convincing, since it depends on the admission that the state does indeed do better than the family and the church in meeting human needs, which is hardly surprising given that it has financial and administrative resources that vastly exceed those of its competitors. Rational agents are likely to prefer greater material benefits, consistently provided as a matter of law, to lesser rewards offered as charity, particularly when such charity may put one under an obligation to those providing it. The welfare state might well thus "force out" the family and the church as providers of material welfare because the former is a better provider. The welfare state should thus unambiguously provide greater happiness, presuming that we accept the thesis (discussed at length in Chapter 4) that the principal determinant of happiness is the objective conditions of one's life.

There is, however, a stronger argument within the logic, which depends upon the issue of obligation. Rather than focusing on how the church and family provide a qualitatively better kind of support, one can look to the consequences for these institutions when the material benefits they previously provided are instead supplied by the state. These are not difficult to imagine: when deprived of the psychological and emotional power over individuals that comes with being the only suppliers of financial security available to the ordinary person, these institutions decline in importance. People are thus less tied to their families, and their churches, because they are no longer as dependent upon them. Having to rely on them less for their material needs, they become less tied to them in other ways.[3] As we have good evidence that exactly the kind of social connectedness that family and church provide is intimately related to happiness (e.g., Lane, 2000; Putnam and Campbell, 2010), a decline in the social significance of these institutions is likely to depress a society's overall degree of happiness. This is perhaps the most significant, and certainly the most theoretically compelling, of the arguments predicated on the deleterious "unintended consequences" argued to accompany the welfare state.[4]

Of course, the question is the balance between the effects of these processes. The welfare state provides a higher standard of living and less insecurity, at the cost of diminishing the salience or availability of the social connections that the extended family and the church might provide. Whether the welfare state results in a net positive contribution to human happiness depends on its relative effect on both the positive and negative sides of the ledger.[5]

IN DEFENSE OF SOCIAL DEMOCRACY

The first task in considering the social democratic alternative to the pure-market approach to maximizing human well-being is to offer a critique of the argument from efficiency that is the foundation of pro-market thinking.

The Critique of Market Efficiency

It would not be sensible to enthrone the market as the institution to which we entrust human well-being because markets are efficient if (a) markets are not, in fact, generally efficient or, (b) efficiency was not a normatively appropriate criterion. I argue that neither condition obtains.

There is a long research program in economics on the concept of "market failure" – which is defined, of course, as the failure of the market to produce

---

[3] For both an axiomatic treatment of the relationship between religiosity and the welfare state, as well as strong empirical evidence that the welfare state does indeed reduce religious observance, see Gill and Lundsgaarde (2004).

[4] The same argument would of course apply to the labor union: the union becomes an emotional focal point for the individual, given its centrality to both the work that consumes so much of one's life energies, and to one's financial well-being. To the extent that unions succeed in being fraternal organizations, they become seen as both a source of protection from the market and of emotional support for the members, and must of necessity limit the energy and commitment one can make to church and family. Put differently, unions may shift social connection away from the church and the extended family and toward fellow workers. It is not obvious which actually provides greater psychological benefits, but to the extent that the former is a superior supplier of such benefits than the latter, unions would, as the welfare state, diminish happiness.

[5] Of course, it should also be noted that the market itself has eroded the importance of the extended family and the church to an enormous extent. Indeed, as Adam Smith suggests, it is the market (as noted in the prior chapter) that produces the individualistic, rational maximizer of utility to whom family and religion are in danger of being reduced to mere sentimentality. It was in this sense that Marx famously observed that capitalism leaves "no other nexus between man and man than naked self-interest, than callous 'cash payment.'" Thus, to argue for the market by appealing to the need for maintaining family and religion seems decidedly odd.

efficient (Pareto optimal) outcomes. This literature is far too long and dense to warrant a review here, but its outline is instantly familiar in the form of public goods, imperfect competition, externalities, and a veritable multitude of informational and rationality problems (for an accessible introduction, see Dutt and Wilber, 2010). Much of this work has been centered on providing "solutions" to these "failures" – meaning, typically, governmental (i.e., political) interventions in the economy. As a matter of principle, political interventions are, of course, precisely what the left-liberal approach to human well-being is predicated on. Thus, if one accepts that the "efficient" market is in fact riddled by market failures that require governmental interventions to fix, nothing remains to distinguish the Left from the Right except for their quibbling over which interventions, in that if we grant that we must intervene in the economy to correct its "failures," all that remains is argumentation over what constitutes a failure. If, for instance, we have to intervene to save financial markets (something done frequently and at enormous public expense throughout the industrial democracies since the beginning of the Great Recession), is there not the same case to be made for intervening to alleviate unemployment (whether on moral grounds or purely economic ones, i.e., to stimulate growth)? The point is too obvious to require long elaboration – it has certainly not been lost on citizens in the United States, Greece, Ireland, Spain, Portugal, and other countries in which the government has financed enormous "bailouts" of private banks at public (i.e., taxpayer) expense while simultaneously allowing unemployment to soar.

The magnitude of the "market failure" involved in these examples is startling for the sums involved – the initial 2008 U.S. TARP bank bailout alone cost 700 billion dollars, a figure equivalent to the gross national product of the Netherlands – but their apparent exceptionalism should not disguise the ubiquity of more conventional market failures in more ordinary economic conditions. This is surely the understanding of markets that emerges from contemporary scholarship, which points toward the fact that market economies generally fail to achieve or even approach the efficiency standard that their defenders maintain is their justification. That is in, any case, the conclusion of the hugely influential Greenwald-Stiglitz Theorem (Greenwald and Stiglitz, 1986), which demonstrates that "whenever markets are incomplete and/or information is imperfect (which is true in virtually all economies," markets are not Pareto efficient. This contention has been verified by much subsequent work, and is now widely accepted by professional economists. It was for this research program, culminating in his *Whither Socialism?* (1994), that Stiglitz was awarded the Nobel Prize in Economics in 2001. The central implication of his work is that "market failure" vis-à-vis the efficiency standard is the norm, so that state intervention in the economy becomes the needed friend rather than the implacable enemy of efficiency.

However important these findings are for academic social science, they have had no moderating influence on the degree to which the Right (especially in the United States, where it exists in this most virulently anti-intellectual form) continues to take the argument from efficiency as a virtual item of faith ("market fundamentalism") and is thus impervious to an explication of its defects from the perspective of economic science. It is unlikely, for example, that the fellows of the American Enterprise Institute, much less Margaret Thatcher, are going to exchange their copies of *The Constitution of Liberty* for *Whither Socialism?* merely because von Hayek, as judged by professional economists, just happens to be demonstrably wrong. As Stiglitz noted in a 2007 interview, the proposition that "unfettered markets often not only do not lead to social justice, but do not even produce efficient outcomes" is not strongly disputed within the field of economics. To again quote from the same interview: "Interestingly, there has been no intellectual challenge to the refutation of Smith's 'invisible hand': individuals and firms, in the pursuit of their self-interest, are not necessarily, or in general, led as if by an invisible hand, to economic efficiency." Still, while the same invisible hand has lost its glamour in serious academic debate, "in political discourse, simplistic 'market fundamentalism' continues to exert enormous influence." Thus, rather than continue to dissect this strand of economic theory, I proceed with an examination of arguments from efficiency judged on their own terms.

When considering efficiency first in the widely used sense of maximizing economic production, rather than its more formal sense of Pareto optimality, two brief observations present themselves. The first is hardly original to me: the market is frequently and obviously not very efficient at all. To take just one painfully contemporary example, the troughs of business cycles, characterized as they are by high unemployment and thus enormous unused human and industrial resources, are periods when the economy produces grossly less than it otherwise might. An economy stabilized by budgetary policies to prevent or soften business cycles, and a welfare state that minimizes the deflationary spiral of falling demand and rising unemployment, will outperform a "self-regulating" boom-and-bust pure market economy. For these and other reasons stressed by Keynes (such as macro-coordination problems, which require more than the "local" price-signal information von Hayek stresses, and yet other information problems beyond those stressed by Stiglitz), it is by no means clear that the "pure" market is as remotely efficient as the managed left-liberal alternatives to it.

A second, and equally inexpensive observation, is this: it seems evident that simply maximizing the total amount that the economy produces, without regard to what is produced or, more importantly, how it is distributed, need not translate into greater human well-being. Clearly, society might well decide – if democratically empowered to make such decisions, contra the "spontaneous order" of the market – that it would be preferable to accept a modestly lower level of production if doing so allowed for a more equitably distributed and consciously planned economy, insofar as such might contribute to a greater aggregate level of well-being. In this situation, society's overall level of happiness would be higher despite violating the principle of efficiency.

It is equally obvious that it may be in the interest of society to violate Pareto optimality, insofar as we are interested in making human life as satisfying as possible. To rely on efficiency in this sense is merely to say that there is no other allocation of goods that everyone would agree to (given that again Pareto efficiency suggests only that no one can be made better off without someone else being made worse off). Thus, efficiency would prohibit making one person slightly less worse off (say, by taxing 10 percent of their earnings over 1 million dollars per year) in order to make one hundred people much better off (say, by providing them with access to health care on the proceeds of such taxes). This is the fundamental weakness in efficiency as a metric by which to judge: it lacks any principle of justice. There are many Pareto efficient outcomes, but not all of them are likely to be considered just by a majority of citizens. Note, for instance, that a distribution that gave the entire product of society to a single individual is Pareto optimal, as are other more realistic but still grossly unequal distributions. Efficiency as a criterion is silent on these matters. By appealing to it alone, we are incapable not only of considering questions of equity or justice, but also of simply not being able to objectively maximize human well-being.[6]

In the same way, appealing to efficiency effectively insulates the market against democracy. We have already noted the inherent tension between capitalism and democracy, and this contradiction appears here as well: to maintain Pareto efficiency in choosing between different allocations of goods (and thus life chances), a majority is not sufficient. Instead, we would need complete unanimity, which is another way of saying that each individual in society has a veto over any proposed policy that might impose costs on them to supply what the majority conceives of as the public good. In essence, the efficiency standard provides what Madison was arguing for in *Federalist 10*: a criterion for making the inherently political decisions about the distribution of wealth (and all that comes from having wealth) that is "objective" and "nonpolitical." Redistribution is thus not merely "wicked and improper" as a matter of political taste, but can be deduced to be so from the laws of economics.

Democracy takes us to von Hayek's obsession with the threat posed to liberty itself by the welfare state, economic regulation, and labor unions. He instinctively views any (non-market) authority structure, including those we would categorize as democratic, as coercive institutions that maintain themselves at the expense of those they allege to serve. At base, what separates von Hayek and his devotees from social democrats is that the former do not believe in the possibility of, or, indeed, the desirability of democracy: it is only a word

---

6 Another way of summarizing this point would be to note that one of the *justifications* for efficiency as a standard is precisely that it ignores notions of justice, as understood in the previous example, in that doing so provides a solution to the problem of interpersonal utility comparisons that is embedded in the redistributive example. This is often justified by appealing to economics as a science which makes no value judgments about justice, but following this course (as is frequently observed) makes the value judgment that efficiency is all that is relevant.

for disguising the self-interested exercise of power in the name of an imaginary popular good. More to the point, this entire style of argument contains an internal contradiction: we object to organizations having power because we as members of that organization cannot control its power. But, at the same time, we do not want citizens to be able to exercise that control, because as rational agents they would utilize that power for their own self-interest. As Madison would put it, the demos, the "majority faction," would be more dangerous still if it could control the state, as they would use the power of the state for their interests, which would result in further market dislocations. In sum, organizations are bad because their members cannot control them, but they would be worse still if their members could control them.

What is objected to, then, is the very idea of political organization itself, in that such are manifestations of what von Hayek thinks of as "collectivism." For the individual to pursue his or her own self-interest, he says, is natural and defensible – but *collective action* to obtain those same goals is unnatural and destructive of the market's "spontaneous order." The logic is self-contradictory, though, in that as a good classic liberal (or libertarian), von Hayek must accept that rational agents have a natural right to form such groups. To achieve the "spontaneous order" toward which humanity is impelled, then, we have to "construct" an artificial order that inhibits or emasculates human organization for collective goals.

The New Right thinking, which finds its inspiration in von Hayek, is fatally compromised in at least one other way: its inability to consider that the seemingly free choices made by seemingly free and equal market participants are strongly affected by the conditions that *precede* market participation. As was discussed in the prior chapter, no one less than Adam Smith stressed the fundamental disparity between worker and employer when they face each other in the labor market. For von Hayek, the issue is liberty, and workers are always at liberty to accept or decline to sell their labor power at an offered wage. For Smith, and of course Marx, their basic relationship is both asymmetrical and antagonistic, making market choices rather less free than von Hayek portrays them. This is important, because it speaks directly to von Hayek's concern with coercion, which is ultimately what he purports to object to in principle and to find in all efforts to change market outcomes. From Smith's and Marx's points of view, he is oblivious to the coercion taking place as a matter of course in the labor market – oblivious, indeed, to the fact that such coercion is the entire basis of the capitalist enterprise to which he is so passionately attached.

If so, the question becomes whether one prefers the coercion of the market or the coercion of the welfare state and the labor union. In one scenario, the ordinary person faces the potential coercion of the government, the regulatory agency, and the labor union. However, each of these is at least ostensibly devoted to the individual's well-being, and is at least ostensibly answerable to them when it fails to devote itself to that goal. In the other scenario, citizens face a corporate profit-making enterprise that views them as a commodity, has no interest in their well-being, uses them as a means to the end of profit for themselves, and is answerable only to the shareholders who enjoy such profits. Which situation would a rational agent prefer? A labor union *might* exploit its membership, if the workers are unable to successfully manage it through the democratic charter that gives it legal force, but a corporation *does* exploit workers, as a part of the wage labor agreement itself, and employees have no say in its operation or management. In terms of the welfare state, to take a tangible real world example, do typical citizens of the United Kingdom prefer the bureaucracy that accompanies the existence of the National Health Service, or would they prefer to purchase medical care themselves? In the United States, do old-age pensioners wish that Medicare would just go away – as the Republican Party has actually proposed – because the services it provides are imperfect and accompanied by rules and regulations that limit doctors and patients? Would they, or the British clients of the National Health Service, prefer that the faceless, anonymous government bureaucrat who decides what kind of care they receive be replaced by a faceless, anonymous insurance corporation bureaucrat who decides what kind of care they receive? A rational agent might well deduce that government bureaucrats are preferable, since at least (a) they have no business incentive to deny care, because they are not making profits by minimizing your access, and (b) they are subject to the enormous political pressure that citizens exert on government to fund and administer Medicare in a conscientious fashion, overseen by elected representatives whose political careers depend upon maintaining public support, while the insurance company bureaucrat is (1) actively charged with minimizing the care provided so as to maximize corporate profit and (2) is answerable to no one but a purely private, profit-driven corporation.

The Grand Argument for Social Democracy

It is easy to imagine the ideal world of the market fundamentalists, in that it consists of subtracting what restraints on capitalism that the political process has established in the Western world. Approximations of such a world are also familiar to us in the form of the period of the Industrial Revolution in Britain, the "shock therapy" transitions to capitalism that came with the end of communism in Eastern Europe and the Former Soviet Union or today's "emerging market" economies. Conversely, the social democratic world, at least for the Anglo-American reader, can only be imagined by the wholesale addition or radical expansion of institutions and practices entirely unknown, earlier abandoned, or only marginally existent. Briefly indulging our imaginations in this way may be an instructive way to begin a discussion of why social democracy, for its proponents, so facilitates the pursuit of happiness.

Recall the context in which economic life takes place. Ordinary citizens, or workers, depend for their living on jobs provided by corporations or other entrepreneurs who employ the workers' labor for profit. The two are thus involved in a mundane, micro-scale, but nonetheless real struggle over the degree to which the value created by the worker is retained or taken. The worker is by definition in a subordinate position in this struggle, dependent as they are upon obtaining employment. The corporate employer attempts to take natural advantage of its superior position to minimize compensation, and to control the workplace as a means of maximizing productivity.

The obvious recourse for workers is organization. Through the labor union, they are able to improve their position by bargaining collectively over wages and working conditions. More, they are able to establish through the union a recognized, if still inferior, alternative basis of power and authority within the business enterprise. Through their collective-bargaining agreement, they are able to establish rules that limit the authority of the employer to dismiss or otherwise discipline them arbitrarily. This same agreement institutes grievance procedures, which establish protocols by which individual workers may challenge the authority of the employer, thus providing the worker with a sense of "voice" – the ability to express complaints on matters of interest and principle, rather than to either meekly accept what they perceive to be unfairness or injustice or to surrender their position in the hope of obtaining better treatment elsewhere. These conditions have three important consequences: (a) they improve the worker's standard of living (by increasing their salaries and benefits); (b) they provide the psychological benefit of some degree of job security, an essential resource for those whose financial solvency depends upon maintaining employment; and (c) they reduce the extent to which the worker is a powerless, and voiceless, "biological machine."

Once established, unions also become a political resource for workers, particularly when they coordinate their activities through federations. Such unions use their financial and human resources to facilitate the creation and election of political parties committed to their interests. To the extent that these parties are incorporated into governing coalitions, they pursue public policies with two chief aims. First, they endeavor to make it easier for workers to organize (to maximize their own electoral potential). Second, they attempt to create national labor standards applicable to all or most workers that reflect the same agenda in the workplace that unions themselves pursue: higher wages (fostered through a variety of means, such as establishing minimum wages), more job security (by imposing monetary and legal costs on industry for dismissing workers), better standards of safety (and compensatory schemes for those nonetheless injured), legally mandated sick and vacation time, and so on. They may also press for a formal arrangement in which workers are given some minimal influence over corporate governance through co-determination schemes (e.g., whereby workers nominate representatives to serve on a company's board of directors). In any event, the result is to provide the same benefits – material, psychological, and emotional – to workers in general, rather than merely the organized per se.

The political power of unions will manifest itself in other ways. As we saw in Chapter 2, the most important of these is championing a welfare state that provides income maintenance for the unemployed, pensions for the elderly, and, ideally, a variety of noncash benefits to which everyone in society is entitled, such as medical insurance. These institutions limit the degree to which workers are commodified, which again improves their bargaining position with business (so as to raise wages and improve working conditions), provides security against the vagaries of the market for their labor power, and contributes to their self-esteem and sense of autonomy.

The value of all these goods for human well-being requires no elaboration: people who enjoy a higher standard of living, who work in more agreeable circumstances, who are more secure, and who feel that their dignity as a person is respected are more likely to enjoy rewarding lives than those who do not. But their true value can be appreciated only when considering how these work- or market-related outcomes affect the nonwork, nonmarket part of our lives, which, as Robert Lane (2000) reminds us, are likely the most important sources of human happiness. Standard of living and job satisfaction are certainly crucial, but, the argument goes, more important still are the things that neither any amount of money nor the right kind of job or career can provide: close and fulfilling interpersonal relationships. Happiness, then, is most readily found in the form of close friends and a satisfying personal and family life, rather than in either one's work or the monetary rewards such work provides.

It is tempting, then, to think that the focus here on the economic is excessive, but to do so is to miss the connections between the economic and the personal. Although it is doubtlessly true that money buys neither friendship nor romantic love, and that making work or a career substitute for these things generally fails, it remains the case that financial security and a satisfying work life make these more valuable things easier to find and maintain. Surely the individual who is relatively affluent, and who is, above all, secure in maintaining that affluence, finds it easier to be a good friend and a good spouse, and thus presumably to find that affinity returned to them, than one who lives a precarious existence on the edge of poverty. The reason is obvious: economic deprivation, or the imminent fear of it, imposes psychological costs on the individual that encourages the dispositions that psychologists have identified as inhibiting well-being, such as anxiety and stress, but, less obviously, introversion, pessimism, neuroticism, and loss of self-esteem (e.g., Diener et al., 1999). Although it is sometimes convenient to conceive of these last characteristics as personality traits, they are surely inhibited or promoted by one's life experiences. Thus, as Lane (2000) puts it, they are the "malleable" aspects of the human personality, being largely a product of the material circumstances of life, and thus of the sociopolitical structures that affect those circumstances.

To take two archetypical extremes, it seems certain that the tenured college professor, who is well paid and secure in her position, and who enjoys the free time, autonomy, and social status that her profession confers, is less likely to display the negative personality dispositions just discussed than is the blue- or pink-collar worker, whose life energies are more completely absorbed by the day-to-day struggle to make ends meet on a minimal income with low or nonexistent benefits (perhaps even without medical insurance for herself and her children), and who spends eight or more hours of her day as a powerless, voiceless cog in work that is unrewarding, underpaid, and undervalued. The

Same is true of workaholism

higher level of financial- and job-related dissatisfaction faced by the pink-collar worker cannot but help make it harder, at the very least, to devote the time and attention (in either quantity or quality) to friends and family that she might otherwise, should she enjoy the economic and career privileges of a professional, for the good reason that so much of her emotional and psychological resources are spent on work and financial solvency. As this example illustrates, financial security and social status may not buy happiness, but they doubtless make it easier to obtain, given that they provide the emotional space to better avoid stress, introversion, and pessimism.[7]

The importance of the relationship between the structure of the economy and the quality of the individual's personal relationships and private life in general was stressed by Albert Einstein ([1949]2002) in his essay on "how to structure society so as to make human life as satisfying as possible" with which this book began. He observes, familiarly, that humans have two primary "drives." One is "private" or egotistical; it encourages one to "to protect his own existence" and "to satisfy his personal desires." The other is "social"; it suggests seeking "to gain the recognition and affection of [one's] fellow human beings, to share in their pleasures, to comfort them in their sorrows." Both are always present and necessary, of course, and "their specific combination determines the extent to which an individual can achieve an inner equilibrium" in which he or she lives life to its fullest. Crucially, the "relative strength" of these two drives in most persons is in turn determined less by inherent traits of the individual, but rather "by the structure of society" in which they live. Some institutional arrangements push one or the other of the drives to dominate in an unhealthy way over the other. Thus, the extent to which people find the correct "inner equilibrium" necessary for a good life is greatly influenced "by the types of organizations that predominate in society."

Here we come to what Einstein sees as the central problem with capitalism: whatever its many commendable aspects, as an institution it encourages the

---

[7] It is clear how social democratic institutions might equalize the quality of life these two abstract persons enjoy: they would provide the working-class citizen some of the advantages enjoyed by the professional. If represented by a union, the wages and benefits of our hypothetical worker improve, reducing her levels of stress and anxiety, to say nothing of simply allowing her to better provide for herself and her family. She would face less fear of losing her job on short notice, perhaps without severance of any kind. If living in a country with public policies favored by that union, she would be further protected from dismissal by laws that discouraged redundancies and she would enjoy reasonably generous unemployment compensation while searching for a new position if she were to lose her job. She might also have guaranteed medical insurance for herself and her dependents, whatever her employment status, as well as state subsidized day care or even cash payments (family allowances) to help support children. Her job itself might be at least somewhat more rewarding if, through labor laws and her union, she felt more represented and better treated in the workplace. She may also feel the social equal of the financially better off, given that she has the means to provide for her children, she has medical care, she has job security, and is treated at work, and (through labor law and the welfare state) by the society in which she lives, with dignity and respect. By equalizing the life-chances of individuals across different places in the status hierarchy established by the market, social democratic institutions profitably may be conceived of as embodying the democratic ideal of *fraternité*, meaning the unity of all citizens as valued members of a true community.

individual to see society not "as a positive asset, as an organic tie, as a protective force, but rather as a threat to his natural rights . . . such that the egotistical drives . . . are constantly being accentuated, while his social drives, which are by nature weaker, progressively deteriorate." This, then, is Einstein's view of "the real source of evil" in contemporary society: market economies make individuals "prisoners of their own egotism," so that "they feel insecure, lonely and deprived of the naïve, simple, and unsophisticated enjoyment of life." It is in this vein that Max Weber (1958) concludes that the ultimate symbol of the "spirit of capitalism" is an "iron cage" of soulless materialism, in which the individual is reduced to a "nullity."

What make people unhappy is thus the loneliness and the materialism that capitalism cultivates by encouraging individuals to see themselves as atomistic self-interested utility maximizers. Einstein ([1949] 2002), like Lane, agrees that happiness is more readily found by pursuing a different path: "Man can find meaning in life . . . only through devoting himself to society." By this he means simply an emphasis on the "social drive" to build connections with others, in order to escape being "a prisoner of egotism."

This takes us back full circle to the metaphor of the "market as prison" that we have already encountered. The metaphor suggests, and Einstein forcefully argues for, a different kind of economy, one characterized by the social democratic institutions I have repeatedly stressed, in that they are the only effective countervailing institutions for limiting the market's potential for converting human beings into commodities. These same institutions provide some check on capitalism's propensity to reduce all human interaction to what Marx famously called "the cash nexus" of the market – the same process that conservative economists, such as Schumpeter and von Hayek, would celebrate as a definitively positive development. To the extent that the welfare state and labor unions help limit the hegemony of the market over human relationships, they open the door to Einstein's prison of egotism, and thus, potentially, to a richer and more rewarding life.

In sum, then, the institutions of what I have labeled as social democracy – the labor union, the welfare state, and labor market regulations to protect workers – can be argued to positively affect overall quality of life because they provide a higher standard of living, reduce insecurity, improve satisfaction with one's work, and promote one's sense of dignity and equality with one's fellows. These things in turn help to nurture positive emotional and psychological well-being, which spills over from work life to personal life, facilitating the creation and maintenance of the close interpersonal relationships that so contribute to a satisfying life.

OTHER ARGUMENTS FOR SOCIAL DEMOCRACY

Democracy is impaired by the market. There are inevitable tensions between the principles of democracy and the principles of a capitalist or market society, as we already had much occasion to see. These take many forms, but two are of special importance. The first and most obvious is the "privileged position" of capital in its political competition with workers (and consumers), which is a result of the fundamental power disparity between the groups: capitalists own (i.e., monopolize) society's productive resources, leaving both citizens and the nominally democratic state dependent upon them. When capital finds it in its interest to invest and produce, the economy functions, people have jobs, the governments collect taxes, and citizens support incumbent political parties at election time. Should capital be displeased, the economy slows, unemployment soars, wages decline, and voters turn to opposition parties that promise to restore prosperity by rescinding the recessionary policies of the governing party. The state naturally acquiesces in protecting the conditions of profitability on which everything depends, making the nominally democratic state dependent on pleasing the economic interests of the capital-owning class.

A more basic problem with markets from the point of view of democracy is that a market ideology defines and limits the definition of the political in ways that further privilege the wealthy. This was one of the central insights of Polanyi. Part of *The Great Transformation* (1944) he identified was the way in which capitalism relegated to the private, rather than the public or political sphere, the most important and fundamental aspect of the entire economy: the commodification of labor, and as he saw it, consequently, the commodification of human life itself, in the form of the wage-labor relationship whose characteristics we have already examined. This had the consciously desired effect of separating "people from *power* over their own economic life" (1944: 225, emphasis added). Put differently, market ideology delegitimizes the interpretation of the struggle between owner and worker as a political one. The inevitable conflict of interest between the two classes is denied, given that the worker freely enters into the contract, such that the exploitative nature of the relationship, as Smith himself so clearly saw, is obscured. The experience of work, which features so prominently in determining the quality of one's life, is removed from consideration as a political issue, severing the ability of citizens to exercise control or influence over the single most important aspect of their day-to-day existence. This diminution of the scope of democracy has negative consequences for satisfaction with life both directly – it reduces the extent to which individuals feel in control of their own lives – and indirectly, in that it ensures that the actual terms and conditions of work (and the consequences of being unable to obtain it) are defined by owners rather than workers, to the self-evident disadvantage of the latter.

What is at stake from the point of view of democratic theory is thus indeed power: the capitalist economy ensures that some people have more of it than others do. The shell of electoral democracy is predicated upon one person, one vote, but the economic system it shelters offers no such equality. That realm is to be the "self-regulating" and "spontaneous" order that has to be protected from political meddling. Thus, Polanyi summarizes the kind of argument that von Hayek or Friedman would rely on: "only such policies and measures are in order which make *the market the only organizing power*" in society (1944: 68–9, emphasis in original). Stated differently, the role of the state, following

Madison, is to use its coercive power to ensure that "the majority faction" is not able to organize itself to challenge the power of the market. Quasi-libertarians such as von Hayek implicitly endorse precisely this view: their "spontaneous" social order which enshrines "liberty" as the ultimate goal depends in fact upon the state to enforce the sanctity of the market (or, in Madison's terms, property) against the natural and predictable efforts of the working and middle classes to "stop the mill of the market which ground the lives of the people" (Polanyi, 1944: 226).

Thus, Madison's realization that the state was needed to provide this vital function anticipated Polanyi's suggestion that society would of necessity react against this kind of world – that the market's attempt to impose itself on society would prompt a dialectical response in favor of social protection against the market in general and the commodification of human life in particular. What was at stake, in Polanyi's view, was not merely the idea of democracy, which to be meaningful had to have more connection to the reality of people's lives than the market allowed, but what we might call the "social fabric," meaning the idea that life consists of more than production and trade and that individuals had connections to one another that extended beyond self-interest. In this view, there is, contra Mrs. Thatcher, something called society, whose existence depends on limiting the extent to which the market alone dominates human life. That in turn can be achieved only by subordinating the market to democratic principles, rather than the reverse.

We come thus full circle back to the alternative vision of the kind of society proposed by Madison and von Hayek that were first systematically articulated by Tom Paine during the adolescence of the market society: to privilege democracy over the market when the two conflict. To the extent that democracy contributes to greater quality of life, the ability of citizens to democratically regulate or control the market should increase satisfaction with life. Put in different terms, the democratic process is itself an alternative form of power, in principle independent of the market. It thus stands in opposition to the political Right's view of the world for precisely that reason: it constitutes another organizing power beyond the market. This opposition becomes immediately apparent when we consider the specific institutions that inarguably serve as independent sources of power for workers in market societies: the welfare state and the labor union.

The market reduces social capital. Social scientists are much enamored of the idea of "social capital," meaning generalized norms of interpersonal trust and reciprocity that are encouraged by the immersion of individuals in social networks. Much evidence suggests that this kind of social "connectedness" is associated with greater levels of emotional and physical well-being (e.g., Putnam, 2000a; Helliwell and Putnam, 2004). In other words, individuals embedded in rich social networks, who as a consequence tend to be more trusting of, and more willing to cooperate with, others lead healthier and more satisfying lives than those who are not. Social democracy in turn encourages social capital in two ways. The first is via the labor union, which as Putnam

(2000a) stresses, is an ideal type of institution for helping to create both the social connections and the cooperative norms of trust and reciprocity that constitute social capital. Putnam (2000a) goes so far as to use the extent of labor organization as an empirical measure of how much social capital actually exists in a community. It might be just as accurate, from this point of view, to say that the degree to which workers are unionized is one of metrics by which we measure the extent to which there is genuine community or solidarity. Similarly, extensive social protection programs, as we discussed previously, tend to reduce introversion and a narrowing of one's concerns to the momentary and financial, making room in life for more prosocial behaviors. Putnam (2000a) famously used the phenomenon of individuals increasingly forgoing the collective (and thus in his view more emotionally rewarding) practice of bowling in leagues tied to the workplace or community organizations in favor of the isolating practice of "bowling alone" or, indeed, just staying at home. If the safety net provided by the welfare state, particularly the universalistic sort associated with social democracy rather than the stigma-inducing means tested version practiced in the United States, reduces the stress and anxiety that an insecure position in the labor market clearly produces, it will also discourage the inward-looking, fearful social withdrawal we associate with introversion. As a consequence, a generous welfare state promotes the maintenance of social connections, and thus the attitudinal and behavioral norms such connections facilitate, and increases social capital, and, with it, human well-being.[8]

[handwritten marginalia: really?   evidence?]

The Market Promotes Anomie and Imposes the Resulting Costs on Society

A familiar complaint about capitalism is the problem of externalities, best exemplified by the phenomenon of industrial pollution. Producers have no wish to poison the air or the water with the waste products of their enterprise, but they also have no incentive, unless compelled by regulation, to bear the costs of avoiding or containing the pollution for which they are responsible. There are other and ultimately more fundamental externalities to the market system itself, of which the broadest and most significant is captured in the notion of anomie. In simple terms, anomie refers to a state of personal isolation from society, which manifests itself in a disregard for socially relevant normative restraints on personal behavior. Individuals, in other words, are less bound by the social imperative to "play by the rules," and are thus prone to antisocial behaviors.

---

[8] For a detailed and insightful discussion of the role the universalistic welfare state plays in fostering higher levels of social capital (and, for related reasons, decreasing levels of corruption), see Rothstein (1998, 2010). For an empirical assessment of the conservative contention that the welfare state "crowds out" volunteering and similar nonstate forms of participation, see the OECD report on social capital, which notes (2001: 51) that evidence for this phenomenon is "weak" and that indeed "levels of volunteering, informal socializing, and participation in community projects are relatively high" in countries with expansive welfare states compared to those with more modest public welfare systems.

This tendency is especially pronounced given the inherently competitive nature of market society. Not only are workers involved in conflict with their employers, they compete with other workers for positions, just as capitalists compete with one another. Thus, as Heilbroner (1985: 57–9) puts it, capitalism "encourages – even requires – an antagonistic stance toward [all] other participants in the market," resulting in a "form of social war; and social war brings a new intensity to the drive for wealth in the substratum of behavior I am calling human nature." We come, then, to the conventional argument that a pure market economy lessens the power of normative constraints on behavior, resulting in a more violent, Hobbesian kind of world, in which people more readily treat each other merely as means to their own ends.

We have already encountered the spirit of this view in Einstein's ([1949] 2002) discussion of the conflict between our "social" and "egotistical" drives, and, of course, the ways in which different kinds of economic arrangements encourage one over the other. For Einstein, the market, if unchecked by other institutions, encourages an excessive focus on the egotistical, to the determinant of the individual's inner emotional life. If we need not necessarily concur with Heilbroner's equating of this process as one affecting "human nature," we must certainly concede that it may affect the "malleable" aspects of the human personality. The contemporary sociological theory of "institutional anomie" considers how these effects on the personality affect behavior, which in turn affects the lives of others. As Messner and Rosenfeld (1997: 1396) explain,

Markets presuppose a materialistic goal-orientation among actors . . . When these orientations develop to an extreme degree, anomie . . . is likely to ensue . . . In such an anomic environment, actors are preoccupied with outcomes . . . and the efficiency rather than the legitimacy of the means governs [their] behavior. The resulting attenuation of normative controls is likely to lead to high levels of deviant behavior, including crime.

As before, the key factor in determining how strong anomic pressures in society become is the "institutional balance of power" between, as Polanyi (1944) might put it, the market and society. In the terms I have consistently relied on, the issue is the relative strength of those forces promoting and those resisting the commodification of the individual. To the extent that the latter retain sufficient life, anomic pressure is resisted, and the market economy will function relatively smoothly. When commodification is unchecked, anomie will flourish, bringing with it crime and other forms of antisocial behavior. This is precisely what Messner and Rosenfeld (1997, 2006) find when examining the relationship between decommodification and rates of "criminal homicide" across the world: "the degree of commodification is negatively related to homicide rates, net of controls for other characteristics of nations" (1997: 1393).

Thus, insofar as people are likely to find life more satisfying when there is less violent crime, decommodification should contribute to greater levels of satisfaction. Further, if decommodification can be shown to reduce levels of violent crime, it seems plausible that it would tend to reduce other social pathologies that are also commonly thought to accompany anomie, such as drug abuse or domestic violence. Just as high crime rates are likely to reduce the overall level of happiness in a society, not merely that of the immediate victims of crime, so with other similar "pathologies": they impose costs on society in general, thus decreasing the overall level of happiness.

WHICH ARGUMENT IS EMPIRICALLY CORRECT?

The forgoing discussion has attempted to clarify the nature of the deductive arguments for and against the two basic approaches to political economy that have existed since the dawn of the market society. I have purposely avoided any explicit summary judgment about which is more likely to contribute to individuals leading satisfying and rewarding lives, being content with specifying the logics of these competing theoretical viewpoints in the form that proponents of each are inclined to understand and espouse them. The reason is self-evident: the purpose of this book is to offer an empirical assessment of these matters, predicated upon the same kind of replicable, public evidence used to study other aspects of human thought and behavior. Reasonable individuals can, and will, always differ so long as we are limited to abstract debates over the relative veracity of the intangible assumptions that drive both market-oriented and the social democratic strategies toward maximizing human happiness. We may avoid this kind of unprofitable and endless academic debate by providing an empirical and thus "objective" answer about which approach does indeed provide the greatest happiness to the greatest number, providing only that we can in fact measure and study happiness in a scientifically rigorous fashion. We begin that investigation in the following chapter.

4

The Scientific Study of Happiness

Before we can begin our empirical appraisal of the effects of political out-comes on human happiness, we must first familiarize ourselves with the social scientific literature on subjective well-being. This chapter is thus devoted to developing the intellectual infrastructure needed to approach well-being in the way we study more conventional topics in the human sciences. I begin with the obvious question of measurement, considering if such a seemingly complex and multifaceted issue as happiness can be studied with survey data. As we shall see, it is now widely agreed that subjective appreciation of life can indeed be approached using such methods.

Given that we can measure subjective well-being, we are in a position to pro-pose and to test theories about its nature and causes, using both individual- and national-level factors as our explanatory variables. I review two types of such theories, before providing the synthesis which informs the present analysis. The first suggests that happiness is largely a function of inner psychological pro-cesses, depending variously on genetic inheritance, general personality struc-tures, adaptation to environment, or social comparison. The other suggests just the opposite by maintaining that our happiness depends in the main on the extent to which our needs as human animals are gratified. Although these approaches are sometimes sharply contrasted (see, e.g., Veenhoven, 2009), I argue that they are, for present purposes, complementary.

I then turn to the chapter's final and most practical task: reviewing the exist-ing empirical research on the causes and correlates of happiness, with the goal of providing an inventory of the factors agreed to play a major role in deter-mining levels of happiness. My purpose in specifying the other known causes or predictors of happiness is to be able to account for them – to control for them – in the statistical analyses that follow. In terms of the "variable language" in which testable hypotheses about the observable world are typically stated, then, our dependent variable, the phenomenon to be explained, is life satisfaction.

The independent variables, the conditions which are argued to affect satisfaction, are political variables representing the competing public policies of the Left and Right. The control variables, which this discussion identifies, are the essential nonpolitical factors that we must simultaneously consider to have the greatest possible confidence in the causal relationships that the subsequent chapters seek to establish.

THE MEANING OF HAPPINESS

It may be instructive to reflect on the meaning of happiness before considering how to measure it. However intangible or ineffable philosophers or poets may find the idea, for social scientists the concept is agreeably straightforward: it refers simply to the extent that people enjoy their lives, taken as a whole. As we move into the labyrinth of conflicting theories and interpretations of happiness, it is necessary to keep this definition in mind. What we hope to measure and eventually to explain is nothing more – and nothing less – than the *degree to which people enjoy their lives*.

We can distinguish this kind of general life satisfaction from what are called "domain" measures, which focus on some particular aspect of life, such as job satisfaction. Life satisfaction may also be distinguished from other equally partial elements of one's internal life, such as mood, which may vary from day to day or hour to hour. We conceive of life satisfaction as involving a more generalized and enduring attitude toward one's life. Psychologists thus sometimes refer to life-as-a-whole measures as "global" measures of well-being, in that they focus on the overall, total quality of one's life (rather than on a specific domain of life), which is presumed to be relatively stable over time (rather than merely a transient mood).

Although subtle distinctions are sometimes made between life satisfaction and happiness, wherein the former is argued to offer a cognitive and the latter an emotional appraisal of one's life, these terms are more often used interchangeably. This is for two reasons: (a) the theoretical distinction between cognition and emotion when evaluating how one evaluates one's life is a precarious one, and in any event, (b) the correlations between the two questions (and, as noted in the following, other measures of well-being) tend to be very high (and especially so in the advanced industrial democracies that are my focus), suggesting that they are measuring the same underlying concept. In general, happiness, satisfaction, and similar indicators capture the same basic dimension of subjective well-being. While the distinction between happiness and satisfaction may be of interest to psychologists, for whom the parsing of internal mental states has a natural appeal, I adopt the convention of most scholars working in sociology and political science in treating these terms as synonymous. Whether we call it life satisfaction, happiness, or, as some prefer, subjective well-being (SWB), we are speaking of the same theoretical and empirical entity: the extent to which the individual enjoys life.

MEASURING HAPPINESS

There is a simple, efficient, and well-understood method for generating data on how individuals evaluate the quality of their lives: survey research. This method allows us to readily generate data from representative samples of persons sufficient to make statistically meaningful conclusions about who is happy and why. Recent decades have witnessed the explosion of this kind of survey data, the most familiar of which are provided from the World Values Surveys, which provide high-quality data for several dozen countries for the last three decades. They contains a number of items on subjective well-being, including what has become the standard question in the field: "All things considered, how satisfied are you with your life as a whole these days?" Respondents are asked to reply on a scale from 1 (*very dissatisfied*) to 10 (*very satisfied*). Minor variations on this wording, and in the number of response categories, are used in other familiar surveys, such as the General Social Survey (for the United States) or the Eurobarometer (for the European Union), but the common and essential point is to solicit a subjective appraisal of the quality of one's life in general.

The subjective aspect is crucial, in that ultimately one's inner life is just that – an inner, subjective experience – rather than something that can be assigned to the individual by others, based upon the attainment of income or other presumed life goals. To the extent that we are interested how much people actually enjoy their lives, we must of necessity rely upon subjective measures of exactly this type. The goal in measuring subjective well-being, then, is avoiding the unnecessary, arbitrary, and, as we now know, frequently entirely mistaken assumption that we can presume to know how satisfied someone is with their life by deducing how satisfied that we think they should be. To understand how happy people are in general, we need to measure that concept itself, using survey items such as those noted earlier.[1]

Whatever the advantages of relying on survey data, their use contains obvious pitfalls. However, these relate not so much to the peculiarity of happiness per se, which as a matter of principle should present no unique measurement problems compared to any other personal "attitude," but rather only to the cautions appropriate when using any survey indicator. For a survey item to meet the conditions for scientific utility, it needs to meet two basic criteria: it has to be "valid," meaning that it actually has to measure what it purports to measure, and it must be "reliable," meaning in effect that the question elicits consistent and thus meaningful answers. When applying the same survey question across different countries (and thus cultures and languages) there is also the related question of comparability across these contexts. I examine each in turn.

---

[1] A variety of other constructs beyond ordinary survey data have been proposed, notably Kahneman's attempt to compute an "experienced happiness" score for individuals by having them keep daily inventories of their "affective experiences" (Kahneman et al., 2004). Commenting later on this enterprise, Kahneman (2008) conceded that while the exercise was "interesting and useful" it did not produce the revolution in methodology that had been hoped.

Validity

For a measure of subjective well-being to be valid is to say that it genuinely elicits the respondent's true inner feelings about how happy they are. There are a number of ways which one might suspect such a question to fail. The most obvious are that individuals do not understand the question, somehow misinterpret its meaning, or do not know themselves how happy they are. There is a simple way of testing this proposition: compare self-evaluations with external criteria. When doing so, we find exactly what we would hope to find if self-reports of happiness are valid. Thus, people reporting to be happier than average have been demonstrated (among many other things), to laugh and smile more than others during social interactions, to be less likely to attempt suicide or to become depressed in the future, to be more likely to recall positive rather than negative life experiences, to be less introverted and shy, and to be more optimistic about the future. Crucially, self-assessments of happiness also correlate highly with external evaluations from friends and family members, as well as with clinical evaluations (for reviews, see Myers and Diener, 1995; Veenhoven, 1996; Frank, 1997; Diener et al., 1999; Frey and Stutzer, 2002, chap. 2). The fear that individuals cannot adequately report how happy they are because they themselves do not know can thus be dismissed. As Veenhoven (1996: 3) rightly summarizes the situation, "Most people know quite well whether or not they enjoy life." In the end, the utility of the survey data depends on nothing more than the veracity of this commonsensical proposition.

A further potential problem for the validity of self-reports of happiness depends on the degree to which people are in fact willing to be entirely honest in their answers because of what is called the social-desirability bias: individuals answer the question in the way that they believe they should as opposed to how they really feel. Thus, respondents might feel social pressure to not admit to unhappiness, and thus to overreport how happy they feel. The literature gives strong reasons to believe that this is not a particularly troublesome issue in the study of life satisfaction. Perhaps the strongest evidence on this score is provided by Veenhoven (e.g., 1996). He reviewed, first, evidence from studies that have attempted to demonstrate a social desirability bias in survey measures of happiness by comparing the results of a single direct question asking the individual to rate their own happiness to the evaluations of the same persons from professional, clinical evaluations (using "in depth interviews and projective tests"). Given that both methods produced very similar results, it seems improbable that the expected kind of bias is present. Just as one would expect to discover, say, homophobia or racism through in-depth interviews and clinical psychological evaluations that an individual might deny in the context of a single survey question assessing his or her attitudes toward the relative target groups, one would also expect the clinical methods to discover unhappiness that one might decline to admit to a simple survey question asking them how happy the person is, if he or she were in fact answering the survey question in response to social pressures not to disclose their unhappiness.

Veenhoven also provided original statistical evidence against the idea that social desirability effects plagued responses to happiness questions. He found that there was no correlation between how important people thought it was to be happy and how happy they actually reported themselves to be. Surely, if people's responses to happiness questions are colored by how important happiness is thought to be, we would find evidence of that in this way. At the aggregate, we would expect societies in which individuals believe that it is more important (and thus socially desirable) to be happy to have higher levels of self-reported happiness. The fact that Veenhoven (1996, 1997a) finds no such thing is compelling evidence that social desirability bias is not a major concern when appraising self-reports of happiness.

We also see evidence in support of the validity of self-reports in the technical characteristics of responses that survey researchers look for. Validity tends to be confirmed when the response time, the refusal rate (the percentage of respondents refusing to answer the question), and the number who do answer selecting the "don't know" option are all small. This is the case with subjective well-being questions (Veenhoven, 1996: 4).

A final test of the validity of self-reports is temporal stability. Given that satisfaction with life is defined such that it is neither a transient mood that should swing dramatically from day to day or even week to week, or a completely fixed and unalterable characteristic that is impervious to life-events, an individual's answer to the question of how satisfied they are should show reasonable stability over time, but also vary in a predictable fashion in response to changes in circumstances, such as illness, divorce, or unemployment. These are again precisely the patterns that we observe (e.g., Veenhoven, 1996).[2]

Reliability

In its strictest sense, reliability means that if asking the same question repeatedly one receives the same answer. An unreliable survey question is thus one that people appear to respond to randomly, either because the question is badly worded (such that they do not understand it) or because it is attempting to tap an underlying attitude or opinion that just does not exist. A classic example in the study of public opinion is asking citizens arcane questions about the details of public policies about which they know nothing and consequently have no real opinion about. They may nonetheless answer the question precisely because it was asked of them, but will answer in a way that reflects, say, the lingering

---

[2] There is, to be sure, a debate in the literature (to be encountered shortly) about whether such changes are temporary (with individuals returning over time to their natural "set-point"), though even the strongest proponents of this view now admit that such adaptation is not always complete (e.g., Diener et al., 2006). In any case, as a question of measurement per se, the survey item responds as it should, which exhausts our present concerns.

effects of questions asked earlier, the characteristics of the interviewer, or merely their own passing whims. More generally, reliability implies that those being interviewed find the questions they are asked meaningful, have actual opinions about them, and are able to articulate those opinions through the survey response categories.

We have already touched on one way of accessing reliability: the stability of responses over time. This is because for happiness questions, where the underlying attitude being examined is presumed to be relatively stable, reliability and validity equally require such stability. Another approach is to consider stability not across time, but across similar questions. Thus, if we ask the same basic question in substantially different ways but obtain similar results, we can think of the indicators as being reliable. This approach can be readily applied in the present context by asking about one's subjective well-being in different ways. The World Values Surveys, for instance, contain a number of different survey items that we would presume measure the same underlying disposition. The three most common of these are the satisfaction question introduced earlier, a similar question which asks explicitly about "happiness" rather than satisfaction, and another that invites the respondent to compare their present life to hypothetical "best" and "worst possible" lives. Responses to these three items (each purposely spaced at some distance from each other in the order of questions) show very high correlations (e.g., Veenhoven, 1996; Diener et al., 2010) that in the aggregate approach unity (Schyns, 1998), suggesting that they do indeed measure the same thing: the individuals' appraisal of how much they enjoy their lives. If so, we can be confident that the survey items are reliable, for if individuals were responding randomly, or as an artifact of how or where in the survey the questions were asked, we would not find such correspondence.

While the happiness items are thus widely agreed to be generally reliable, it is important to understand what the implications of less than perfect reliability are, and thus why the issue is of lesser importance than validity. If our measures are invalid, the conclusions we draw from them may be entirely wrong, in that the data do not measure what they are supposed to measure. Unreliability, on the other hand, most commonly manifests itself as imprecision or "noise" in the data. A simple example of this is a respondent who is uncertain as to whether they are "very satisfied" or only "fairly satisfied," and who may thus choose different answers at different times (or, similarly, report they are "very satisfied" but only "fairly happy"). That they are at least "fairly" satisfied is not at issue, but only whether they would go as far as "very satisfied," so that the measure does not really distinguish between these different states. The result is not, as with invalid data, to lead us to make wrong conclusions, but only to be less sure, so to speak, in making right ones. In statistical terms, the correlations between happiness and other factors will tend to be attenuated (making the connections between happiness and other factors appear less strong than they might be), which in turn makes it more difficult for them to achieve statistical significance (i.e., making us less sure that the connection exists). Unreliability, then, poses a very different "threat" to data analysis: it makes our job more difficult. When we find otherwise statistically (and, of course, theoretically) compelling results in the face of potential unreliability, we can remain confident about results. In this sense, unreliability is merely a nuisance in data analysis, not an insurmountable abstract problem.

Comparability Across Countries

Two major potential problems in comparing survey data on happiness across nations present themselves. Veenhoven, in a series of papers (summarized in 1996), has considered each. The first relates to linguistic barriers. As words like *satisfaction* or *happiness* have subtleties and connotations that differ across languages, it is natural to wonder if these differences hinder comparison. Veenhoven concludes that there is little reason for concern, in that the rank ordering of countries are virtually identical when considering national means on questions about "life satisfaction" with the alternative questions referred to earlier about "happiness" and "best and worst possible lives." He (as well as Inglehart, 1990) finds too that average levels of satisfaction within multilingual countries do not differ by language group. In the most telling example, the German-, French-, and Italian-speaking Swiss do not differ dramatically from each other – and, further, do differ from their colinguists in Germany, France, and Italy. This strongly suggests that neither language narrowly conceived, nor language group extended to represent a de facto culture, colors survey responses to questions about well-being.

A second issue returns to social desirability: if the social pressure to over-(or under-)state happiness differed across countries, this would obviously render meaningful comparison difficult. Such a concern seems especially relevant given that some cultures, such as the Japanese, may actually discourage expressions of happiness, as such might appear to violate norms of modesty. Among several other tests, Veenhoven looked for evidence of this propensity by comparing average satisfaction in countries where surveys indicate that happiness ranks high in value hierarchies to satisfaction in countries where it does not. He found no differences, suggesting that our data are not polluted by cross-national differences in the degree or direction of social desirability bias.

Summary Assessment of Measurement Issues

The available evidence suggests that we can both measure life satisfaction in a scientifically rigorous fashion as well as compare its levels across nations without great difficulty (for a general summary and evaluation, see Bok, 2010, chap. 2). This is certainly the conclusion offered by the two scholars most associated with the appraisal of self-reported measures of happiness. Veenhoven has examined in detail a large number of concerns over the scientific utility of self-reported satisfaction in a number of papers, concluding in the end that most doubts "can be discarded" (1996: 4). As he puts it, the "literature on this point can be summarized as saying that simple questions on happiness and life-satisfaction measure subjective appreciation of life quite validly" (1997b: 157). Similarly, Diener et al. (1999: 4) summarizes the scholarly consensus on "global" (meaning life-as-a-whole) self-reports, typified by the conventional questions on life satisfaction and happiness: "these measures possess adequate psychometric properties, exhibiting good internal consistency . . . stability, and appropriate sensitivity to changing life circumstances." We have, then, the essential ingredient – valid, reliable, comparable data – necessary to proceed with a rigorous investigation into the question posed by Einstein: "how to structure society so as to make human life as satisfying as possible." The next step along that path requires an analysis of the theoretical approaches advanced by scholars for understanding how socio-political conditions affect happiness.

THEORIES OF HAPPINESS

There are two major approaches to explaining variations in happiness across individuals or countries. Pressing them to their extremes so as to best illustrate their logics may be helpful. One relies on what psychologists like to call a "bottom-up" process, in which happiness is largely determined by events and situations external to the individual's inner mental processes. In this view, happiness will be affected by observable characteristics of the individual, such as their health; by the social and material conditions of their lives, such as whether they have a life partner, how much they enjoy their job, and their income; by behavioral characteristics that mimic personality traits, such as the extent to which they worry or suffer from chronic anxiety (activities which are themselves at least in part determined by external circtumstances); and by aspects of their socio-political environment, such as the crime rate or level of political freedom. This view is associated with the idea that happiness is determined by the extent to which universal human needs are met, with greater need gratification producing greater happiness.

In contrast, "top-down" theories suggest just the opposite: happiness is a product of the individual's inner psychological processes more than the external world. Just as the bottom-up metaphor suggests that particular life events are aggregated or summed to produce some given level of happiness, top-down theories suggest that one already has a preset internal happiness level, and that this in turn almost entirely colors one's day-to-day experience. There are a variety of such theories. One is predicated on the notion that individuals have genetically or experientially determined "set-points," which are akin to such physical characteristics as eye-color or height, or that humans routinely and automatically acclimate themselves to whatever external conditions present themselves through the process of "adaptation," which produces much the same lack of correspondence between happiness and the conditions of life as set-points. Another and highly influential theory of this type is social comparison, which is predicated on the assumption that happiness is determined relatively through a comparison of one's own life situation to that of others (Easterlin, 1974, 1995).

Before proceeding, it is necessary to consider what is at stake. The bottom-up interpretation is the obvious, commonsensical approach to understanding happiness, and in particular for understanding how differences in happiness across countries are to be explained. People are happier when more of their needs are met; ergo, societies that develop sociopolitical structures that best allow people to gratify their needs will exhibit the greatest levels of happiness. The arguments I have reviewed in previous chapters for and against political regulation of the market have all implicitly depended on this supposition, as does nearly all contemporary popular (if not academic) discourse on politics and economics. We may differ in our conclusion about what will make life better, but there is an agreed-on mechanism: life is better when we create the background conditions that best allow human beings to flourish.

By contrast, top-down interpretations, if taken to their logical extreme, and interpreted as being exhaustive in determining happiness, imply that happiness is not a function of the outside world, so that attempts to make the world better by improving living conditions, whether by the political program of the Left or the Right, are doomed to failure. Happiness, it follows, could not be meaningfully increased, because it is not determined by the degree to which human needs are met. What this transparently implies, as Veenhoven (2009) memorably puts it, is that people will "be equally happy in Heaven as in Hell." If so, it can hardly matter whether we pursue the policies of Mrs. Thatcher or those of the Swedish Social Democratic Party.

Fortunately, we are not faced with a choice between these interpretations: our evaluation of life can be determined in part by both top-down and bottom-up processes. We can admit that individuals may have some disposition toward a certain level of happiness, as set point theory suggests, and that individuals in some ways evaluate their position in life relative to others, while still maintaining that the structure of society – the environment in which humans live and attempt to satisfy their needs – is also as important as common sense would suggest. How this is possible is best understood through a closer examination of the logics of the relevant theories.

Happiness Is Determined by the Provision of Human Needs

The most prominent incarnation of this view is "livability theory," as proposed by Veenhoven: "subjective appreciation of life depends in the first place on the objective quality of life," such that "the better the living-conditions in a country, the happier its inhabitants will be" (1995: 3). The basis of this interpretation is the intuitively appealing one "that there are universal human needs" – material, psychological, and social – which emerge from our biological constitution. Human societies, in turn, can be understood "as collective arrangements to gratify these needs," with variation in actual quality of life across countries reflecting nothing less than differences in how effective they are in this respect (1995: 4). In sum: the more people's needs are gratified, the happier they tend to be.

Veenhoven (2009) has recently provided a more formal treatment of livability theory, situating it more firmly in an abstract theoretical language drawn from evolutionary biology. He begins with this central premise: "happiness is a reflection of how well we *feel*, generally" (p. 59, emphasis added). It is for this reason that he labels the theory "affective," that is, one based on human emotional feelings. He quotes Wessman and Ricks (1966: 240–1) to the effect that "[h]appiness appears as an overall evaluation of the quality of the individual's own experience in the conduct of his vital affairs. As such, happiness represents a conception abstracted from the flux of affective life, indicating a decided balance or positive affectivity over long periods of time." Happiness continues to be defined in the conventional way – the extent to which one enjoys life, overall – and is still conceived of as a relatively stable, enduring mental state or attitude. Veenhoven conceives of this state as a kind of running sum total of positive and negative experiences. Although he does not use this language, the suggestion is that we imagine happiness as something like a bank balance, in which positive emotional experiences are deposits and negative ones withdraws. How happy we are at any given time is not, then, the mere fleeting mood of our current or recent affective reactions (or some fixed aspect of our person), but rather our present balance, as it were, taking into account these current or recent states. If so, the key to understanding happiness is clearly to be found in understanding the nature and evolutionary purpose of emotional experience.[3]

"Why," Veenhoven asks, "do we feel good or bad at all?" The answer: emotions "are an integral part of our adaptive repertoire and seem to be linked to the gratification of human needs." He goes on to note that needs are not to be confused with wants; in that needs are those things that are "vital" for surviving and flourishing. We have affective responses to life events because these emotional cues provide guidance to us in our quest to survive and flourish. "Nature seems to have safeguarded the gratification of needs with affective signals such as hunger, love and zest." Thus, we have needs, and the fulfillment or frustration of those needs provides emotional signals that are in turn cues to our behavior.[4] "In this view negative and positive mood function as red and green lights on the human machine, indicating either that there is something

---

[3] To quote Veenhoven (2009: 60–1) "This theory also makes sense in an evolutionary perspective. It is likely that evolution has developed ways of monitoring needs gratification, in particular in organisms that can choose. It is unlikely that rational thinking is the main way, since this developed late in evolution. It is quite likely that adaptation is guided by affective signals in the first place and that all higher animals can feel more or less well. It is unlikely that humans are an exception to this rule. The ability to think was added to an existing affect system and did not replace that. This can be seen in the structure of the human brain, where the affect system is located in the older parts that we have in common with other animals..."

[4] Veenhoven stresses the primacy of affect over cognition for a variety of reasons too detailed to warrant review here. Briefly, he relies upon a long established argument in psychology that affective or emotional appraisals precede cognitive ones; seem to be more fundamental in making choices or forming impressions; and influence cognitive judgments about life much more than the reverse.

wrong or [right]... [T]his is likely to have behavioral consequences, negative mood urging caution and positive mood encouraging going on."

This in turn indicates why, evolutionarily, happiness is a desirable state, and indeed one that is natural for humans to pursue: because it teaches us how best to gratify our needs, which in turn allows us to survive and to flourish. As Veenhoven notes, there is enormous evidence that happy people do in fact live longer and healthier lives, "comparable to smoking or not," with much reason to believe that causality runs from happiness to health (Veenhoven 2006). This point is worth dwelling on, given that competing set-point theories ultimately treat happiness as just another aspect of the person – as Veenhoven notes, as if happiness or unhappiness were merely a neutral and unchangeable characteristic, in the same way that having blue eyes or brown is.

This model maintains the core idea of livability theory as originally articulated: the satisfaction of human needs is the principal determinant of human happiness, such that the program of designing society so as to "create greater happiness for a greater number" remains intelligible through the obvious course of determining what kinds of social, economic, and political conditions maximize the production of human needs. If we accept that happiness can be maximized by maximizing the provision of human needs, two questions present themselves. The first is what, precisely, are the most important human needs; we turn to this question presently. The second is, of course, which of the two basic ideological approaches to human society that we have considered in previous chapters best supplies those needs, and thus best contributes to happiness; this is the empirical question to which the remainder of this book is devoted.

Veenhoven (2009) specifies two ways to advance happiness that provide guideposts toward understanding what he means by human needs: "improving the livability" of a given society and "enhancing individual life-abilities." The meaning of the former is obvious: it refers to creating objective living conditions that most readily allow individuals to fulfill their needs, and might include conditions such as low crime rates, high wages, and liberty. Enhancing "life-abilities" means fostering human development, so as to equip citizens to best take advantage of the resources for meeting needs that high livability implies (or, indeed, providing the skills necessary to improve livability through collective action). Thus, life abilities are the functional equivalent to what Sen (1992) calls human "capabilities," meaning having the positive ability to make real choices about the conditions of one's life. Poverty and inequality, per Sen, can be conceived of as capability deprivation, given that they limit the ability of the individual to develop, as do other social ills, such as the absence of education opportunities, oppression by government, and economically or politically imposed modes of thought or consciousness that discourage free choice. Someone could be deprived of such capabilities in many ways, e.g., by ignorance (i.e., lack of schooling or training), government oppression, lack of financial resources, or, for want of a better phrase, a false consciousness that limits the individual's ambitions or belief in their ability to succeed (such as that identified as "cultural deprivation" by Pierre Bourdieu [1986]).

It is obvious, then, that Veenhoven conceives of human needs broadly. In this he explicitly follows Maslow (1970), who proposed five types of needs, arrayed hierarchically (such that one pursues higher needs only when those lower have been secured). These are physiological needs, safety and security, love and belonging, esteem, and self-actualization. The happiest society would be that which best allows individuals to provide themselves with these needs. We can appreciate what this means by looking more closely at what Maslow included under each category.

Physiological needs are those required for physical survival, such as food, clothing, and shelter. Once these needs are satisfied, individuals move on to focus on their "safety," which might more profitably be conceived as having "security": financial and employment security, security against accident or illness (and for one's family, security in the event of one's death), security for one's person and property against violence or robbery, and so on. Security may also include the idea of justice, which offers a global social commitment to safety in its most expansive sense. Social needs include not only romantic and sexual love, but also friendship and immersion in social networks that provide a needed sense of belonging (as in sports teams, civic or political organizations, labor unions, religious groups, etc.). The absence of close connections manifests itself in loneliness and isolation, which are in turn associated with pathologies such as introversion and neuroticism. Esteem refers to the human need to be respected and valued by others and by one's self (i.e., self-esteem). It is the desire to be treated with dignity and respect by others, and to believe that one is worthy and deserving of such. When these needs are satisfied, the person feels self-confident and valuable as a person in the world. Self-actualization is the need to develop one's potential, to achieve whatever life goals one chooses, and, in sum, to feel in control of one's own life.

To anticipate what is to come, it may be instructive to note the close correspondence between this list of needs and the observed correlates of happiness to be discussed presently, to say nothing of the connections such needs have to the arguments for and against the welfare state, labor unions, and similar market interventions discussed earlier.

Set-Point Theory

We can distinguish two kinds of human characteristics. Traits are essentially aspects of the person, whereas states are conditions that apply to the person. To take extreme examples, height is a trait, whereas poverty is a state. The distinction is of profound importance for the study of happiness, in that if happiness is a fixed trait, there is little point in attempting to change sociopolitical conditions so as to maximize its attainment. Alternatively, if happiness is a state, its level can be affected through obvious means: by public policies that improve the conditions and prospects of people's lives.

Some psychological theories suggest that happiness is in fact a trait, or at least something with enough "trait-like" characteristics to suggest that it is a relatively fixed, internal condition of the person. The common point of such arguments is the contention that happiness is largely the product of "inner causation," something determined by one's mind rather than by one's life circumstances. Some people, it is said, are just happier than others. They have "set-points" to which they naturally gravitate. These set-points represent their normal, long-term equilibrium level of happiness to which external events or conditions move them only marginally and then only temporarily. Everyone is said to be programmed to experience some given level of happiness, which does not in the end depend upon the objective, external conditions of his or her life.

This conclusion can be reached by different paths. The most obvious is to argue that happiness is determined by one's genetic code, such that it is something one inherits from birth.[5] The most compelling evidence for the idea that happiness is a genetic trait comes from the analysis of twins, which found (among other things) that identical twins who were raised apart (and thus faced different life circumstances) showed very similar levels of subjective well-being (e.g., Tellegen et al., 1988, Lykken and Tellegen, 1996). Based upon these analyses (and other, similar studies) it has been argued that as much as 50 percent of the variance in well-being can be explained by genetic inheritance. There is much debate over the exact amount of genetic determination, with some arguing that the level of genetic influence is even higher, while others believe even the 50 percent value to be exaggerated. In any case, though, the consensus view is thus that happiness is partially, but only partially, affected by genetics, leaving, at the very least, a substantial and perhaps a predominant portion determined by the kind of lives that people lead (e.g., Inglehart and Klingemann, 2000).[6]

---

[5] Another possibility, proposed long before genetic evidence was available, focused not on a strict biological source of happiness, but presumes instead that it is an acquired disposition, something ingrained in the individual at a deep level through pre-adult life experiences. Some people, it is said, develop more positive attitudes toward life than others, not so much because of who they are (as in the genetic argument) but rather because what happens to them determines who they are. This ingraining happens easily in one's youth, becoming complete by the end of adolescence. Thus, as Lieberman (1970:74) put it four decades ago: "at some point in life, before even the age of 18, an individual becomes geared to a certain stable level of satisfaction, which – within a rather broad range of environmental circumstances – he maintains throughout life."

[6] Some psychologists put much emphasis on the process of adaptation, in a manner analogous to genetic influences. In this view, people are disposed toward some given level of happiness, which need not be specified – it can merely be assumed that people on average tend toward the mean level of satisfaction in their country (or other reference group). When positive or negative life events occur, individuals may be briefly affected, but ultimately revert to the mean. The seminal contribution to the literature on this subject is Brickman, Coates, and Janoff-Bulman (1976), who purported to find that neither winning a fortune in the lottery nor suffering terrifying accidents leaving victims paraplegics had any enduring effect on happiness. A variety of other studies have since argued for adaptation effects of a more modest nature, suggesting, for instance, that people generally do eventually return over a period of months to their prior levels of happiness following events such as divorce or a large increase in income (see Diener et al., 1999).

Fortunately, this is all that we must establish, in that even if, say, 50 percent of the variance in well-being is genetically determined, this means that 50 percent is not. We are still eminently capable of using statistical tools to determine what factors determine that remaining portion. Were one to determine that, say, doubling the size of the U.S. welfare state would double the amount of happiness, the fact that we are working with only half the variance in happiness would not in any way change our conclusion about the effect of the welfare state. In this example, the amount of happiness in the country would still double. That it might have quadrupled if genetics did not intervene to damper the effect is irrelevant, insofar as we wish to increase happiness.

The reduced variance in reported levels of well-being is thus, like the reliability of the life satisfaction measures, merely a practical obstacle to finding strong results, not an indictment of any statistically significant results that are found. Seen in this light, the prospect that genetics, or any other manifestation of a fixed personality, determines one's satisfaction with life is, again, irrelevant, *if* we find statistically compelling evidence for other, nongenetic effects. Set-point theory thus provides no necessary reason to believe that we should not look to public policies to improve the quality of life that people experience – whether by intervening in the market, or protecting markets from such intervention.[7] Nonetheless, given the prominence of set-point theory in the literature, a further digression into its logic will prove instructive for understanding how personality can affect well-being across nations in ways that are entirely consistent with livability theory.[8]

Personality Traits and Subjective Well-Being (SWB)

More than a decade ago, Diener (Diener et al., 1999) correctly noted that the "working model of researchers in the field [of psychology]" depended upon the notion of set-points. While a more recent survey of the literature notes that

---

[7] Of course, one might be able to make a case for this prospect even if completely accepting set-point or adaptation theories. As Carol Graham (2005: 48) notes, "Even under the rubric of set point theory, happiness levels can fall significantly in the aftermath of events like illness or unemployment. Even if levels eventually adapt upwards to a longer term equilibrium, mitigating or preventing the unhappiness and disruption that individuals experience for months, or even years, in the interim certainly seems like a worthwhile objective for policy."

[8] It is perhaps worth noting that there is much empirical evidence against the idea that happiness is a trait or traitlike characteristic of individuals in the way set-point theory suggests. The most exhaustive and careful examination of this question is offered by Veenhoven (1994; see also 2009). He considers the core empirical predictions of the trait argument: that happiness is stable over time, and in particular that it does not lastingly respond to "fortune and adversity." He also examines the theoretical question of "whether the evaluation of life is largely determined by 'inner' psychological characteristics rather than by 'external' living conditions." In both his own empirical analysis and in his review of the existing literature, Veenhoven (1994) concludes that the trait interpretation fails: "The results are: 1) Happiness is quite stable on the short term, but not in the long run, neither relatively nor absolutely. 2) Happiness is not insensitive to fortune or adversity. 3) Happiness is not entirely built-in: its genetic basis is at best modest and psychological factors explain only part of its variance."

much work that has caused this approach to be strongly "questioned" as the "discordant evidence" about its utility accumulates, it nonetheless remains the "dominant or at least most widely accepted theory . . . in research on subjective well-being" in psychology (Headey, 2008). Still, as Diener himself acknowledged (Diener et al., 1999) even within this interpretation, set-points are not argued to be solely determinant, given that "SWB has both trait-like and state-like properties."

Thus, in this interpretation, it is granted that happiness per se is not a trait, but it is argued instead to be strongly affected by other personality factors that are themselves relatively fixed traits. Such traits in turn could, again, be either a genetic inheritance or something acquired during the maturation process, but in either case, they are thought to affect how we react emotionally to (and, indeed, how we cognitively perceive or categorize) life events. Happiness, then, is indirectly affected by these personality traits, as they become the lenses through which we interpret the world. We have already encountered in Chapter 3 the personality traits most commonly argued to affect satisfaction with life: extroversion, neuroticism, optimism, self-esteem, and efficacy (the sense of being in control of one's own life). The process by which the last three might affect well-being are self-evident: people who feel confident about the future, who respect themselves, and feel in control of their own lives are certainly more likely to interpret day-to-day events in a more positive fashion. The other items have more complex and multiple pathways to happiness (for a discussion, see Diener et al., 1999), but in the end, they also have an intuitive connection to happiness. Extroverts are less likely to focus unprofitably on themselves and to welcome and enjoy human interactions, while neurotics – people who tend toward worry and anxiety – find life less appealing in ways that do not require further elaboration.

The immediate point of this contention is straightforward: happiness is to be conceived of as being partially determined by one's relatively fixed personality "traits" – so that happiness itself is traitlike – but at the same time, happiness is also admitted to be determined partially by conditions external to the individual. But there is a deeper point, not seemingly appreciated by the proponents of trait theories, which flows from the fact that the aspects of personality thought to affect happiness are themselves not entirely fixed and unalterable traits. They may be real dispositions, but they need not be completely immutable: people can become lastingly more or less optimistic, more or less introverted, and so on, over time. They change not merely their behavior, but their underlying personalities. Observing such changes in ourselves and our fellows is a common aspect of human experience. It is easy to imagine that the personality can develop and grow, particularly when the conditions of life encourage such growth. Going to college, for instance, is surely likely to affect personality in a way we commonly associate with growth and development.[9]

---

[9] To illustrate with a political example familiar to students of democratic theory, citizens who are encouraged (or required) to participate in workplace or civic organizations develop greater

We can extend this logic to consider circumstances in which individuals might become more or less optimistic, or more or less neurotic, as external conditions change. For instance, the New Deal programs that offered hope in the face of the deprivations of the Great Depression surely increased how optimistic many people were while also decreasing extreme anxiety and worry (i.e., "neuroticism"). Insofar as these changes in outlook were not merely fleeting changes in mood but were relatively enduring and genuine changes in one's outlook on the prospects for a better future, we can conceive of such changes as being the functional equivalent of changes in the personality "traits" that affect happiness. Major events, such as living through an economic depression, change people; so too does the accumulation of the smaller, more mundane, everyday events that make up a human life.

It follows, then, that these aspects of personality can change in response to changes in the conditions of one's life, so that "innate" personality traits are, like happiness itself, at least somewhat responsive to factors external to the individual. If so, then we may grant that happiness is partially determined by aspects of personality, but we may equally say that these same personality attributes are themselves mutable, so that social policies designed to improve happiness might be directed toward fostering the latent personality traits that are most conducive to happiness. This commonsensical view is, of course, evident in the psychological literature. Emmons, Diener, and Larsen (1986), for instance, long ago suggested that one's environment and one's personality mutually affect one another, in much the way described previously. More recently, Boyce, Wood, and Powdthavee (2012) have provided strong evidence that the personality traits associated with happiness do in fact vary considerably over time, and that these changes correspond with changes in happiness in the predicted direction. It is only a small step from here to equating personality attributes like efficacy or optimism with Sen's (1992) human capabilities, which are obviously affected in powerful ways by forces external to the individual, such as poverty. I would argue that this is, indeed, the most instructive way of conceiving of the kind of personality traits in question, which in turn points us toward the politically determined, objective conditions of life stressed by Sen as the factors producing them.

The idea that personality "traits" can be changed is the same common sense that motivates the entire "positive psychology" literature, which attempts to provide individuals with practical strategies for achieving greater happiness, whatever their set-points or personalities. No one argues with the suggestion that individuals can intervene in their own lives so as to "learn" to be happy, in part by changing their dispositional characteristics – teaching themselves, in effect, to worry less, to be more optimistic, or to be less shy. They can learn to

self-esteem, self-confidence, and efficacy through the process of participating (for a discussion, see Radcliff and Wingenbach, 2000). If so, creating more participatory opportunities, such as those provided by labor unions in the workplace, should foster precisely these kinds of positive personality changes.

foster the behavioral and cognitive traits that promote greater optimism and greater self-esteem. If individuals themselves can make such changes, it follows obviously that societal changes in the conditions of life can have similar effects: we can alter sociopolitical arrangements so as to promote the mental states most conducive to happiness.[10]

This contention is consistent with, if not strictly equivalent to, recent work by Kahneman and his collaborators, who suggest that while happiness is indeed affected by personality, it is equally affected by "the hedonic value of the activities to which people allocate their time." Of course, as Kahneman (e.g., 2008) stresses, again echoing Sen (1992), the "hedonic value" of the "activities" that make up one's life is heavily affected by his or her individual wealth and status, to say nothing of the wider social and economic context in which his or her life is embedded. Put differently, the "activities to which people allocate time" are heavily affected by their life circumstances. Those struggling to make ends meet "allocate time" in ways radically different from the affluent, for reasons that hardly require explication. This takes us to precisely the conclusion our a priori intuitions about happiness might suggest: happiness doubtless depends in part on one's personality, but it also depends on the objective quality of one's life, which in turn reflects in part the objective quality of the society in which one lives.

Happiness is thus not best conceived as a fixed personality trait, but rather as something that emerges from a combination of our life experiences and the interaction between those experiences and particular aspects of our personality. This implies the general conclusion that the set-point or trait approaches reduce in practice – when identifying factors that cause *average* levels of happiness to vary from place to place or time to time – to something very much like the common sense view of "livability" theory. The contribution of the trait approach is thus not to lead us away from the idea that we can improve the amount of human happiness in the world, but to underscore a second, additional level at which we might strive to do so: by strengthening and facilitating those aspects of the human personality that best allow individuals to find the happiness they naturally pursue.

To summarize, it may be useful to compare our conceptualization of happiness to that of obesity – or, to maintain the directionality of preferences over having this attribute, fitness. They are individual level characteristics that vary across both individuals and nations: within any country, some people are fitter than are others, just as mean levels of fitness vary across countries. Each concept is agreed to have a genetic or personality-driven component, but neither is entirely determined by this disposition. People are not obese entirely and only,

---

[10] The malleability of the human propensity for happiness is clearly evident in the experience of immigrants, who, the literature suggests, tend to lastingly adjust their subjective well-being to the general level of the society in which they come to live, rather than maintaining the prior level typical of their country of birth (e.g., Veenhoven, 1997a) and, presumably, their own individual set-points.

or even primarily, because that is just the way they are. Instead, their latent disposition toward a given level of fitness is strongly affected and responsive to their diet and life-style. Similarly, the variation we see in levels of obesity across countries does not reflect so much the shared genetic inheritance of their citizens as the diet typical of the country. The high level of obesity in the United States, for instance, is widely agreed to be mostly a function of the American diet, not of the prevalence of a "fat gene" that somehow dominates the U.S. gene pool. Even if some of the variation is indeed due to genetic structures, much of it, almost certainly most of it, is a function of the "objective conditions" of American life, in the form of the national diet. The same, then, is likely to be true of happiness: genetics and/or similar unalterable features of individuals might play some role, but we can still identify the factors external to the individual, amenable to change, that also play a role. For the student of happiness, the goal is to identify those factors that play the same role as diet or exercise for obesity and, so armed, to suggest public policies that would encourage the appropriate behaviors.[11]

Social Comparison Theory

In 1974, economist Richard Easterlin delivered a now classic paper on the question, "Does Economic Growth Improve the Human Lot?" His answer, subsequently elaborated and defended in much later work, was surprising and disquieting: once a country reaches a minimum level of affluence, further growth does not contribute to greater happiness. The evidential basis for this empirical claim is the absence of any apparent relationship between per capita GNP and average levels of happiness within countries over time: as a country becomes richer, happiness does not increase as a result. Easterlin proposed a theoretical explanation: subjective well-being is a product of social comparison, wherein individuals compare their economic situation (their level of "consumption") to the norm within their society at any given time. Thus, Americans in 2010 are happy when they are above the "consumption norm" for this time and are unhappy when they are below it. That in 2010 all or most are above, say, the 1950 median level of consumption is irrelevant, in that what matters is one's level relative to that of others. Thus, we typically see, as Easterlin notes, that at any particular point in time, those with higher incomes

---

[11] If people are less obese in country A than country B in a way that is consistent with theoretical predictions about which kinds of diets produce more obesity than others, the only way to dismiss this correspondence is to postulate that some third factor affects both obesity and diet, creating the illusion that diet matters. This seems unlikely, to say the least. In any case, no one can seriously believe that Americans are obese just because of their genetic backgrounds, not because of what they eat. The obesity metaphor thus provides a strong intuitive example of the truism that even if genes are important, they are not the only thing that is important. Just as no one could seriously maintain that "there's nothing to do about obesity, it is all in people's genes" it would be equally ridiculous to suggest that "happiness is not affected by the quality of the society in which people live, so we don't have to worry about making their lives better."

do report greater happiness, but only because they are higher in the hierarchy of financial success for their time. Increases in median income over time (of the sort that raising GNP would plausibly be thought to produce) do not change the average level of happiness, because there are by definition always as many people below the median as above it.

Now, it is essential to note that this process of social comparison, as Easterlin himself seems to believe, is usually presumed to apply mostly or only to consumption, and not to other things that promote happiness, such as health, or the quality of one's family life. If so, the obvious conclusion, and arguably the single most important take away point from the argument from social comparison, is that as a society we should encourage individuals to focus less on financial gain in their aspirations for a happier life, in that they will see greater returns from other domains that are not (as strongly) affected by social comparison.[12] Governments are then best advised to concentrate on values other than (or at least beyond) economic growth – security, health, fulfilling and stable interpersonal relationships, job satisfaction, social capital, and so on.

The reasoning is twofold. First, because more money just makes one want to get more money to sustain or improve one's position in a status hierarchy, it leaves one on a "hedonic treadmill" that does not produce lasting improvements in happiness. Second, by pursuing this game, individuals actually make life worse for others, imposing a kind of negative externality on society by providing upward pressure on others to maintain their relative position vis-à-vis others. It is in this spirit, for instance, that the British economist Richard Layard (2005) argues that the narrow pursuit of greater income and career success (the proverbial "rat race") is a kind of "pollution," affecting society in the same way as industrial waste. He suggests social policies, such as special taxation on incomes, to help individuals maintain a better balance between work and other aspects of life. More generally, he makes the entirely reasonable and commendable suggestion that we should focus less on income (and, thus, economic growth per se) and instead consider the process by which happiness is more readily created, which involves the kind of factors we have already reviewed.[13]

---

[12] The sharpest critique of this approach is Veenhoven (e.g., 1991, 2009), who tends to interpret the logic of social comparison as if it did apply to all goods promoting well-being, which would, if true, suggest that "happiness is insensitive to actual quality of life." As this is demonstrably not true, we must either abandon social comparison or limit the range of human concerns to which it applies. The profound divergence between Veenhoven's needs-based approach to happiness and social comparison theory depends on just how many domains of life social comparison does apply to. So long as we limit social comparison to affecting primarily only consumption, it remains compatible with the approach to happiness that Veenhoven advocates.

[13] Layard argues, as most scholars in the field would, that five core domains of life contribute to happiness: family relationships, financial situation, quality of work life, community and friendship, and health. Social and economic policy should thus be directed more specifically toward these goals, rather than narrowly and simplistically on income, and thus, economic growth. The theoretical connections between these priorities and a generous welfare state, strong

Social comparison theory remains controversial (for a general assessment, see Dutt, 2009; Graham, 2009; Frank, 2009). Much attention has naturally focused on the "Easterlin Paradox" per se,[14] but for our purposes Kahneman's (2008) summary of the global pattern contains the essential point: "Humans everywhere, from Norway to Sierra Leone, apparently evaluate their life by a common standard of material prosperity, which changes as GDP increases." Fortunately, we have the liberty of remaining agnostic about the relative consumption hypothesis as a general phenomenon, insofar as its relevance for the empirical analyses that follow is the modest one of controlling for whatever effect relative rather than only absolute income might have on individual assessments of well-being. The empirical literature in economics tends to focus on absolute rather than relative income, with little fear that the resulting models are misspecified by this strategy.[15] In any event, there is a straightforward method of defusing concern over the effects of relative income, which I adopt in the econometric chapters that follow: I include one's subjective level of income satisfaction along with their actual reported income as control variables. If relative income is important to people, it will drive their income satisfaction levels, and including such in the model will capture any potential impact on their appraisal of their lives that operates through this mechanism.

DETERMINANTS OF HAPPINESS

It is to this general question of specifying the empirically established individual- and national-level determinants of happiness that prior research has identified that we now turn. My central purpose is to review what we know about the causes and correlates of happiness on issues other than those regarding state and market, so as to be best able to control for these factors in the empirical models that motivate the chapters that follow.

We must first pause to consider the preliminary question that animated our discussion of set-points versus the gratification of human needs: What does the empirical research say about the basic question of whether conditions external

---

labor unions, and economic regulations that make life more satisfying require no elaboration; nor do the close connections between Layard's domains and Maslow's Hierarchy of Needs.

[14] See, for instance, Oswald (1997). For a detailed exchange between Easterlin and his critics, see Hagerty and Veenhoven (2003), Easterlin (2005), Veenhoven and Hagerty (2006), Easterlin et al. (2011).

[15] To take just one prominent example, Frey and Stutzer (2002) devote a chapter of their notable and important book to reviewing the literature on the effects of income on happiness, where they maintain that "it is not the absolute level of income that matters most, but rather one's position relative to other people" (p. 85). However, they go on in their own empirical analysis of both the effects of income per se (see chap. 4) and on other determinants of happiness for which income is only a control variable (chap. 8–9) to use only a conventional measure of absolute income. How can they do so, if it is relative income that matters? The obvious answer is that one can safely ignore relative income (even if one believes it is all that matters) because absolute income appears to adequately capture the real effect of income (absolute or relative) on happiness empirically (in part because the two covary in an obvious fashion).

to the individual's inner mental processes correlate with, and, thus (given a compelling theoretical argument to expect such a correlation) presumably cause happiness? Whether this is the case is the central difference between livability and trait theories of happiness, and as such the answer offers a way of adjudicating between them.

Does Happiness Have Correlates?

Taken literally, set-point and trait theories suggest that essentially nothing should correlate with happiness in that external conditions are not important, or at least not of lasting importance, as causes of happiness or distress. In large samples, the temporary effects of life events should largely cancel each other out, particularly since the decay function eliminates whatever impact on satisfaction such events might have over fairly short periods. On average, people should all be at or near their set-points, or have largely adapted to whatever living conditions they face. We should see little or no connection between events or conditions external to the individual. Neither individual-level factors (such as income or being married) nor country-level conditions (such as the level of economic development) should matter.

In reality, of course, proponents of these top-down theories do not typically claim that forces external to the individual are completely irrelevant, but that they have only weak or insubstantial effects on well-being. This argument depends on the much-repeated claim that external variables explain only a trivial amount of the variance in subjective well-being (e.g., Diener et al., 1999). This influential contention, providing as it did the initial impetus for top-down models, is problematic in several important ways. The first is that it is overstated, with much current research suggesting stronger correlations than originally reported. Kahneman (2008) notes, for instance, the correlation he finds between life satisfaction and a nation's GDP is "over .40 – an exceptionally high value in social science." His reference to the figure being high "in the social sciences" highlights the general propensity for survey data in the social sciences to yield relatively modest correlations as a hazard of survey data, rather than of the phenomenon being studied. The cause is the unreliability of the data. As discussed earlier, this is a technical problem – meaning, an issue introduced by the survey method itself – which manifests itself as measurement error, which tends to attenuate statistical relationships. It does not cause bias, it only introduces noise, which tends to damper relationships, making them appear weaker than they are likely are. Researchers used to working with survey data are seldom troubled by low explained variance for exactly this reason. In any event, there is a simple expedient by which one can determine if the low correlations are due to random measurement error or to genuine lack of correspondence with external factors: aggregate the data from the individual to the aggregate level, i.e., change the unit of analysis from individual self-reports to the national means. If random measurement error is an issue, it will tend to resolve itself when averaging across large numbers of respondents.

It is, indeed, for this very reason that much research on the sociopolitical determinants of happiness relies on national means rather than on individual-level data.

The results of these studies confirm the suggestion that external factors do explain much of the variance in happiness. To take just three examples, Veenhoven (2004) explains about 75 percent of the variation in average happiness across a wide set of countries using variables representing economic affluence, freedom, and democracy, while Pacek and Radcliff (2008) explain no less than 94 percent of the variance in life satisfaction across the member states of the European Union (from 1975–2002), using economic and political variables, and Helliwell and Huang (2008) report models wherein structural social conditions explain 70 percent of the variation in mean satisfaction in a sample of more than seventy countries. A number of other studies of aggregate satisfaction have produced similar results. In sum, the low correlations between factors external to the individual and happiness appears to be a function of what we have previously referred to as the "nuisance" of unreliability of the survey data. National averaging, which largely eliminates the effects of unreliability, demonstrates exactly the kind of strong relationships that top-down, set-point-type theories deny exist.

The usual interpretation of the low individual-level correlations (that happiness must be determined by factors intrinsic to the individual) does not follow for yet another and more fundamental reason: the level of correlation is simply not the appropriate statistical metric by which to judge the strength of a casual effect. A high correlation between, say, income and happiness emphatically would not imply that there is necessarily a strong relationship between the variables in that sense normally understood, i.e., that a modest change in income would produce a large change in happiness. As Achen (1982: 61) puts it, correlation "measures nothing of serious importance" in this kind of context. What matters instead is the slope of the line (the regression coefficient) connecting income to happiness, which provides precisely what we want to know, viz. how changes in income correspond to changes in happiness. On this question, correlation is silent on everything but direction (whether positive or negative); it does not indicate the strength of the relationship at all. A very high correlation can very easily be associated with a tiny slope, suggesting that, in this example, there is in fact a very weak substantive relationship between income and happiness, in the sense that even very large changes in income would produce only trivial changes in happiness. Conversely, one could have a small correlation but a very steep slope, which would imply that happiness is indeed very elastic with income–which is, of course, precisely the contention denied by set-point theory.

One example, entirely characteristic of the literature in general, is Blanchflower and Oswald (2002), who (confirming much previous research) find a massive and highly significant negative effect of unemployment on life satisfaction in the United Kingdom, which is inconsistent with top-down theories. They report a similar finding for the United States, as well as strong relationships between satisfaction and other variables (such as divorce). At the same time, the explained variance for their models hovers around a tiny 5 percent. To their credit, the econometrically sophisticated authors focus almost entirely on the magnitude and significance of their slope coefficients rather than on the explained variance, rightly concluding that unemployment has an enormous impact on satisfaction. The low R-square is unremarkable because, as so often occurs when using individual-level survey data, explained variance is artificially diminished by measurement and response errors (i.e., unreliability). High explained variance is always a welcome and positive result for the modeler, but it is not necessary. We look instead to the estimates of the independent variables, as these tell us what factors are important statistically (they are "significant") and practically (as reflected by how much they affect the dependent variable, i.e., by the magnitude of the coefficients).

Two conclusions can be drawn from this discussion. First, we can say with confidence that the principal evidence used to support the move from bottom-up to top-down theories is largely irrelevant to the debate between them. Second, using more appropriate statistical evidence – slope coefficients rather than correlations, as well as the use of national averages – provides evidence supporting bottom-up rather than top-down theories. It remains now only to review the individual- and national-level factors which prior research has identified as important determinants of happiness.

Individual-Level Determinants of Happiness

There is an extensive literature cataloguing the factors that appear to determine how happy individuals tend to be. The following discussion draws heavily in its format from the convenient review provided by Frey and Stutzer (2002), as well as other recent surveys of the field (Layard, 2005; Di Tella and McCullough, 2006; Graham, 2009; Diener, Helliwell, and Kahneman, 2010).

Sociodemographic Factors. Age displays a U-shaped pattern with happiness, such that both the young and the old are happier than are those in the middle, with the nadir of happiness (controlling for other factors) appearing to be in one's early forties. There are varying interpretations of why this might be, the most obvious being that youth is a natural font of happiness, which is dampened by the frustrations and compromises of life until one learns how to enjoy life in a more sophisticated fashion.

The effects of gender are less clear, though, on balance, the collective evidence seems to suggest that women are marginally happier than are men overall. This is easily reconciled with the fact that women also appear to suffer from anxiety and other mood disorders more frequently than do men because women may simply experience both more extreme positive emotions and more extreme negative emotions (for a detailed review off all aspects of the mental health of women, see Nolen-Hoeksema and Rusting, 1999). More generally, either because of a biological difference or because of socially assigned gender

NO – age – H correlations don't say anything about causation roles that encourage this propensity, women may on average have a marginally higher level of emotionality. So long as the relative balance of emotion favors the positive in the long run (as, again, the evidence suggests), women would experience greater overall average happiness.

Race has the predictable effect on well-being in the United States: persons of color have lower levels of subjective well-being than do whites. The magnitude of the difference in some studies is less than one might expect because some of the effects of race are absorbed by other variables, such as income, or psychological factors, such as self-esteem, both of which we might, sadly, expect to be lower among groups that have been traditionally discriminated against. It also appears that the difference between races, at least in the United States, has been declining over time, as one would hope, given that the degree of discrimination has declined in recent decades. Cross-nationally, race has been less studied (in part because of limitations in the World Values Study, which provides most of the data for cross-national comparisons), though the data seem to suggest the same pattern as in the United States: in South Africa, for instance, blacks report lower happiness than do whites, but the difference becomes small when we control for factors (like income) through which their inferior position in society manifests itself. From a statistical point of view, the fact that the effects of race nearly disappear when relevant statistical controls is convenient, in that it allows the estimation of models that omit race itself as a control variable when the data do not allow for it.

Education shows inconsistent effects vis-à-vis happiness, varying across model specifications, in part because its effects are, again, channeled through other variables like income. Equally, higher education may not provide greater happiness because it also raises aspiration levels, which make it more difficult to be happy. Education might also encourage a more obsessive interest in one's work, which becomes more literally a career, which in turn may lessen the energy invested in other aspects of life, such as friends and family, to the detriment of one's happiness.

Income. Income is understandably one of the most studied and discussed determinants of happiness. The conventional wisdom in the literature is the familiar admonition that "money does not buy happiness," given that income is argued to have a relatively modest effect on well-being. Thus, one does consistently find that greater income is associated with greater happiness, but the amount of variance explained tends to be small. As we have seen in the previous discussion, however, considering only explained variance is not the best way to determine the relative contribution a given variable makes to the value of another. Frey and Stutzer (2002: 82) provide some simple evidence to illustrate that the role of income might be larger than the psychologists suggest. They note, for instance, that in the United States (using data from 1994), "the proportion of persons rating themselves to be "very happy" rises from 16 percent for those with incomes below $10,000 to 44 percent for those with incomes above $75,000." We see the same pattern at the other extreme: "the proportion of persons considering themselves to be "not too happy" falls from 23 to 6 percent" when moving between these same income groups. These differences are dramatic and similar to what common sense might suggest, yet the correlation between happiness and income with the same data was only a modest .20. As before, the reliance on correlations tends to make relationships look less pronounced than they are.

There is also considerable evidence that the effect of income on happiness displays diminishing returns, though it is unclear how quickly the relationship flattens, such that additional income starts to provide very little additional benefits. Frey and Stutzer (2002: 83) provide a graph of subjective well-being versus income which shows only a very modest leveling toward the upper end of the measured maximum income of $100,000 per year or higher. It is very likely that the relationship does eventually become quite flat at higher incomes not included in the study – say, by $200,000 or $300,000 – but the pattern for the more reasonable levels of income, which account for 95 percent or more of Americans, shows only a tiny bit of variation from linearity. This is important for our understanding of income – diminishing returns exist, but they only begin at very high income levels – as well as for how we model the effect of income statistically. Given the small variation from linearity within the income ranges actually included in the typical survey, we can presume that happiness is effectively linear with income.

As we have seen, economists sometimes argue that income should be measured in relative rather than absolute terms (for a review, see Frey and Stutzer, 2002, chap. 4), such that people exhibit more satisfaction with life when they perceive themselves to be better off than others. As noted, there is a simple method for controlling for this possibility in statistical models: include one's subjective level of income satisfaction along with their actual reported income as control variables. If relative income is important to people, it will drive their income satisfaction levels, and including such in the model will capture any potential impact on their appraisal of their lives that operates through this mechanism. As with all the "control variables" discussed in this section, my purpose is not to specifically appraise whether they affect satisfaction, but merely to control for them as potential alternative explanations that must be statistically accounted for to ensure that my statistical results could not be artifacts of failing to consider these other possible causal factors.

Employment Factors. It is convenient to quote Frey's and Stutzer's (2002: 10) summary directly on the kind of work issues that are known to affect happiness: "employment and working conditions, the stress involved at the workplace, [and] interpersonal relations with work colleagues." A large body of literature attests to the great (and growing) importance of work in most people's lives (e.g., Lane, 1991; Hochschild, 1997). Indeed, one scarcely need appeal to an authoritative scholarly literature to realize the centrality of work to life: no one could doubt that people's general feelings about their lives are affected by their relationships to their jobs. It should consequently not surprise us that work-related issues are important contributors to well-being. In prior chapters, we have focused on precisely these kinds of issues, and how they may be linked to the quality of one's life. The existing literature has tended to jumble these matters together into a single construct of job satisfaction. Although this oversimplifies, it remains constructive, in that studies show job satisfaction (even using the simple correlational criterion I have been at pains to criticize) to be a strong predictor of overall happiness. Of more interest still, students of job satisfaction have identified some aspects of work which determine how satisfying it is. These include, beyond pay and benefits, some of the specific issues discussed in prior chapters as directly affecting happiness: job security, physical safety at work, social status provided by the job, opportunities for personal self-direction at work, ability to actively use one's skills and abilities, nonmonotony, and opportunities for friendship and other personal connections among workers (Frey and Stutzer, 2002: 104–5).

Even more important than these multiple aspects of job satisfaction is the fact of having a job, that is, not being unemployed. Few things could be more clearly related to a worker leading an agreeable life than having a job, given that one's (and perhaps one's family's) financial security depends upon possessing one. Given, as we have seen, that in market societies, workers depend for their livelihoods on selling their labor power as a commodity, workers' inability to find a buyer for that commodity will of necessity be associated with distress. We see this clearly in the literature: being unemployed is one of the strongest correlates of unhappiness. It frequently emerges as the single most important factor in determining levels of happiness.

Marriage and Other Social Connections. If unemployment has any competitor for being the leading determinant of subjective well-being, it is in having close interpersonal relationships. Marriage, or an equivalent form of life partnership, is in turn widely agreed to be the most important interpersonal relationship. We thus find that marriage raises happiness, everywhere and at all times. The relationship holds for both men and women and is robust in the face of simultaneously including other controls, including unemployment, income, age, and so on.[16] The importance of marriage requires little elaboration: at least when successful, marriage supplies strong protection against loneliness or isolation (which clearly diminishes well-being), while also being for partners a vital source of self-esteem by providing (Frey and Stutzer, 2002: 57–8) "an escape from stress in other parts of one's life (in particular, one's job)." That marriage provides enormous emotional benefits of this kind is also suggested by evidence implying "that marriage brings marked advantages in terms of mortality, morbidity, and mental health" (Lee, Seccombe, and Shehan, 1991, quoted in Frey and Stuzter, 2002: 57).

---

[16] Marriage can sometimes be reduced to statistical insignificance when including simultaneously a control variable for the quality (or satisfaction with) "one's home life," which illustrates the general point that broader, more inclusive controls can reduce the apparent affects of more particular or narrow controls (through multicollinearity), but this does not always imply, as with marriage, that the more specific factor is not intrinsically important.

Other kinds of personal connection also produce greater levels of well-being, with the magnitude of the effect roughly equivalent to the emotional closeness provided. Close relationships with friends or other family members would come first after marriage, followed by more casual friends, neighbors, work colleagues, and so on. All kinds of positive personal connection appear to benefit the quality of one's life.

We thus see the social connections in general as being a source of happiness. Individuals who are immersed in the kinds of cooperative interpersonal networks that proponents of "social capital" are concerned with – such as social and civic clubs, neighborhood associations, and other voluntary associations – display higher levels of happiness. Thus, Putnam (2000a), among others, has demonstrated that individuals who are immersed in such networks (i.e., who volunteer and join such organizations) show higher levels of happiness, though it is not clear in which direction causality runs, i.e., do people become happy by joining, or do people join because they are happy? In the same way, the other principal benefit argued to accrue to individuals with high levels of this kind of "social connectedness" – the development of "norms of trust and reciprocity" (typically measured by a survey item asking how trusting of other people one abstractly tends to be) – also shows a positive correlation with happiness (and other measures of physical and mental well-being).[17]

Health. Like (un)employment or marriage, health would be an obvious suspect for any list of the determinant of happiness. The data bear this out: self-reported health is another consistent and powerful predictor of happiness. It is true that the effects of physician assessments of health are smaller, but this hardly changes the fundamental conclusion that people who feel healthy enjoy life more than do those who do not feel healthy.

Religion. The principle aspect of religion that is commonly studied in the happiness literature is attending religious services, which generally shows a positive association to happiness. The problem is that it is difficult to disentangle the social effects of attending church (increasing social connections) from any spiritual benefit. Inglehart (e.g., 2010; see also Norris and Inglehart, 2004) has explicated a number of pathways via which religion might improve well-being net of its effect on social connection (e.g., by providing meaning and purpose in an uncertain and dangerous world or, perhaps less felicitously, by "dampening aspirations" for a better earthly life), though as he notes these connections are likely to be weaker in countries with developed welfare states (for the reasons we have observed in prior chapters). In what is likely the best work done on this subject, Putnam and Campbell (2010), using panel data, which allow a

---

[17] There is also some evidence, principally Helliwell (2003), confirming what we might expect, viz. that the mean level of interpersonal trust within a country, as well as the mean number of memberships per person in voluntary organizations, have positive effects on overall levels of well-being, net of the effects accruing to the specific individuals trusting or volunteering themselves.

better dissecting of causality than the cross-sectional data typically used, offer strong evidence that the connection between religiosity and happiness is due to social connections made through one's religious congregation, i.e., they find no evidence that religious *beliefs* explain happiness. Happily, as we are interested in religion only as a control variable, we may remain agonistic on the nature of the benefits that attending religious services provides, and merely include such a variable in our econometric models.[18]

Cognitive and Emotional Dispositions. As we have noted in passing earlier, the literature suggests that there are a number of personality characteristics that relate to happiness: extroversion, neuroticism, optimism, efficacy (i.e., sense of having control of one's life), and self-esteem. Why these dispositions should promote happiness is largely self-evident (for a discussion, see Diener et al., 1999). Extroverts are happier than introverts because the latter are more inward looking, socially withdrawn, and less likely to seek out or to enjoy companionship; lacking the excessive self-focus of introverts, extroverts are also better able to invest emotional resources in others, and to have more rewarding marriages and other interpersonal relationships. Neurotics are less likely to be happy because the anxiety and other mood disorders that plague them negatively affect their well-being and interfere with their ability to build and maintain nurturing relationships; neurotics also tend to focus on, and be more adversely affected by, negative life events. Optimists confront a world in which they expect mostly positive experiences, and thus are more likely to experience just that; they are also less easily dissuaded from pursuing goals than are pessimists, who, expecting defeat, are less persistent, and thus more prone to failure. People with high levels of efficacy are happier, as they do not feel themselves to be victims of powers beyond their control, and thus channel frustration or disappointment into positive action rather than resignation; in effect, such persons feel that they possess autonomy and so lead self-directed (and thus fulfilling) lives. Finally, individuals with high self-esteem not only feel good about themselves and their abilities but have also apparently developed the cognitive skills to defend their self-image in the face of life's setbacks and failures; furthermore, to say that one has self-esteem is also to imply that one feels respected and valued by society.

National-Level Determinants of Happiness

Relatively little attention has been paid to how the characteristics of the country in which one lives affects one's level of well-being. The relative paucity

[18] Other survey questions have sometimes been used to gauge the significance of religious devotion, notably that from the World Values Survey asking respondents "how important God is" in their lives. The difficulty with this question is that the meaning of "God" is unclear even with a given religious tradition (would a Unitarian Christian recognize the God of a Pentecostal?), and becomes even more unintelligible cross-culturally (is it likely, for instance, that "God" means the same thing to a Buddhist, a Hindu, or an Animist as it does to a Christian or Muslim?).

of the literature on this subject, compared to the enormous body of work at the individual-level, leaves us with a less clear understanding of national-level determinants of happiness. The situation is made worse by a tendency of different scholars to use different control variables, to operationalize concepts in different and incommensurate ways, and to rely on wildly different samples of countries, which often pool heterogonous sets of countries without adequate considerations of the consequences (e.g., when pooling developing and industrialized countries). That said, the literature does identify a number of factors which are widely agreed to affect cross-national levels of well-being (for reviews, see Pacek, 2009; Graham, 2009).

Economic Development. Of all variables studied, a country's level of economic development or modernization emerges as the most important. This is hardly surprising, given that richer countries provide a number of advantages over poorer ones. The most obvious is the standard of living itself, which however unevenly distributed remains relatively high, even for the disadvantaged, compared to developing countries. Thus, however difficult life is for the urban poor in the United States or the United Kingdom, there are not shantytowns surrounding Los Angeles or London. Equally important are the ancillary effects of development, which also affect quality of life, manifested in institutions and practices that Westerners may take for granted, but which are less well established in poorer parts of the world. It is, as Inglehart and Welzel (2005) note, this wider set of qualities, often labeled "modernization," that contributes to greater subjective well-being: civil and political liberties; the rule of law; political stability; relatively low rates of violent crime; the relative absence of corruption; relatively low rates of economic inequality; relatively accessible medical care of a relatively high nature; relatively open educational opportunities; and economies that are (even in the face of such events as the global economic crisis current of this writing) relatively stable (given the resources and political structures to ensure such).[19] Richer countries are, in sum, just nicer places to live. As Frey and Stutzer (2002: 76) put it, "It has been established that essentially all social indicators are more positive in nations of higher income: richer countries enjoy more and better quality food, cleaner drinking water, better and more widely spread education, better health services, higher longevity, more parity between the sexes, and more respect for human rights."

It is for this reason that, as Veenhoven (1997a, 1997b) and Schyns (1998) suggest, the correlations between many specific, individual measures of the social conditions tend to disappear when controlling for per-capita GDP (or, equivalently, when considering the rich and poor countries separately), suggesting that the more refined indicators are simply tapping a more generalized dimension of development.[20] If so, the most profitable way to proceed is to

---

[19] For an accessible and enlightening discussion and general review of the connection between these factors and well-being, see Graham (2009).

[20] In an otherwise thoughtful and meticulous paper, Helliwell (2003; see also Helliwell and Huang, 2008) puts much emphasis on the explanatory power of a measure of what its proponents call

consider those national characteristics that appear to show a separable and independent effect on happiness when controlling for development. A discussion of such factors follows.[21]

Democracy. As noted earlier, democracy and economic development tend to covary, such that more development implies more democracy. While democratic institutions and practices do tend to be better provided as the size of the economy increases, their provision is sufficiently affected by other factors, and sufficiently important for happiness, that their attainment appears to have the kind of separable effects from development noted above. Thus, a large literature documents the connection between democracy and happiness. As Inglehart (2010: 354) succinctly puts it in his review of the literature, "happiness is strongly related to democracy," though there is also disagreement as to the magnitude of the relationship, whether the relationship is the simple linear one usually supposed, and, above all, to the direction of causality (i.e., does democracy foster satisfaction more than satisfaction fosters democracy (e.g., Lane, 2000: 265–6; Inglehart, 2009)). Fortunately for purposes at hand, we need not take sides on such questions, or even consider variation in levels of democracy as a matter of statistical control, given that our attention in

---

"good government" developed by the World Bank (Kaufmann, Kraay, and Mastruzzi, 2005), going so far as to suggest it "dominates" the importance of economic development. This is hardly surprising, given that the index, constructed for any given country from an average of twenty-five different variables, not only correlates very strongly with development (as its creators are quick to point out) but also covers the correlates of economic development which are in turn thought to explain the association between development and satisfaction. The index includes, for example, measures of democracy (covering "political, civil and human rights"), political stability, the professionalism of the police and courts, the actual "likelihood of crime and violence" within a country, the control of corruption, and so on. It is difficult to interpret this index, given that it covers such a large range of concerns, being again an amalgam of twenty-five indicators that cover everything from political structures to social and economic outcomes. It is thus unclear what it represents, unless we interpret it, in the main, as just another measure of development. That approach, however, is invalidated by the fact that the index also contains hidden ideological presumptions which further limit its utility, particularly in having one of its six (equally weighted) dimensions devoted to "measuring the incidence of market-unfriendly policies" (as defined by the Heritage Foundation). To first define deference to the market as evidence of "good" government and then to lump it together with a score of other variables, as if they all represented the same underlying construct is methodologically mistaken, implying as it does that a low level of welfare spending is the equivalent of a low rate of violent crime. This ideological bias renders the "good government" variable inappropriate and unintelligible. For a general assessment and critique of these measures, see Kurtz and Schrank (2007).

[21] As with individual-level income, there is some evidence that the aggregate level of affluence (development) carries diminishing returns, such that increases tend to produce little improvement in happiness beyond a certain point, usually thought to be approximately the level of the poorer West European countries such as Portugal or Greece. Although there is much to commend in this view when considering all countries simultaneously, GDP per capita shows a statistically significant and linear (if smaller) relationship with happiness when considering only the richer OECD countries. Radcliff (2001), for instance, finds this pattern when considering only fifteen such countries, while Inglehart (1990) also did for twenty-four (nearly all developed) countries.

subsequent chapters is focused on Organisation for Economic Co-operation and Development (OECD) countries, in which democracy is so firmly and uniformly established that empirical measures of it do not meaningfully vary over the time frame in question, making its inclusion in the analysis unnecessary (and, indeed, econometrically impossible given the democracy variable would be a constant).[22]

Culture. There are two kinds of arguments typically made regarding the effect of culture on subjective well-being. The first, best exemplified again by Inglehart (e.g., 1990), conceives of variation across nations in levels of satisfaction with life as reflecting accumulated national experiences, absorbed in pre-adult socialization, that form a "national character" that is largely (though, admittedly, not entirely) immune to changes in the objective conditions of life. In this view, culture becomes the national equivalent of a relatively fixed personality, affecting the overall level of satisfaction in a country in precisely the same way that human individuals have set-points that predispose them toward a given level of happiness. In this view, national culture is the extension of the idea that happiness is a personality trait, in this instance a collective rather than an individual one. Veenhoven (e.g., 1994) argues passionately and convincingly against the idea that countries, any more than persons, have rigid and all-encompassing set-points. Radcliff (2001) suggests that the difference between Inglehart and Veenhoven is largely one of emphasis, because the former does not deny that observable conditions do affect satisfaction but only imagines the magnitude of the relationships to be more attenuated than does Veenhoven.

Others have sought to connect international differences in satisfaction with variation not in ideographic national cultures, but with more particular cultural characteristics. By far, the most successful of such attempts is the effort to show that the fundamental cultural dimension relevant to happiness is that between "individualistic" as opposed to "collectivist" value orientations (e.g., Diener et al., 1995; Veenhoven, 1996, 1997b; Pacek and Radcliff, 2008). The basic distinction is between the prevalence of cultural norms that encourage citizens to define themselves as either essentially autonomous individuals or as members of nested superordinate groups (e.g., family, religion, ethnicity, region, nation, etc.).[23] In collectivist cultures, individual freedom is subordinated

---

[22] The potential for democracy to affect SWB may instead draw our attention toward "smaller" democratic institutions and practices that allow the individual to attempt to exercise some control over their lives through political participation. Thus, we might find that other participatory institutions below the national level promote happiness. Frey and Stutzer (2002) find that happiness in the Swiss cantons varies directly with the amount of participatory, direct democracy present. Others have pointed toward work-focused practices that increase the amount of participation in the day-to-day decisions of the workplace (e.g., Layard, 2005; Radcliff, 2005). The most important and most institutionalized form of workplace democracy is, of course, the labor union, which is a variable that we consider at length in subsequent chapters.

[23] There is a long tradition in comparative politics of considering the special importance of what scholars conceive of as a specific "Catholic culture." This implies the existence of social norms,

to the customs, practices, and perhaps needs of the reference group, with consequently greater emphasis on conformity and obedience to authority, and thus
less freedom for individuals to lead lives that maximize their own personal
satisfaction.

In terms of statistical modeling, I adopt the strategy of Pacek and Radcliff
(2008), who refrain from any final judgment over the utility of either approach,
but attempt to include appropriate statistical controls to account for either
possibility, to the extent the data allow.[24]

National Unemployment. Unemployment, as we have seen, is one of the
strongest individual-level determinants of happiness. Given that the unemployment rate represents not only the experience of those unemployed, but acts as
a barometer of the level of social anxiety about the prospects of their own job
security, as well as of general, short-term economic performance, the national
level of unemployment is often argued to affect happiness, net of the direct
impact of personal unemployment (e.g., Frey and Stutzer, 2002: 100–2).[25]

CONCLUSION

This chapter was devoted to an overview of the scientific study of happiness. It had three specific goals. One was to review the intellectual infrastructure that allows us to measure happiness, and thus to study it using familiar survey research methods. The standard measures, much scrutinized by
skeptics and advocates alike, were concluded to display the essential characteristics (validity, reliability, and cross-national comparability) the researcher
requires.

The chapter also sought to explain and to evaluate the major theoretical
approaches to understanding happiness: the "commonsense" view that happiness is ultimately determined by the degree to which human needs are satisfied,

ethics, and modes of life that are shaped by the historical legacy of the Catholic tradition, which
can be roughly but adequately captured in comparative research by focusing on the percentage
of the population that self-identifies as Catholic (for an example in the literature on subjective
well-being, see Bjørnskov Dreher, and Fischer, 2008). I thus consider this cultural dimension in
subsequent chapters.

[24] The first approach to culture can be accommodated by fitting separate intercepts for each
country, which is generally feasible only when using pooled time-serial data (i.e., countries over
time). The second is easily accounted for simply by including as a control variable a measure of
the individualism of culture, such as that suggested by Veenhoven (1996). These econometric
details are discussed in more detail as necessary in subsequent chapters.

[25] Another probable determinant of life satisfaction that may not be reducible to economic development is, of course, communal violence, interstate or civil wars, and similar incidents of
violence and disorder (though rich countries certainly have experienced less such strife in recent
decades). Relatively little attention has been devoted to this issue, in part because the negative
effects of such conflicts need little documentation (see Veenhoven [1984] for some evidence
of the commonsense expectation that civic disorder produces lower levels of satisfaction). The
exclusion of such factors is, however, a problem in studies that attempt to be global in their
inclusion of all possible countries, without, as noted previously, considering the possible model
misspecification which fails to consider such factors.

versus the alternative approach in which happiness is effectively determined by internal psychological processes of the individual rather than by the objective conditions of their lives. I argued that these perspectives are not mutually exclusive, such that we can accept that happiness is partially determined by one's genetics, personality, or set-point, and quite possibly affected by a process of social comparison, while still maintaining that cross-national differences in subjective well-being will be largely determined by the extent to which societies are successful in gratifying the material, social, and psychological needs of their citizens.

Finally, I reviewed the literature on the individual- and national-level determinants of life satisfaction as the background for the empirical appraisal of the effect of Left and Right public policies on human happiness. It is to this endeavor that I turn in the chapters that follow.

5

The Size of the State

For too many of us life was no longer free; liberty no longer real; men could no longer follow the pursuit of happiness. Against economic tyranny such as this, the American citizen could appeal only to the organized power of government.
                                        – Franklin Delano Roosevelt (1936)

Government is not the solution to our problem; government is the problem.
                                        – Ronald Reagan (1981)

In this chapter, we commence our empirical analysis of the political determinants of happiness, beginning with the most obvious and significant question in the traditional debate between Left and Right: Does "big government" improve or impoverish human life? Given the metric of life satisfaction adopted here for assessing quality of life, this seemingly imponderably complex philosophical question reduces itself to a relatively simple empirical question that is within our means to answer: Does a large, activist state tend to make people more or less satisfied with their lives? To use the formula frequently evoked in the United States over this question, is government the solution or the problem?

The size of government, in turn, can be conceived of as having three aspects. The first is the scope of the welfare state, which directly transfers income from its a priori market distribution to a politically determined distribution. The welfare state dispenses unemployment and sickness benefits, family allowances, pensions, and other kinds of income maintenance to those in need. By decommodifying persons in this way, it fundamentally alters, as we have seen, the basic relationship between workers and employers, with what both defenders and detractors agree are profound consequences for individual and society. It remains for us to determine whether, and how, the changes affected by the welfare state influence human happiness.

The second aspect of the size of the state comprises the multitude of other state activities beyond simple redistribution. These involve the ability to manipulate economic outcomes by the presence of the state as an actor within the economy – an actor which, unlike most others, is not directly or immediately motivated by market calculations of profit and loss. Both the social democrat and the libertarian can conceive of the share of the economy that is publically appropriated by – and thus controlled by – the state as the share that is "democratically" allocated, as opposed to being left to the private sphere; the issue is whether private or public is more consonant with satisfying lives. One way of approaching this concept is to consider what is conventionally called "government consumption": the share of the economy the state sector "consumes," that is, the amount that it spends, on matters other than transfers. Thus, having considered how actively the government redistributes income (through, for example, unemployment benefits and old-age pensions), we can also consider how much it spends on other activities. Here we would consider the total value of all the things the government pays for (and thus administers and controls), ranging from public education to health care to the maintenance of roads to the enforcement of workplace safety and consumer protection laws, and so on. The larger the amount of such spending as a percentage of the economy, the larger is the state as an economic actor.

A final way of approaching the size of government is by considering the tax burden the state imposes on society. This measure is intuitively appealing and easily understood: the tax burden is simply the sum total of the portion of the economy that the government collects as taxes. From this perspective, we can readily imagine placing societies along a dimension in which one end is a a purely "socialist" economy implying one-hundred percent taxation and the other a purely libertarian one having zero taxation. This dimension captures the final size of the state's "footprint" on the economy, reflecting, however crudely, the sum of everything government does, with a larger state size implying a more active and thus potentially a more "controlling" state.

We see, then, three means of measuring the role of government. The best, because it has the most immediate and tangible effects on citizens, is the generosity of the welfare state. It is here that we find the most direct evidence of the degree of the state's effort at providing for human needs, through its provision of cash payments to individuals and families. As we shall see, our empirical measures are always, when possible, attempts to capture the actual benefits that people receive, rather than merely relying on simple dollar amounts of taxing and spending that inform other methods of determining the degree to which a country suffers (or enjoys) "big government." This chapter seeks to determine how these various dimensions of "big government" affect the quality of life that citizens actually experience. I proceed as follows: the next section reviews the connections between human needs and governmental activity previously discussed, which form the basis of the theoretical expectation that a more generous welfare state, or a larger state sector in general, contributes to greater levels of happiness. I then introduce the standard measures used in political economy to operationalize the dimensions of state intervention in the economy that are our concern, before turning to the statistical methodology that informs the empirical analysis that takes up the remainder of the chapter.

PUBLIC POLICY AND HUMAN NEEDS

Articulating the connections between human needs and the welfare state, and by extension other aspects of the size of the state, is not a task that need detain us long. Prior chapters have discussed the arguments for and against political interventions in the economy designed to improve the provision of human needs in some detail. It is necessary here only to provide a brief review and summary, focusing for the sake of brevity on the arguments in favor. According to proponents of the welfare state, there are several mechanisms through which it increases the level (and equitable distribution) of the provision of human needs.

The Welfare State Reduces Poverty and Generally Increases Living Standards

While there is of course much dispute over the ultimate consequences of the welfare state – it is that controversy which in part motivates this book, given that one of its goals is to determine if in the end, the welfare state makes human life more satisfying – there is little doubt that the welfare state succeeds in its immediate and narrow goal of improving the material conditions of life. Despite occasional attempts in the popular press to discredit even the antipoverty consequences of a state commitment to social security, of which Charles Murray (1984) is the most famous and influential example, the actual peer reviewed literature generally confirms that the welfare state achieves its immediate goals of reducing poverty and inequality (for a general discussion and review, see Kenworthy, 1999; Bradley et al., 2003; Scruggs and Allan, 2006).

That the welfare state does reduce poverty has enormous implications for the well-being of individuals and families. The scholarly literature documents a multitude of destructive and injurious effects of poverty too numerous to catalogue. We know, for instance, that poverty is associated with lower self-esteem, lower efficacy, higher rates of depression, and other deleterious psychological states (e.g., Brenner, 1977; Galea et al., 2007; Simmons et al., 2010). It is also well established that poverty is highly correlated with, and a demonstrable cause of, poor physical health (e.g., Porter, 1999), greater rates of alcoholism (e.g., Valdez, Kaplan, and Curtis, 2007), domestic violence (e.g., Gonzales de Olarte and Gavilano Losa, 1999; Heise, 1998), divorce rates (e.g., Buckingham, 2000), and – if any further evidence of its negative effects on human life is needed – shorter life expectancy (e.g., Haan, Kaplan, and Camacho, 1987).

The specter of poverty, or similar if less extreme forms of financial distress that haunt so many working people, thus imposes physical and emotional costs on the individual, which can in turn have secondary consequences that further reduce quality of life. Thus, people who live in the persistent and structural financial insecurity that is inherent in being "commodified" suffer from the persistent and entirely rational fear of future (if not present) financial disaster – the inability to pay the rent, pay their credit card bills, put food on the table – that always threatens to appear over the next horizon. This perpetual and real insecurity is not only emotionally costly, it is also insidious, in the sense that it tends to affect other domains in life besides the financial. For instance, as we have discussed in earlier chapters, the stress and anxiety that poverty causes tends to progressively shrink the individual's world down to a rational obsession with the self, and with security, leaving less room for the nurturing human relationships that are themselves essential human needs. This causes not only a decline in the quality or survival of one's emotional relationships – manifest in the most extreme form, and illustrative precisely of the mechanisms in question, through divorce – but also damages other less intimate but equally supportive kinds of relationships. These are most readily seen in the decline of the bowling leagues that Putnam (2000a) uses as a symbol of a general decline in human connections that come when individuals withdraw from both public life (e.g., civic organizations) and even social life (in Putnam's small but telling example, no longer inviting friends to one's home, as emblematic of less time or interest in building or maintaining relationships). It thus comes as no surprise that poverty is known to lower both membership in voluntary organizations and to reduce levels of social trust (e.g., Kawachi, Lochner, and Prothrow-Stith, 1997).

These same tendencies are documented in the extensive literature on the effects of unemployment (and the fear of it) on individuals: the general effect is a closing-in of one's world, with all attention and energy focused on "keeping body and soul together." It is beyond question that the unemployed are more likely to develop depression, as well as anxiety disorders and other kinds of mental illness, to say nothing of a variety of serious forms of physical illnesses (e.g., Linn, Sandifer, and Stein, 1985; Warr, 1987; Blake, 1995; Mossakowski, 2009).

The Welfare State Reduces the Insecurity Inherent in the Market System

Poverty, unemployment, underemployment, and other forms of financial insecurity reduce human well-being, but (as already noted) so does the chronic apprehension that such conditions may come to plague one at any time. Franklin Roosevelt famously expressed the need for human beings to be free from both need and from fear of need. These represent the most fundamental and important elements in Maslow's (1970) hierarchy of needs: their attainment are necessary conditions for meeting other needs. The fear that Roosevelt spoke of was not merely as a special condition of the time, but a consistent feature of capitalism: the rational anticipation of adverse economic consequences to oneself that are endemic in a market economy characterized by commodification. People are naturally insecure, given that they depend for their financial survival on the sale of their labor power as a commodity, the market for which is beyond their ability to control. In the absence of accumulated wealth that most people utterly lack, market participants live in fear of unemployment or under-employment. This insecurity is an unremitting structural condition of a market economy. It will manifest itself in the individual's psychology as a milder version of the actual effects of poverty or unemployment, creating a similar if less pronounced version of the same psychological issues. Thus the market creates insecurity, making it a seemingly natural part of life. The welfare state, according to its proponents, reduces or limits this pervasive fear and should thus contribute to greater human well-being.

The Welfare States Reduces the Social Pathologies that Accompany Poverty and Insecurity

Economic deprivation is also associated with innumerable social pathologies, which impose costs on society in general, not merely the poor per se. This is most obvious in the study of crime rates. It takes little insight to realize the consequences for society when a portion of its members live in poverty or have a life lived on the perpetual edge of poverty with little hope of a better life. The communities suffering such deprivation are prone to an arguably rational disregard for either law or social norms, breeding the conditions that produce unsafe cities inhabited by people who feel unsafe. If in fact the welfare state reduces poverty and the social desperation that accompanies it, it will also reduce the crime and other antisocial behaviors that follow poverty and desperation. There is ample evidence that is in fact the case. To take but one example, the criminology literature demonstrates that rates of criminal homicide decline as the amount of decommodification increases. As Messner and Rosenfeld (1997) summarize their econometric analysis of criminal homicide rates across the world, "levels of homicide vary inversely with the [level of] the decommodification of labor... The degree of decommodification is negatively related to homicide rates, net of controls for other characteristics of nations." In sum, the welfare state reduces crime, and thus the fear of crime, which in turn is certain to improve the general quality of life in society.

From here it is but a short jump to the generalized social problem of what Durkheim (1893) called "anomie," meaning the decay of the individual's adherence to social norms. Individuals suffering from anomie are prone to alienation from society, thinking themselves separate or apart from it, and inclined thus to behaviors that lack the moral "regulation" societies inevitably depend upon. They are thus prone to "deviant" behaviors, as they lack the moral compass that society presumes is common to its members. Market forces are often argued to promote anomie for reasons that are not hard to fathom. No one denies that the market encourages the rational pursuit of self-interest. The market economy tends to produce citizens with a rational tendency toward goal-seeking behavior that ignores the effects of their activity on others. It seems clear that people will find life less agreeable as the number of people they share their city or country with behave in this fashion. If the welfare state performs its function of protecting people from market forces, it should thus serve to reinforce social norms and thus reduce anomie. Surely the less anomic a society is, the more satisfied with their lives people should be, such that, again, the welfare state and other state interventions in the economy should themselves promote greater satisfaction.

The Welfare State Promotes Agency

For social theorists, agency refers to the ability of individuals to control their own lives, in the sense of being able to make free choices. One has agency when one can act independently. This capability is a human need – to feel in control of one's life, rather than being a powerless cog in the social machine. It is from agency, too, that we trace an important source of dignity of the individual – the recognition by the self and by society that the individual is deserving of respect. Although the market contributes to agency in obvious ways, it also limits it in others. In particular, the central feature of capitalism – the commodification of labor and thus of persons – must by definition reduce agency. The welfare state, by reducing commodification, limits this tendency. Simply put, one is more in control of one's life if one has more security, such that to the extent that the welfare state does provide such security, it contributes to agency (see Rothstein, 1998), which contributes to greater satisfaction with life.

CONCEPTUALIZING AND MEASURING THE SIZE OF THE STATE

In Chapter 4, how subjective well-being can be profitably subjected to empirical measurement was considered. By comparison, measuring the various dimensions of the size of the state introduced earlier in this chapter is straightforward. As we shall see, most of these are directly prepared by (or, in any case, closely based upon) mundane accounting figures routinely prepared by the statistical bureaus of the OECD, the European Union, the United Nations, the International Monetary Fund (IMF), and the World Bank. We begin with indicators designed to tap the generosity of the welfare state, the most complicated and nuanced of the questions at hand, before turning to the simpler measures of general state spending and tax burden. Finally, a summary measure of all aspects of the size of government is briefly considered.

While it is typical to speak casually about "the welfare state," it is not a concept that lends itself to casual measurement. Until fairly recently, the literature on the development of the welfare state relied on simplistic measures based purely on spending, or as it has sometimes been suggested, just the "quantity" rather than the various qualities of the social security system. For decades, scholars assessing the welfare state used aggregate spending levels, typically the share of a country's economy (as measured as a percentage of its GDP) devoted to public welfare programs. While that work certainly contributed to our understanding of the welfare state, more recent scholarship has expressed enormous skepticism about our ability to rely on nothing but raw expenditure levels insofar as we are interested in the actual effects of the welfare state on society, as opposed to a mere fiscal phenomenon. Esping-Andersen (1988: 18–19) puts it this way:

Most of these studies claim to explain the welfare state. Yet their focus on spending may be irrelevant or, at best, misleading. Expenditures are epiphenomenal to the theoretical substance of welfare states... by scoring welfare states on spending, we assume that all spending counts equally.

Two years later, he would give substance to the call for a better method of "scoring" the welfare state in his hugely influential *The Three Worlds of Welfare Capitalism* (1990). In that book, Esping-Andersen directs our attention to the tangible consequences of welfare effort on people's lives by focusing on the decommodification of labor, a theoretical concept that has occupied much of our attention in prior chapters. In Esping-Andersen's succinct definition, "labor is decommodified to the degree to which individuals or families can uphold a socially acceptable standard of living independent of market participation" (1990: 37). As I have been at pains to demonstrate, it is the commodification of citizens that is the core institution of the market economy. It is the degree of decommodification a welfare state provides, not the amount of money it spends, that produces the positive consequences in security, agency, and the provision of other human needs that are our theoretical focus as determinants of happiness. Simply but aptly stated, the level of decommodification in a society is, in the eyes of its social democratic proponents, really the level of "emancipation" from the deleterious consequences of the market that their political struggle against the interests of capital has been able to achieve. If those of a more conservative perspective may reasonably distrust the idea of "emancipation," seeing the market as they do as itself a source of empowerment for the individual, they cannot quarrel with the logic. Whether we think of decommodification as the amount of liberation from the market, or, as von Hayek might put it, the level of subordination of individual workers and employers to an inefficient, wasteful, and even coercive conceit of the state, both would agree that the level of decommodification represents a valuable metric by which to evaluate how closely a society conforms to free market ideals. As such, an objective, empirical indicator of decommodification is the ideal explanatory variable for the present study. We thus rely upon it extensively in the analyses that follow.

Computationally, Esping-Andersen's (1990) measure is a summary index that assesses the extent of social insurance in three specific domains: pensions, income maintenance for the ill or disabled, and conventional unemployment benefits. The scoring on each dimension is built from multiple indicators (five for old-age pensions, four each for sickness and unemployment) to capture the relevant aspects of each program. The details of the complex operationalization are not readily summarized, but perhaps the most concise description is offered by Messner and Rosenfeld (1997: 1399):

Esping-Andersen's measure of decommodification encompasses three primary dimensions of the underlying concept: the ease of access to welfare benefits, their income-replacement values, and the expansiveness of coverage across different statuses and circumstances. A complex scoring system is used to assess [the amount of decommodification provided by] the three most important social welfare programs: pensions, sickness benefits, and unemployment compensation. The scoring system reflects the 'prohibitiveness' of conditions for eligibility [e.g., means testing], the distinctiveness for and duration of entitlements [e.g., maximum duration of benefits], and the degree to which benefits replace normal levels of earnings. The indices for these three types of . . . programs are then aggregated into a combined [additive] index.

At the risk of repetition, three aspects of the definition should be stressed. First, the individual indices are weighted by the percent of the relevant population covered by the given programs ("coverage"), so that the more universal a program, the higher is the scoring; thus, an unemployment scheme covering all or most workers receives a higher score than does one covering only certain types of employees. Second, the formula is sensitive to how generous the programs are: for unemployment, a system is more decommodifying the greater the percentage of the individual's prior income it provides (the "replacement rate") and for how long benefits are available ("duration"). Finally, the approach eschews spending levels and instead focuses on the nature and extent of "entitlements" to state support, which make it immune to a final problem with spending levels, which is that variation in spending may reflect merely greater need among persons (e.g., because there might be a greater number of the unemployed drawing support during recessions) rather than greater state generosity toward persons.

Originally provided by Esping-Andersen (1990) for just one year, the decommodification score is now available in time serial form (courtesy of Scruggs, 2005). These data cover eighteen advanced industrial countries from 1971 to 2002, utilizing the same basic computational methods as Esping-Andersen (1990). Since our main dependent variable under investigation, subjective well-being, is available over time, such longitudinal data are ideal for our purposes. In a subsequent paper, Scruggs also offered a modification of the original Esping-Andersen scoring system, which included an alternative method of scoring individual programs that he argues is more sensitive to their real impact on citizens, which he labeled the "generosity index" (Scruggs, 2005). We thus use this indicator, available for the same countries and years, as well as the original decommodification index. Although we take seriously the difficulties in relying on spending noted earlier, it remains the fact that spending, given its intuitive appeal and easy intelligibility, remains a common focus of public and scholarly discourse. It would thus be foolish to ignore it entirely, in that whatever conclusions we draw about decommodification (or the sibling measure of the "generosity index") can only be strengthened if they also obtain when considering conventional measures of social spending. We thus also consider "net total social spending," defined as the total of public spending (including that publicly mandated in the private sector) across all the main areas of social policy, covering old-age pensions and survivor benefits, medical incapacity supplements, public health spending, family allowances, unemployment benefits, housing subsidies, and so on, as a share of GDP. Data are from the OECD (OECD, n.d.), and are available from 1980 to 2007 for all OECD countries.

This last measure is an ideal bridge to the second aspect of the size of government, that of government "consumption." As noted earlier, this refers to the amount of governmental spending on all activities beyond the provision of the income transfers that we associate with the welfare state. Net social spending reflects primarily such transfer payments, being dominated by mathematical necessity by precisely the kind of insurance-style programs that Esping-Andersen focused on, but also contains those elements of government consumption that are most directly related to social welfare. The paradigmatic examples are public spending for housing, education, and health. While this combination of services with entitlements has obvious appeal, it is also instructive to consider each separately, particularly as the social-spending data purposely exclude so many governmental activities. In the end, the "size of government" has to focus on the totality of governmental activity. Here, too, there is general agreement that, conceptually, spending is in fact the appropriate indicator. We thus utilize the most commonly used measure of general government consumption: the total amount of all such spending (i.e., at all levels of government), expressed as a share of a nation's GDP (using data from the Penn World Tables, version 6.3) again from 1980 to 2007. Higher values indicate, of course, a large state sector, or a more "socialistic" economy.

The other side of government spending is of course taxation. For reasons elaborated earlier in this chapter, if we wish to assess the impact of the size of government, it is certainly sensible to focus on the tax burden that citizens face. Like government consumption, this idea is readily operationalized as the share of a nation's GDP that government (at all levels) collects as taxes. Data are from the OECD (Stat Extracts, n.d.) from 1980 to 2007.

Finally, we consider a summary index of the "size of government" developed by the Fraser Institute (Gwartney, Lawson, and Norton, 2008). It consists of five components, which are standardized into a single summary score: government spending on transfers (the pure money equivalent of the more appropriate decommodification indices discussed previously), the level of government consumption, government spending on public enterprises and investments, and, finally, the top marginal tax rate on income. Data are available from 1980 to 2008. While such indices have to be used with caution, given that they are produced by an interest group with an explicit ideological agenda, they are nonetheless assembled in an entirely transparent and professional manner. The Fraser data have also become so ubiquitous in the political economy literature to warrant their consideration for that reason alone. The ideological orientation (not to say bias) in the data are reflected by the coding scheme, which treats higher values on each of the components as intrinsically undesirable, so that larger scores on the summary index represent a smaller government. We thus expect to see a negative relationship between this measure and life satisfaction, if the arguments of progressives in favor of what their opponents call "big government" are correct. A positive relationship would suggest the conservative conclusion of precisely the opposite.

DATA AND METHOD

As is conventional in the emerging literature on the cross-national determinants of life satisfaction, I rely upon the World Values Surveys. Available in five waves between 1981 and 2007, it provides survey data with representative national samples for all OECD countries over time.[1] Our dependent variable, *life satisfaction*, is the standard question utilized in nearly all prior work in the study of subjective well-being across countries: "All things considered, how satisfied are you with your life as a whole these days?" There are ten response categories, with higher values suggesting greater satisfaction.

I analyze these data in three ways. First, I simply take the satisfaction item noted above as the dependent variable, modeling it as a function of both individual- and national-level factors, using individuals themselves as the units of analysis. Second, following an equally familiar convention of the literature, satisfaction is aggregated to the level of national means so as to explicitly identify those country-level factors that affect the average level of happiness per se; here the unit of analysis is the country-year. Finally, I aggregate country means in a different fashion, considering not the general average but the average of paired social groups (such as women and men, and those of low and high income), with the obvious goal of determining if the same explanatory factors identified earlier affect the major subgroups of the population equally; the unit of analysis remains, of course, the country-year.

While estimation technique and other details of the analysis vary as appropriate, the fundamental method is the same. Satisfaction is modeled as a function of the measures of the size of government discussed earlier, plus a set of theoretically and econometrically appropriate control variables. These statistical models thus provide an estimate of the marginal effect of the political variables of interest, controlling for the effect of the other factors. The resulting regression coefficients thus lend themselves to a ready and intuitively appealing interpretation: as partial slope coefficients, they indicate, if they are statistically significant, the predicted effect on satisfaction of a one unit change in the value of the variable in question. Simply stated, a positive and significant coefficient

---

[1] The analysis focuses on the twenty-one traditional, core member states of the OECD: Australia, Austria, Belgium, Canada, Denmark, Finland, France, Germany, Great Britain, Greece, Ireland, Italy, Japan, the Netherlands, New Zealand, Norway, Portugal, Spain, Sweden, Switzerland, and the United States. The small states of Luxembourg and Iceland are effectively eliminated from the analysis due to missing data on many of the independent variables. Portugal, Spain, and Greece are also missing in some models due to missing data on certain indicators.

suggests increasing values of the given variable produce greater life satisfaction, whereas a negative and significant coefficient suggests just the opposite. Interpreting the magnitude of the coefficients – the elasticity of satisfaction to changes in the independent variable – is less transparent, requiring as it does sensitivity to the units of measurement, among other things. I am thus at pains to interpret the substantive, rather than the merely statistical, significance of the results.[2]

Individual-Level Analysis

When considering the individual-level, my approach to model specification is straightforward, and, I would argue, the most econometrically powerful, for isolating the effect of the political variables from other factors. I specify, first, a set of individual-level controls, which account for the conditions that prior research (reviewed in the prior chapter) has established as important predictors of satisfaction. I account for long term national-level factors, such as a country's culture, history, and level (and type) of economic development by including dummy variables for each country (excepting a reference category). The effect of the dummy variables is, of course, to fit separate intercepts for each country, thus accounting for the large and sustained differences in satisfaction that one might expect to result from different cultural and economic contexts. Thus, the inclusion of these "fixed effects" absorbs the general impact on a person's satisfaction that comes from living in any particular country. The use of these variables as controls allows us to say with confidence that the reported impact of a given political variable on satisfaction holds when accounting not only for the individual-level factors (such as a person's income) that affect their satisfaction but also the sum, net effect that comes from living in their particular country. We further insulate our results from other extraneous factors of a short-term nature by also including dummies for each year (again, of necessity omitting a reference category). By controlling for the particular year, we are also able to say that the estimated impact of the political variables of interest on satisfaction account for the year in which the survey was conducted. In sum, the statistical results provide an estimate of the impact of a given measure of the size of government on a person's satisfaction with life, when controlling for all other possible determinants of their satisfaction, whether these be their

[2] Because the response set for life satisfaction has a wide range (1–10), and the wording of the question asks for a numeric score rather than a verbal ranking (of the "somewhat satisfied," "very satisfied" variety), we assume a constant distance between response categories and treat the dependent variable as interval rather than ordinal (e.g., Heady, 1993). This is the standard approach in the literature, with much evidence confirming its validity (e.g., Helliwell, 2003). However, all reported results are similar if using ordered probit (the more strictly appropriate estimator). Indeed, the principal result of using this method is to increase the significance of the reported coefficients in almost all cases. We report the more conventional OLS results both because they are easier to interpret and because they are the most commonly used in the literature.

personal characteristics or those of the country and year in which they are living.

It remains only to specify the precise individual-level characteristics to include as controls. Our principal guide is of course the existing literature, which is fairly clear in documenting the main candidates for inclusion. However, we also face a practical limitation of the availability of data, in that we must be sensitive to the effects such choices make on the size of the sample: some individual-level variables are simply not available for some nations or years, such that as we expand the number of individual-level determinants the more cases are excluded. We thus begin with a model that contains the minimal number of demographic controls, which minimizes the amount of missing data, and then move on to more completely specified models which provide some extra controls at the cost of excluding some countries. As we shall see, the results are comfortably similar regardless of which individual-level variables are included.

Research on individual-level determinants of subjective well-being consistently shows that the same basic characteristics tend to affect individuals similarly across countries. We thus treat life satisfaction as a function of *gender*, *age* and *age-squared* (to account for the curvilinear relationship between age and life satisfaction), household *income*, as well as one's *income satisfaction* (to reflect, beyond greater control over the adequacy of income, any possible effect of income being relative), whether the household's chief wage earner is *unemployed*, whether the respondent is *married* (or living as married), self-reported *health*, the respondent's level of interpersonal trust (as a measure of *social capital*), and the frequency of attending religious services (*church attendance*).[3] We also include an interaction term between income and each of the political variables, to account for the possibility that the impact of the political terms is conditioned by an individual's income. One might expect, for instance, that the higher one's socioeconomic status, the fewer are the benefits (if any) they might receive from a more generous welfare state or a larger state sector; the interaction term accounts for this possibility. In the expanded models, we add several additional variables: *education*, whether the respondent has *children* living at home, and a set of dummy variables for religious denominations (*Protestant*,

---

[3] Income is measured in ten categories in ascending order; employment status is a dummy coded 1 if the household's chief wage earner is unemployed and zero otherwise; gender is coded 1 for males, 2 for females; church attendance is the frequency with which respondent attends religious services in eight descending categories; income satisfaction is from the survey question ascertaining level of agreement with the statement "Our family income is high enough to satisfy nearly all our important desires"; personal health is based on agreement with the survey item "I am in very good physical condition"; age is measured in years; social capital is measured by the item asking whether one agrees that "most people can be trusted" (coded 1) or no (coded 2), such that higher levels indicate less interpersonal trust. The indicators for church attendance and social capital are recoded from the World Values Survey default so that their expected signs are positive.

Catholic, Orthodox, Jewish, Muslim, Buddhist, Hindu, and *Seculars,* leaving the other small religious groups as the collective reference category).[4]

Estimation is with Huber-White robust standard errors, correcting for the pooled structure of the data (i.e., country-clustered). This procedure yields estimates that are robust to both between-country heteroscedasticity and within-country correlation (i.e., robust to error terms being neither identically distributed nor independent).[5] For those unfamiliar with the econometric jargon, it is necessary only to note that this method accounts for any potential impact on the results that might come from the pooling of data across countries and years.

Aggregate Analysis

When turning to the analysis of mean levels of satisfaction across countries, where the units of analysis are no longer individuals but instead country-years, we rely upon a different but equally conventional and obvious econometric approach: a random effects model. Whereas we before attempted to control for national-level conditions using country dummy variables (fixed effects), we here substitute in their place a set of substantive controls and rely upon the estimator to control for the pooled structure of the data (i.e., via random effects). Among the advantages of this method is greater econometric efficiency, which is decidedly helpful when the number of observations per country is small (about three, depending upon model specification). In any event, all of the main results (reported in Table 5.4) also obtain when returning to the use of country dummies (fixed effects), such that the results do not depend upon the choice of estimator.

When modeling the national mean level of satisfaction, we utilize the following rather obvious controls: a nation's general level of economic development, in terms of real *GDP* per capita in purchasing power parity; the immediate-term level of economic prosperity, as reflected by the *unemployment rate* and

---

[4] Education is measured in the age intervals in which one completed formal education (ranging from less than twelve to twenty-one or more). Results are substantively identical when including yet additional control variables, which we do not report in that (a) they don't affect the reported results, and (b) they often consume many thousands of cases from the analysis because of missing data. I experimented with nearly every item in the World Values Survey that might plausibly be thought to affect satisfaction, but found the results to be exceedingly robust. Among the obvious candidates for omitted variables, I considered still more religious variables (whose effect, if any, would appear to be accounted for by the church attendance and/or confessional variables) and individual's self-reported ideology, given some evidence that self-described conservatives exhibit greater satisfaction with their lives than liberals or leftists. These (and other) variables had no effect whatsoever.

[5] Results are similar when using hierarchical linear modeling (HLM). We report conventional regression models rather than HLM for the same reasons we do not report ordered probit models, as discussed above. The sensitivity of the results to the choice of estimator (including HLM) and a variety of other econometric issues are discussed at length in the Appendix to this chapter.

the given year's rate of *economic growth*; the level of *social capital* (the national mean value of the interpersonal trust variable used earlier); and two dimensions of a country's culture: the extent of *ndividualism* rather than collectivism in attitudes and values (Veenhoven's (1999) measure of "individualization"), and the size of its Catholic population (as a percentage of the total population), to account for the possibility, much discussed in the literature on culture, that countries may exhibit a greater or lesser degree of a distinctive *Catholic culture* independent of an individual's religious beliefs (or lack of them).[6] Finally, to account both for any potential unmodeled year-specific or time-trend effects on satisfaction, such as the downward trend in satisfaction over time passionately argued for by Lane (2000), we retain the dummy variables for years.

RESULTS

Having detailed the estimation procedures, the results may be presented more succinctly. As we shall see, they require little elaboration or commentary, in that they eloquently speak for themselves.

The individual level results are presented in Tables 5.1 through 5.3. Considering first the basic results for the welfare state, we see (Table 5.1) that the decommodification index is positive and significant in both the initial (column a) and the expanded model (column b). The implication is, of course, that greater levels of decommodification are associated with higher levels of satisfaction, controlling for other factors. The same conclusion applies for the related generosity index (columns c and d). We see, thus, that more expansive, universalistic welfare states contribute to a higher quality of human life.

The data for net social spending and the general level of government consumption are also consistent with underlying logic that happiness is best served by limiting the power of the market, as documented in Table 5.2. As before, the coefficients of interest are uniformly positive and statistically significant. The greater the state's footprint in the economy, as expressed by the share of the economy it spends on social services per se, or the amount it simply "consumes" for its general operations, the more satisfied with life people tend to be, other things being equal.

Table 5.3 (columns a and b) presents the results for taxation. Depending on which side of the ideological coin one wishes to focus upon, the share of GDP taken as taxes is either the tax burden the state imposes on society or, just as correctly, the share of the economy that is democratically allocated through free elections and representative government. Whatever our preferences in normative interpretation, the results of the estimation suggest precisely the same empirical conclusion: higher levels of taxation suggest higher levels of satisfaction with life. Surely no one enjoys being taxed, but it is via taxation that the effects – as we have seen, the apparently positive effects – of governmental

---

[6] The data for GDP and growth are from the Penn World Table version 6.3; unemployment is from the ILO, http://laborsta.ilo.org/STP/guest (accessed January 19, 2010).

TABLE 5.1. *The Welfare State and Life Satisfaction: Individual-Level Data OECD Countries (1981–2007)*

	(a) Base Model	(b) Expanded Model	(c) Base Model	(d) Expanded Model
Decommodification	.047**	.058***	n/a	n/a
	(.019)	(.015)		
Decommodification Interaction w/Income	−.001	−.001	n/a	n/a
	(.001)	(.001)		
Generosity Index	n/a	n/a	.062***	.059***
			(.012)	(.014)
Generosity Index Interaction w/Income	n/a	n/a	−.000	−.000
			(.001)	(.001)
Financial Satisfaction	.349***	.349***	.349***	.350***
	(.022)	(.024)	(.022)	(.023)
Social Capital	.267***	.275***	.268***	.276***
	(.022)	(.026)	(.022)	(.026)
Gender	−.051**	−.050*	−.057**	−.050*
	(.034)	(.034)	(.031)	(.034)
Age	−.033***	−.041***	−.033***	−.041***
	(.005)	(.006)	(.005)	(.006)
Age-squared	.000***	.000***	.000***	.000***
	(.000)	(.000)	(.000)	(.000)
Married	.466***	.408***	.467***	.411***
	(.030)	(.032)	(.030)	(.032)
Personal Health	1.272***	1.353***	1.277***	1.356***
	(.176)	(.194)	(.174)	(.193)
Unemployed	−.317***	−.272***	−.318***	−.272***
	(.073)	(.090)	(.073)	(.090)
Income	.001	.006	−.011	−.009
	(.036)	(.040)	(.035)	(.039)
Church Attendance	.039***	.032***	.038***	.032***
	(.005)	(.006)	(.005)	(.006)
Children	n/a	.045***	n/a	.045***
		(.007)		(.007)
Education	n/a	−.000	n/a	.000
		(.006)		(.006)
Muslim	n/a	−.347***	n/a	−.351***
		(.131)		(.132)
Catholic	n/a	−.030	n/a	−.037
		(.057)		(.058)
Protestant	n/a	.082	n/a	.073
		(.074)		(.075)
Hindu	n/a	.058	n/a	.043
		(.285)		(.281)

	(a) Basc Model	(b) Expanded Model	(c) Base Model	(d) Expanded Model
Buddhist	n/a	.010 (.065)	n/a	.003 (.065)
Jewish	n/a	−.044 (.136)	n/a	−.040 (.136)
Secular	n/a	−.031 (.067)	n/a	−.038 (.068)
Constant	4.153*** (.524)	3.353*** (.661)	3.810*** (.396)	4.100*** (.452)
Observations	39,808	32,236	39,808	32,236
R-squared	0.2674	0.2659	0.2676	0.2660

*significant at .10. **significant at .05 level. ***significant at .01 level.

Note: Dependent variable is life-satisfaction. Table omits country and year dummy variables. Entries are unstandardized regression coefficients (country-clustered robust standard errors).

spending are made possible. At least within the context of the relatively prosperous, democratic societies we are considering, greater government control over the product of society through taxation has laudatory consequences for the quality of life that citizens experience.

A final judgment about the role of "big government" is offered in the remaining models reported in Table 5.3. The independent variable is now a summary index of the "size of government" developed by the Fraser Institute. As previously discussed, it subsumes into a single score spending on transfers, general government consumption, public investment, and the top marginal tax rate on income. Given that the index is constructed such that higher scores represent greater "economic freedom" – which, is to say, *smaller* government – this variable should show a negative regression coefficient, if the results are consistent with the findings presented above. This is precisely what we find (columns c and d).

Before continuing to the aggregate data, two observations are in order. First, in regard to the interaction terms with income, in most of the models they are either of the wrong sign, statistically insignificant, or trivial in magnitude. If we interpret the coefficients, and thus compute the effective slope of the given measure of state size on satisfaction for any particular level of income, we always find only a very modest decline in the slope as income increases (because the coefficient of the interaction term is tiny), such that the slope remains positive even at the highest income level. Greater decommodification and a large state sector appear to make life better for everyone, rich and poor alike.

Second, an inspection of the coefficients of interest suggests, that the political realities they represent have not merely *statistically* significant but also *substantively* important effects on the degree to which individuals tend to find life rewarding. This is perhaps most readily seen when comparing the predicted

TABLE 5.2. *Social Spending and Government Consumption: Individual-Level Data OECD Countries (1981–2007)*

	(a) Base Model	(b) Expanded Model	(c) Base Model	(d) Expanded Model
Social Spending	.030** (.013)	.025** (.011)	n/a	n/a
Social Spending Interaction w/Income	−.000 (.001)	−.001 (.001)	n/a	n/a
Government Consumption	n/a	n/a	.052*** (.017)	.033** (.019)
Government Consumption Interaction w/ Income	n/a	n/a	.003* (.002)	−.004** (.002)
Financial Satisfaction	.344*** (.019)	.346*** (.021)	.341*** (.019)	.343*** (.021)
Social Capital	.254*** (.026)	.265*** (.028)	.254*** (.026)	.262*** (.027)
Gender	−.038 (.031)	.027 (.037)	−.040 (.031)	−.027 (.037)
Age	−.033*** (.004)	−.041*** (.005)	−.032*** (.004)	−.040*** (.005)
Age-squared	.000*** (.000)	.000*** (.000)	.000*** (.000)	.000*** (.000)
Married	.449*** (.027)	.417*** (.027)	.454*** (.027)	.424*** (.028)
Personal Health	1.283*** (.143)	1.311*** (.161)	1.282*** (.141)	1.310*** (.158)
Unemployed	−.322*** (.073)	−.320*** (.087)	−.326*** (.074)	−.326*** (.090)
Income	−.005 (.027)	.001 (.031)	.030 (.021)	.037* (.025)
Church Attendance	.037*** (.006)	.028*** (.007)	.037*** (.006)	.028*** (.007)
Children	n/a	.039*** (.008)	n/a	.039*** (.008)
Education	n/a	−.002 (.006)	n/a	−.002 (.006)
Muslim	n/a	−.380*** (.130)	n/a	−.369*** (.131)
Catholic	n/a	−.059 (.057)	n/a	−.049 (.059)
Protestant	n/a	.054 (.070)	n/a	.070 (.072)

	(a) Base Model	(b) Expanded Model	(c) Base Model	(d) Expanded Model
Hindu	n/a		n/a	.040
		(.283)		(.290)
Buddhist	n/a	−.031	n/a	−.019
		(.067)		(.067)
Jewish	n/a	−.071	n/a	−.071
		(.131)		(.133)
Secular	n/a	−.077	n/a	−.066
		(.075)		(.076)
Constant	5.317***	5.081***	4.989***	5.391***
	(.315)	(.300)	(.241)	(.283)
Observations	57,345	38,893	58,155	39,479
R-squared	0.2626	0.2603	0.2624	0.2607

*significant at .10. **significant at .05 level. ***significant at .01 level.

Note: Dependent variable is life satisfaction. Table omits country and year dummy variables. Entries are unstandardized regression coefficients (country-clustered robust standard errors).

impact on satisfaction for an individual who moved from the country-year with the lowest amount of decommodification to the country-year with the highest level (i.e., moving from the time and place with the least generous welfare state to that with the most generous) with the same change that would be predicted by a change in what are usually agreed to be the most powerful individual-level determinant of satisfaction: marriage and unemployment. Using the base model reported in column (a) of Table 5.1 suggests that moving across the range of decommodification from lowest to highest country-year would produce a full one point increase in a person's level of life satisfaction. As it is difficult to interpret movement along ordinal scales, comparison to the aforementioned benchmarks offers perspective: the change in question is more than twice the benefit that comes from being married and three times the cost to happiness that results from unemployment. Clearly, these impacts are enormous, dwarfing as they do the relative contribution to a satisfying life made by marriage or avoiding unemployment.[7]

It is worth dwelling for a moment upon how profound the effects of decommodification are for human happiness. In our day-to-day lives, we understand intuitively what scholars have long documented: marriage (or equivalent long term committed cohabitation) contributes dramatically to a better life, while being unemployed detracts enormously from one's quality of life. Indeed, it

[7] The effect on satisfaction of unemployment or marriage, given that they are merely dummy variables, is the value of the coefficient itself: unemployment reduces satisfaction by about a third of a point, while being married increases it by about half a point. By comparison, if we compute the predicted change in satisfaction moving across the observed range in decommodification, we find a value of about 0.98. Using the expanded model in column (b) of the same table suggests an even greater effect of decommodification equal to more than three times marriage and four times unemployment.

TABLE 5.3. *Tax Burden and the Size of Government: Individual-Level Data OECD Countries (1981–2007)*

	(a) Base Model	(b) Expanded Model	(c) Base Model	(d) Expanded Model
Tax Burden	.026***	.042***	n/a	n/a
	(.009)	(.009)		
Tax Burden Interaction w/ Income	−.001	−.001*	n/a	n/a
	(.001)	(.001)		
Smallness of Government	n/a	n/a	−.108***	−.099***
			(.042)	(.037)
Smallness of Government Interaction w/ Income	n/a	n/a	.003	.003
			(.003)	(.004)
Financial Satisfaction	.341***	.343***	.339***	.343***
	(.020)	(.021)	(.020)	(.021)
Social Capital	.256***	.265***	.255***	.262***
	(.026)	(.028)	(.025)	(.028)
Gender	−.040	−.027	−.042*	−.028
	(.031)	(.037)	(.030)	(.037)
Age	−.032***	−.040***	−.032***	−.040***
	(.004)	(.005)	(.004)	(.005)
Age-squared	.000***	.000***	.000***	.000***
	(.000)	(.000)	(.000)	(.000)
Married	.456***	.423***	.451***	.420***
	(.027)	(.027)	(.026)	(.028)
Personal Health	1.281***	1.310***	1.286***	1.315***
	(.143)	(.160)	(.141)	(.158)
Unemployed	−.326***	−.329***	−.335***	−.323***
	(.073)	(.086)	(.077)	(.089)
Income	.031	.039	−.025*	−.029*
	(.035)	(.040)	(.017)	(.020)
Church Attendance	.037***	.029***	.036***	.028***
	(.006)	(.007)	(.006)	(.007)
Children	n/a	.030***	n/a	.039***
		(.007)		(.008)
Education	n/a	−.004	n/a	−.002
		(.005)		(.006)
Muslim	n/a	−.369***	n/a	−.370***
		(.130)		(.131)
Catholic	n/a	−.043	n/a	−.048
		(.058)		(.059)
Protestant	n/a	.071	n/a	.065
		(.072)		(.072)

	(a) Base Model	(b) Expanded Model	(c) Base Model	(d) Expanded Model
Hindu	n/a	.051 (.289)	n/a	.049 (.292)
Buddhist	n/a	−.008 (.066)	n/a	−.014 (.067)
Jewish	n/a	−.064 (.132)	n/a	−.059 (.134)
Secular	n/a	−.057 (.075)	n/a	−.062 (.077)
Constant	4.225*** (.155)	4.360*** (.361)	6.236*** (.321)	6.303*** (.292)
Observations	58,155	39,479	59,080	39,479
R-squared	0.2623	0.2610	0.2614	0.2605

*significant at .10. **significant at .05 level. ***significant at .01 level.
Note: Dependent variable is life satisfaction. Table omits country and year dummy variables. Entries are unstandardized regression coefficients (country-clustered robust standard errors).

does not seem an exaggeration to say that for most people, having a life partner and having a job rank at or very near the top of their list of values and life needs. We need only imagine the profound psychological distress that comes from unemployment to understand how emotionally rewarding the finding of a job means to those who need one; we need only imagine the loneliness and isolation that comes from wishing to love and be loved – to wanting someone to share our lives with – to appreciate how fulfilling the finding of love and companionship can be. Now, consider that the effect of moving from the least to the most decommodifying welfare state would produce three times the improvement in one's quality of life than that achieved by escaping from unemployment. Or consider that this same difference in the welfare state would provide one with twice the increase in life satisfaction that finding a life-partner would. Seen in this light, it seems difficult to overstate the significance of the welfare state as an agent for human happiness.

National and Group Means

Turning to the second method of analysis introduced above, the data tell a story very similar to that we have already seen. The results for the national level of satisfaction (for the given country-year) are displayed in Table 5.4 for the core variables of interest. As is apparent, the average level of life satisfaction, controlling for the other factors that may have an impact on satisfaction, is affected in the hypothesized fashion by decommodification, general government consumption, and the tax burden: in each, the relevant coefficient is significant and of the predicted sign.

TABLE 5.4. *The Size of Government and Life Satisfaction: Aggregate-Level Data OECD Countries (1981–2007)*

	(a) Decommodification	(b) Government Consumption	(c) Tax Burden
Decommodification	.035***	n/a	n/a
	(.011)		
Government Consumption	n/a	.020*	n/a
		(.014)	
Tax Burden	n/a	n/a	.013**
			(.007)
Social Capital	.752**	.711**	.618**
	(.429)	(.431)	(.432)
Unemployment	−.000	−.020**	−.022***
	(.014)	(.012)	(.012)
Real GDP	.000	.000	−.000
	(.000)	(.000)	(.000)
Individualism	.649***	.506***	.493***
	(.153)	(.096)	(.099)
Catholic	.321*	.282*	.226
	(.240)	(.179)	(.177)
Economic Growth	.014	.023*	.022*
	(.013)	(.016)	(.015)
Constant	6.972***	8.577***	8.336***
	(.950)	(1.007)	(.995)
Observations	51	73	73
R-squared	0.7685	0.7471	0.7538

*significant at .10. **significant at .05 level. ***significant at .01 level.

Note: Dependent variable is life satisfaction. Entries are unstandardized regression coefficients (standard errors). Table omits year dummy variables (GLS random-effects model).

To illustrate the substantive importance of the political factors, I introduce another method for interpreting the results beyond the comparison to unemployment or marriage. In this approach, we express their effect in terms of the variability in satisfaction we observe over space and time, rather than their impact relative to other factors. This method is especially helpful when considering variation in the mean level of satisfaction across countries (or groups of people, such as those with low or high incomes), in that comparison to individual-level factors such as marriage makes little sense. To do so, we merely compute the expected change in levels of satisfaction expressed in terms of what are called "standard deviations."

For those unfamiliar with thinking in terms of this metric, the logic is straightforward. When determining how to think about the impact of some independent variable on a survey item, such as life satisfaction, we can interpret things relatively – as we did when comparing the welfare state to marriage and unemployment – or we can do so in terms of the observed dispersion of the survey question itself. This is because something like life satisfaction lacks an absolute method of interpretation, in the way something like poverty rates do. If we were studying the percentage of the population living in poverty, we could determine that a given change in the generosity of the social security system would produce, say, a 5 percent reduction in the share of the population in poverty. There is no equivalent with most survey items on opinion, life satisfaction included. We can accomplish the same goal, however, simply by expressing change not in the absolute amount of satisfaction in the 1–10 scale on which it is measured, but in the standardized amount of variation in satisfaction that exists across countries and over time. Such standard deviations are readily interpreted, reflecting how much higher (or lower) satisfaction is for a given person relative to the overall mean. Thus, a predicted change of one-half of a standard deviation would be considerable, one standard deviation would be very large, and two standard deviations would be enormous. This can be readily seen in this way: if a change in some variable produced a change in satisfaction sufficient to move us from the mean in the distribution (the 50th percentile) of satisfaction to one-half of a standard deviation above the mean, this would take us to the 69th percentile in the distribution of satisfaction; one standard deviation above the mean, we are at the 84th percentile; and two standard deviations above the mean would imply the 98th percentile.

If moving from the minimum to the maximum observed value of decommodification, the results suggest a predicted change of 1.53 standard deviations in mean life satisfaction. Moving across the range of government consumption or tax burden also implies a large impact on satisfaction (about one standard deviation, and about three-fifths of a standard deviation, respectively). These effects are large, by any standard, particularly when considering that the model contains a plethora of control variables, whose effect is likely to underestimate the effect of the coefficients of interest in service of being certain of their independent and separable effects on satisfaction. We may thus conclude once again that the political variables have an extremely powerful, not merely a statistically significant, impact on the degree to which people find life to be satisfying.

The reliance on using average levels of satisfaction as the dependent variable has the added advantage of providing an intuitively appealing and econometrically simple method of determining if the relationships we have been examining are constant across different subgroups within the general population. We have already touched on the constancy of the effects across income, which we may further examine here through the obvious expedient of computing the mean satisfaction for those with high- and low-incomes, and repeating the core analysis on each group.[8] Table 5.5 presents the results for the basic decommodification model for each income category (columns a and b). The coefficient is positive and significant for both groups, suggesting once more that the welfare state

[8] The high income group is defined as those in the top three of the ten categories of income, but equally strong results obtain using categories 1 through 5 as low and 6 through 10 as high.

TABLE 5.5. *Decommodification and Life Satisfaction: Mean Satisfaction by Social Groups Aggregate Level Data OECD Countries (1981–2007)*

	(a) Low Income	(b) High Income	(c) Men	(d) Women
Decommodification	.038***	.031**	.037***	.040***
	(.012)	(.014)	(.012)	(.013)
Social Capital	.562	.795**	.748**	.516
	(.527)	(.459)	(.417)	(.536)
Unemployment	.001	.031**	.010	.003
	(.017)	(.015)	(.014)	(.017)
Real GDP	.000	.000	.000	.000
	(.000)	(.000)	(.000)	(.000)
Individualism	.676***	.511***	.663***	.649***
	(.153)	(.214)	(.172)	(.172)
Catholic	.290	.056	.394*	.086
	(.260)	(.322)	(.268)	(.285)
Economic Growth	−.007	−.024**	.008	.017
	(.016)	(.014)	(.013)	(.017)
Constant	6.393	7.524***	6.707***	6.414***
	(1.136)	(1.032)	(.929)	(1.168)
Observations	49	49	49	49
R-squared	0.7750	0.6105	0.8005	0.7106

*significant at .10. **significant at .05 level. ***significant at .01 level.

Note: Dependent variable is life-satisfaction. Entries are unstandardized regression coefficients (standard errors). Table omits year dummy variables (GLS random-effects model).

benefits both the affluent and the less-well-off. To be sure, we do so see, as we might expect, a modestly stronger effect for the lower-income group, but the difference between the coefficients is extremely modest. This is consistent with the individual-level results, which also suggested a small (and generally insignificant) reduction in the benefits of welfare spending as income increased. This makes perfect sense from a social democratic point of view: the less prosperous have more to gain in an immediate way from a generous welfare state, but, according to this logic, the secondary effects on society in general (such as the reduction in crime, anomie, and other social pathologies that economic adversity fosters) benefit everyone.

Comparing decommodification for men versus women (Table 5.5 columns c and d) suggests that, again, both benefit from it. While the coefficient for women is nominally larger, the difference is negligible, suggesting no tangible difference between genders in the degree they benefit from the welfare state. The lack of a difference is, perhaps, contrary to expectations, given this is usually agreed that women generally are (to at least some degree) less economically privileged than are men (as evidenced by, among other things, persistent differences in earnings, as well as women's concentration in less secure and less well-paying jobs), and thus might have a greater stake in the social safety net. I do not wish to make too much of failing to confirm that here – one might be able to tease out greater female sensitivity to the provision of social rights (by considering, for instance, differences between single and married women, number of dependent children, education, and so on) – but such matters, however potentially important in their own way, are beyond the scope of this study. The essential point here is not to ponder the lack of difference in how much men and women find their lives improved by the welfare state, but to note that the welfare state does indeed appear to contribute to both groups enjoying better lives.[9]

I would like to consume whatever patience the reader may still possess for yet more statistical results by briefly presenting a final exhibit from the case-file of evidence connecting the redistributive efforts of the state to the well-being of its citizens. This takes the form of a last table further documenting prior conclusions by introducing an additional empirical indicator of the generosity of the welfare state. Table 5.6 provides models relying on the OECD's official measure of the "social wage," showing that the result for the average level of happiness across countries, as well as for the mean levels for income and gender groups, survive yet more statistical tests. The concept of the "social wage" is used in different ways by different scholars, but it is essentially a synonym for the state's commitment to income maintenance – the "social wage" being a metaphor, implying the "wage" one can receive, when in need, by virtue of one's status as a member of society. Thus, for the OECD statistical bureau, the social wage is the name given to their index of a country's system of unemployment compensation.[10] As the table illustrates, this analysis confirms the prior results: in each case, the social wage is positive and significant, suggesting that a more robust system of unemployment insurance is associated with higher levels of well-being.

CONCLUSION

The analysis above has provided compelling evidence in support of the contention that "big government" promotes human happiness. In presenting the results, I have relied upon the strategy of making the evidence genuinely compelling by showing that the same basic results obtain across a range of different measures of state size, across its three dimensions of transfer payments that

---

[9] In the Appendix to this chapter, we consider two other possible subgroup differences in response to the welfare state: those on the left versus the right of the political spectrum (according to the conventional left-right ideological placement survey item) and those who are accepting of versus those who disapprove of gays and lesbians. The results suggest no dramatic differences between groups.

[10] The measure is defined "as the average of the gross unemployment benefit replacement rate for two earnings levels [median-income and the 67th percentile of the income distribution], three family situations, and three durations of unemployment." Data are available at http://www.oecd.org/dataoecd/25/31/34008592.xls (accessed October 10, 2009).

TABLE 5.6. *Social Wage and Life Satisfaction: General Population and Social Groups Aggregate Level Data OECD Countries (1981–2007)*

	(a) General Population	(b) Low Income	(c) High Income	(d) Men	(e) Women
Social Wage	.009***	.010***	.009***	.008***	.010***
	(.003)	(.003)	(.003)	(.003)	(.003)
Social Capital	.707**	.384	.738*	.342	.741*
	(.398)	(.469)	(.479)	(.451)	(.466)
Unemployment	−.023**	−.021*	−.003	−.022**	−.015
	(.011)	(.013)	(.014)	(.012)	(.013)
Real GDP	−.000	−.000	.000	−.000	−.000
	(.000)	(.000)	(.000)	(.000)	(.000)
Individualism	.540***	.542***	.416***	.519***	.549***
	(.068)	(.091)	(.078)	(.091)	(.076)
Catholic	.195*	.138	.0540	.224*	.068
	(.145)	(.177)	(.169)	(.175)	(.165)
Economic Growth	.015	.017	.028*	.017	.024*
	(.016)	(.017)	(.018)	(.016)	(.018)
Constant	8.838***	8.170***	8.542***	8.137***	8.578***
	(.795)	(.985)	(.990)	(.950)	(.965)
Observations	73	69	69	69	69
R-squared	0.7995	0.7964	0.7258	0.7988	0.7913

*significant at .10. **significant at .05 level. ***significant at .01 level.

Note: Dependent variable is life-satisfaction. Entries are unstandardized regression coefficients (standard errors). Table omits year dummy variables (GLS random-effects model).

provide direct decommodification, the share of the economy that the state "consumes" and thus directs and controls in the presumptive public interest on all other activities beyond the direct provision of welfare payments, and the tax burden that the state imposes on a society for the payment of all that it does. I have also endeavored to show that these conclusions are consistent across different model specifications, different levels of analysis, different econometric methods, and different sub-groups within society. My purpose has thus been to illustrate that the statistical results are, in the jargon of econometric modeling, "robust." More simply stated, by presenting model after model showing that the same substantive results obtain when changing any detail of the statistical analysis that might conceivably affect those results, I have attempted to show the results cannot be attributed to peculiarities of the data or the method of analysis. The Appendix to this chapter continues that endeavor by demonstrating that the reported results survive a variety of other methodological and theoretical objections.

Throughout this chapter, my goal as author has been that of the skeptic of my own findings, placing myself in the role of an adversary whose goal was to find a weakness in the empirical analysis sufficient to raise doubts about the stability or "truth" of the results. I have gone to such lengths because of the importance of the questions at hand. What I claim to have provided is an "objective" empirical answer to the ideological question of whether big or small government is most conducive to human happiness. This is no small thing. As its validity depends entirely upon the evidence from which it is based, I have amassed and tested that evidence in what I hope is a rigorous and compelling fashion. The more controversial and consequential a conclusion, the greater is the evidence needed to support it. The reader must judge for him- or herself the degree to which I have been successful.

If the evidence is indeed found convincing, there are two obvious implications. The first is for the study of well-being, in that the test of whether the welfare state and other political interventions in the market implied by a large state sector is also a test of the theory that happiness is largely determined by the provision of human needs. Surely if happiness were purely or mostly a product of the individual's genetic or psychological makeup, or if it were merely a process of social comparison, the results presented here simply could not obtain. That the welfare state makes for more satisfied lives clearly suggests that it is the material and emotional preconditions for a good life that the welfare state provides that are what drive international differences in quality of life.

More important, and more obvious still, are the implications for social policy. These are difficult to overstate, given that they provide clear instructions on how to proceed if we truly do wish to build a society in which "human life is as satisfying as possible." The way to maximize the degree to which people find their life to be positive and rewarding is to create generous, universalistic, and truly decommodifying welfare states. Similarly, human well-being is best served by a relatively large state sector, which brings more of the productive capacity of society under political – which is to say, democratic – control. In the same way, we see that human life is best served by a larger share of the economy being absorbed through taxation to pay for the services and protections governments provide or guarantee, in that this can be profitably conceived of as increasing the reach of democracy into the economy.

These themes are further developed in the next chapter, where attention turns to how two other and more basic forms of democratic "intrusion" in the economy affect satisfaction with life. One involves the labor laws that regulate the market relations between employer and employee so as, ostensibly, to protect workers from the negative effects of being (as we saw in Chapters 2 and 3) in an inferior power position vis-à-vis employers. The other is the role of labor unions, which (as we have again had occasion to see in earlier chapters), serve as vital engines for giving political expression to the interests of wage and salary workers.

APPENDIX: DETAILS AND OBJECTIONS

My purpose here is to address some econometric details and potential objections that may interest readers concerned with methodology. The object is both to acknowledge such concerns and to illustrate why they do not pose a threat to my substantive conclusions.

Reverse Causality

It is of course possible that the causal relationship between leftist policies and life satisfaction is reversed, that is, that individuals with high levels of life satisfaction are more inclined to be left-liberal, so a concentration of liberals within a state produces liberal governments that pursue liberal policies. In this view, liberal citizens are happy citizens, and the apparent connection between liberal policies and happiness reflects merely this. Elsewhere I have explicitly considered this possibility (Pacek and Radcliff, 2008) by modeling support for the Left as a function of satisfaction and a set of individual- and national-level controls. I found "that greater [subjective] well-being does not seem to foster greater support" for the Left. Indeed, much evidence suggests just the opposite. A study by the Pew Research Center (2006), for instance, found that self-identified conservatives in the United States are consistently happier than are liberals (in every year since 1972), even when controlling for income. Bjørnskov, Dreher, and Fischer (2008: 137, table 2) report a similar result across a sample of seventy countries, finding that conservatives are happier when controlling for an entire battery of demographic controls. When applying this approach to the present data, similar results obtain: regressing ideological self-identification (coded such that the variable measures how conservative one is) on satisfaction plus the controls reported in either the base or expanded models in Table 5.1 produces a positive (and significant) coefficient, suggesting again that it is conservatives – presumptive opponents of "big government" – who are more satisfied. If so, the results can hardly be the result of a reverse causality that depends on happy liberals supporting liberal policies. As a final check, I replicated the results in Tables 5.1 through 5.3 while including as a control the respondent's ideological self-identification. There were no material effects on the reported results (and, again, the ideology coefficient was itself positive, contrary to the reverse causality hypothesis). Given, thus, that the relationship between opinion liberalism and satisfaction is actually negative, and that, in any case, the inclusion of the individual ideology in no way affects the results, I feel comfortable in concluding that it is unlikely that these findings could be driven by reverse causality.

Testing for Robustness

I have been at pains throughout my analyses to demonstrate whenever possible that the results I obtain are robust, meaning that they do not depend upon any particular modeling specification, variable definition, estimation technique, or other details of the analysis. It was in the interest of demonstrating that the results were highly stable in the face of all such choices that I have presented an analysis using multiple measures of the size of the state, using different estimators, different model specifications, and different units of analysis. At every step in the process where a choice in statistical strategy has to be made, I have endeavored to show that similar results obtained when making other reasonable choices. I here briefly consider some additional ways to demonstrate the robustness of the results reported earlier.

First, the stability of the empirical findings was examined in two additional ways. The individual-level models reported in Tables 5.1–5.3 were also estimated with HLM; the substantive conclusions are unchanged from those reported above. The stability of the aggregate level results were also examined by considering various confirmatory tests performed on the final summary empirical model (relying on the social wage as the indicator of the state's effort as market intervention, Table 5.6, column a), including, among others: (a) results are unchanged when using robust regression (a technique that is designed specifically to show that the results are not affected by either outliers or other especially influential data points); (b) results are again stable when removing the three countries with the highest level of satisfaction, given the suggestion that sometimes any apparent effect of the welfare state might be driven by extreme cases only; and, similarly, (c) unchanged when removing the three countries with the highest levels of decommodification.

Second, some recent work (e.g., Helliwell and Huang, 2008; Ott, 2010) has highlighted the importance of the efficiency and professionalism of government in the bureaucratic sense, using a World Bank indicator of "good governance" (the six dimensions of this concept averaged into a single indicator, from Kaufmann, Kraay and Mastruzzi, 2005). As I noted in Chapter 4, this variable is highly problematic, in that it actually contains as elements of "good" government ideologically contested aspects of policy (such as a low level of transfer payments) that are anything but the coldly technical and non-partisan concepts the index purports to cover. It also suffers, from the point of view of the analysis offered here, in being available for a limited number of years, so that including it in any model here would drastically reduce sample size, even to the point of making the analysis impossible in its present form. In any event, the relevance of this "variable" to the OECD countries that are our focus is highly questionable, given that it scarcely varies at all. The index was really designed for use across developing and developed countries. Thus, while Helliwell and Huang (2008) apply it profitably to a mixed sample of seventy-five such countries, it makes little sense to use it when considering only the OECD. Within the highly institutionalized and professional administrations of these industrial democracies, there is very little variance across countries, reflecting the fact that (to the extent the index does measure non-partisan subjects, such as corruption) these countries all have extremely high "quality" of government. Further, as Ott (2010) notes, "good government" in the sense of a professional, efficient system of administration would be an intervening variable between the size of government (or the level of taxation) and life satisfaction, such that in corrupt or grossly inefficient countries, government intervention would not have the positive effects we do expect in the OECD where the administration of government conforms to the standards of "good governance." So long as one has reasonably "good" government, which all OECD countries do, even according to the World Bank index, this concept is not relevant to present purposes. Indeed, when looking at the data for the countries considered in this study, the mean of the variable is 1.6, while Helliwell and Huang (2008) report that the mean for their seventy-five countries is .68 (with a range of −1.3 to 2.0). When looking at the data for countries considered in this study, there are only two countries that are meaningfully below the high OECD mean: Greece and Italy. The simplest and the most powerful way of ensuring that the reported results are robust to any possible failing to control for the lack of homogeneity in the sample vis-à-vis this variable is simply to remove these two countries from the sample and repeat the analysis. As in the examples noted earlier, doing so produces results that are substantively identical to those reported.

Finally, I considered the stability of the results across two other sets of subpopulations beyond income or gender. One is those who express animosity toward gays and lesbians as opposed to those who do not, on the logic that the persistence of antigay attitudes offers a good approximation of the general "traditionalism" of value structures, being correlated as it is with a panoply of other social attitudes. The second is self-identification along the conventional left-right economic ideological divide, given the importance some economists have put on this distinction as it relates to happiness (and in particular, how it might relate to ideologically charged governmental policies, such as those studied here).[11] For both sets of groups, we find, as we did when comparing women with men, that the welfare state affects each subgroup, and does so with a comparable magnitude.

As with income, there is a very modest difference, such that the satisfaction of those on the left, and those who do not disapprove of gays and lesbians, is marginally more elastic with the social wage than those on the right. The reasons for this effect, however modest, is unclear; it might reflect differences in social class, gender, or even generation (whose main effects, but not their interactions with welfare, are controlled for), but it is not my purpose to consider such tangential issues. It is sufficient, as with gender or even income, merely to note that this distinction (suggested by some economists as a basic

---

[11] Ideology is measured in the World Values Survey on a 1–10 scale with higher levels indicating greater conservatism. I defined those on the left as being in categories 1 through 5 and conservatives as those in categories 6 through 10 (thus dividing the ideological range precisely into two halves). Similarly, attitudes toward gays/lesbians is also on a 1–10 scale (asking how "justifiable" the respondent believes "homosexuality" to be); I have similarly coded it in 1–5 and 6–10 categories.

distinction between people, akin to gender or income) does not seem relevant in assessing the impact of the welfare state. It should be noted, further, that I see no theoretical reason to expect ideological self-placement to condition the effect of state policy on satisfaction in the way income might. Given that happiness (or at least, that portion of the variation in happiness that can be attributed to conditions outside the individual's genetic or personality makeup) is argued to be determined by the extent to which an individual's human needs are met, and that ideological congruency between the self and the government is not a human need in the way that things like personal and financial security are, we should expect no conditioning effect of ideology. Surely one may think that big government is a bad idea, yet find their lives positively affected by the family allowance (or old-age pension) they receive every month, by their ability to see a doctor when ill due to a state mandate, by the unemployment check the government provides when they are unable to find work through no fault of their own – just as they may benefit in ways that may not discern from the lower levels of criminality and other forms of antisocial behavior that the provision of such benefits to others produces.[12]

Exceptions to the Pattern?

What about countries with relatively high levels of satisfaction but modest welfare states? In particular, critics of the argument when it has been discussed at professional conferences are quick to point out two countries that appear to stand out as examples of just this: Ireland and Switzerland. Both score high on satisfaction, but are middling welfare states. Do they represent outliers in the analysis, thus forming deviations from the presumed pattern, and, ergo, evidence against the arguments advanced here? The first thing I would note in considering this suggestion is that neither Switzerland nor Ireland is in fact an outlier or leverage point in any statistical sense. In the final summary aggregate results I have used for testing robustness (those in Table 5.6, column a), no observations from either country shows a large dfbeta (an influence statistic, i.e., a test of the extent to which the given observation has a disproportionate influence on the results) nor a large standardized residual (a statistic that measures the distance that the case is from the regression line). Second, although it is true that the satisfaction rates for Switzerland and Ireland are somewhat higher than a simplistic bivariate argument that satisfaction is determined entirely and only by the welfare state would imply, I have never advanced simple bivariate arguments of any kind. A country's level of satisfaction is determined by many things, which is why the models contain multiple control variables. One

---

[12] Further, the fact that the well-being of those who self-identify as conservative is slightly (but only slightly) less affected by the welfare state must be considered in light of the fact that those who disapprove of gays and lesbians also receive the same marginally smaller benefit from the welfare state. Whatever might be driving this small difference it is unlikely to be a principled objection to the welfare state, since antigay feelings work as a substitute indicator.

could interpret the data as saying that the modest size of the welfare state in these countries is offset by other factors, some modeled explicitly (as in Tables 5.4–5.6) and others implicitly (through the dummy variables, as in Tables 5.1–5.3).

Further, while these countries have welfare states that are modest compared to the Scandinavian standard, they are also not welfare "laggards" such as the United States or Australia: their decommodification scores are in fact about average for OECD countries. Further, the history of changes in satisfaction and the welfare state in recent decades are actually highly instructive for how they do, in fact, confirm the arguments being made here. Ireland's mean level of satisfaction has increased substantially over the time covered by the WVS data (which, of course, ends just before the 2008 global economic disaster) while Switzerland's has declined drastically. Curiously, their decommodification scores show exactly the corresponding pattern I would predict: Ireland's increased while Switzerland's declined precipitously. In sum, rather than being counterexamples, these cases nicely illustrate the relationships I argue for.

The Endogeneity of Politics and Economics: Considering the Indirect Effects of the Welfare State on Happiness via its Negative Consequences for the Economy

I have attempted to demonstrate that an expansive welfare state (or, equally, government consumption or taxation) contributes to life satisfaction. In the aggregate analysis, the statistical analyses devoted to that demonstration included as control variables measures of the state of the economy. The reported models do not, thus, consider the possibility that economic conditions may themselves be partially determined by the same political factors that affect satisfaction. It could thus be that while social democracy promotes life satisfaction directly, it could have indirect negative effects by adversely affecting the economy. The *net* effect of social democracy could thus be zero or even negative. Similarly, modest welfare states could have strongly positive but indirect consequences for happiness that occur through the greater economic prosperity they might conceivably contribute to. Put another way, the price of explicitly controlling for economic conditions is to raise the possibility that the total effect of the welfare state is hidden by its indirect effect on the control variables. A neoclassical economist might agree that, yes, it is likely that the welfare state per se makes people happier, but it also makes them unhappy through its unanticipated, negative consequences on the economy. Thus, the suggestion that the welfare state contributes to "making life as satisfying as possible" is potentially misleading.

This is indeed a legitimate concern, which I address in two ways. First, it must be noted that while the negative economic consequence of the welfare state is a hobgoblin of conservative ideology, the literature offers little reason to believe that the welfare state or other variables considered here actually have anything remotely like the clear and powerful negative effect on the economy the objection presumes. The empirical as well as the purely theoretical research on the topic is completely inconclusive, with as many (or more) studies finding no effects (or even positive effects) of government spending on economic performance as those finding negative ones. Thus, in her exhaustive review of this literature, Mares (2007) concludes that "the predictions of negative relationship between higher levels of social protection and growth have not been borne out" and that the "empirical studies also fail to uncover a consistent negative relationship between larger welfare states and the level of employment."[13] In any event, however one wants to mince the evidence, it cannot be denied that the failure to find anything remotely like consensus, even among economists, that public spending does erode economic growth suggests at the very least that any corrosive effect of state spending on the economy must be very modest, if it exists at all. Further, as noted in Chapter Three, the fact that the Nordic countries with their huge welfare states are consistently given high scores by economists for the quality of their business environments (Rothstein, 2010) demonstrates that generous, universalistic welfare states are not incompatible with a thriving and dynamic market economy.

In any event, there is one obvious and definitive strategy for testing the overall argument about endogeneity disguising the net total effect of the welfare state with the present data. This is simply to confirm the basic results when excluding the economic controls. In this approach, the resulting coefficient for the welfare state would reflect the total, final, net effect of that variable on satisfaction. Doing so (for the final model in Table 5.6, column a, as well as in all of the models reported in Table 5.4) produces results that are as before: the coefficients of interest remain significant, of the expected sign, and of about the same magnitude. This evidence makes clear that the argument about indirect effects being masked by holding economic conditions constant when assessing the impact of the welfare state is simply not true: the total effect of the welfare state, including its potential indirect effects via economic performance, remains positive and statistically significant.[14]

---

[13] Other reviews come to similar conclusions. In an influential paper on the determinants of cross-national growth, Levine and Renelt (1992) attempted to isolate factors that have stable, robust effects on economic growth. It was motivated by the fact that the existing literature produced wildly different conclusions. While they do not consider welfare spending per se, they do examine several variants of governmental consumption of GDP (e.g., total consumption, total defense spending) that are certain to correlate highly with welfare state generosity. None of these variables prove to have robust effects on growth. Similarly, Atkinson (1999) carefully reviews ten major studies of the impact of social transfer spending on growth. He reports (1999: 34) that of the ten, two find an insignificant effect, four a negative effect, and four a positive effect. His review of the literature on how the provision of social security affects unemployment comes to similar "agnostic" conclusions (1999:43–9). One could continue reviewing more recent and definitive studies (e.g., North, Wallis, and Weingast, 2009) that find no evidence for believing that public spending and taxing depress economic performance.

[14] Another, rather more econometrically elaborate possibility is to use a system of equations using instrumental variables (two-stage least squares). I have applied this methodology to the problem elsewhere (Radcliff, 2001) to results identical to those noted earlier.

6

Labor Unions and Economic Regulation

The market economy is the central institution of the modern world, affecting the nature and quality of human life more than any other. Consequently, it is the internal structures of the market that draw our attention in the search to understand how human well-being is produced and distributed. This in turn takes us to the essential, and in large measure, defining features of the capitalist economy, which we have already had ample occasion to see: economic activity depends on an inherent asymmetry in power between two classes of persons, one of which depends for its livelihood on the sale of its labor power as a commodity, and another who purchases that commodity in order to so profit by. To be sure, the latter class relies on the labor of the former in order to generate the riches it enjoys, but it remains in a superior position because its very ownership over the capital resources that allow production ensure that it itself need not engage in wage or salary labor in order to survive or flourish.

To say that capital enjoys an asymmetrical power relationship with the wage and salary workers it hopes to profit by is not, of course, to say that workers are entirely powerless. Indeed, the theoretical and practical integrity of the market system requires that workers cannot be compelled to work in the way that serfs, slaves, or indentured servants are. Instead, workers and employers must negotiate the wages and other terms of work, through contracts that are enforceable by law. That employers enjoy a natural advantage in the negotiation of the terms of employment by no means suggests that such terms are anything other than the process of a genuine negotiation. The "struggle" between worker and employer, each of whom wishes to maximize his or her position relative to that of the other, then, takes places first and foremost in this process of negotiation, in which not only wages and benefits but also the conditions, hours, and other rules of work are determined. If so, it is natural to look to such details of the labor market itself as a principal aspect of people's lives, and thus, potentially, of the quality of their lives.

At the level of social structure, the most important aspects of labor market negotiations are the conditions that precede or mediate such negotiations. The welfare state is surely the most influential (because it is the most structural) of such conditions, and we have already documented its positive influence on quality of life. But there are more direct aspects of the background environment in which individual workers negotiate terms with individual employers that are also likely to have profound impacts on individuals. For our purposes, these involve the nature and extent of political regulation of the labor market. Thus, for instance, if the law stipulates a reasonable maximum number of work hours per week or legally mandates and enforces procedures to guarantee safety in the workplace, these issues become relatively less important in the process of negotiation, in that they may be taken as given. This in turn allows employees to focus their limited bargaining power on other aspects of the employment agreement. The net result, of course, is to increase the relative bargaining position of the worker. Thus, just as workers attempt to improve their relative power vis-à-vis employers through the welfare state that limits the degree of commodification of labor, workers also attempt to use the political process to (from their material and ideological vantage point) institute laws that govern the terms of employment in ways that further mitigate their relative disadvantage vis-à-vis employers. Rather than depend entirely upon their ability to negotiate with employers, they use the power of the state to create legally mandated minimums that promise to make work more lucrative, safe, rewarding, and secure.

A second and more general way in which employees seek to advance their interests in negotiations with employers is to form their own cooperative organizations, which allow them to negotiate not as individuals but as a collective. Such labor unions have ever been the initial and most basic method by which the atomized, anonymous "workers" attempt to improve their bargaining position with employers. Through unions, workers create an independent political organization that acts, in effect, as their agent in their dealings with employers. Once represented collectively, through such political organizations, workers are able to negotiate better terms of employment than lone individuals are capable of, in terms of: (a) better wages and salaries, (b) greater security, such as guarantees against arbitrary dismissal or generous severance packages in the event of losing their position, and (c) maintaining agency, as in consultation over the rules of work that may thus better adapt work to the individual (rather than the reverse), or in the creation of official grievance procedures (with independent mediators) that further empower workers by making them something more closely approximating "citizens" rather than mere "subjects" in the workplace. Indeed, while the power structures created by unions are as prone to corruption and other principal-agent problems as any other institution, their very existence as representative democratic institutions is likely to provide psychological benefits to the workers they represent for the same reason that other democratic institutions, however imperfect, are widely agreed to be preferable to authoritarian systems.

Unions provide not only these kinds of immediate benefits to their members, but also, once organized, form, as was discussed at length in Chapter 3, the basis for a more general political program in support of workers. These workers, organized or not, find that unions serve not only their abstract ideological interest (as advocates, at least ideally, for wage and salary workers in general) but also their particular interest, insofar as political programs – such as a minimum wage – are known to raise the wages of higher-paid, organized workers who are already above the higher minimum. Organization, in sum, provides the basis for mobilization in the electoral and policy-making processes, wherein unions make financial and human (i.e., activist and volunteer) contributions to progressive parties and movements, so as to become, potentially, an organized interest that sees itself as representing all workers. Through both their influence on the economy and the political process, then, unions may play a role – positive or negative in their final consequences – on the life satisfaction of all, whether members of unions or not.

This chapter thus considers the impact on life satisfaction of a state's regime of labor market regulation (that is, the extent to which a nation's system of laws "protects" workers) and the degree to which workers have organized themselves into labor unions – what we call the level of union "density," meaning the percentage of the workforce represented by unions.[1]

LABOR MARKET REGULATION

The political program of the Left has traditionally put enormous emphasis on regulating the labor market, for the obvious reason that from this ideological vantage point, human well-being is best served by an explicit social commitment to the well-being of persons, which is to say, by the conscious elevation of the individual's inherent right to protection by society. It is entirely possible that the Right is correct in its contention that the generalized, long-term consequences of labor regulations are in fact deleterious to the economy; it is hard to deny that as rational, self-interested utility maximizers, individual workers in real life situations are likely to favor market regulations that promise higher wages and greater job security. This chapter, of course, addresses empirically which perspective is correct, but to do so we need both a way to measure the extent of "pro-worker" labor market regulation and a better understanding of what, precisely, such regulation might entail.

A general understanding of the issues involved can be seen in the indicators used by conservative think tanks, such as the Heritage Foundation or Fraser Institute, which we encountered in Chapter 2. In the Heritage Foundation's *Index of Economic Freedom* (2008, chap.4: 53–5), they suggest four key components in a country's system of regulation: (a) the level of a country's minimum wage, presuming it has one; (b) "the rigidity" of the rules regulating the number of hours employees can be required to work; (c) the "difficulty of firing

---

[1] Union density data used in this chapter are from the OECD, http://stats.oecd.org/Index.aspx (accessed August 29, 2009). These data rely on the methodology of Visser (Visser, Martin, and Tergiest, 2009), which is generally accepted as the most reliable.

redundant employees"; and (d) the "cost of firing redundant employees." These are indeed the core issues about which workers and employers differ; it is entirely obvious which is in the interest of each class.[2]

A similar but more methodologically sophisticated and generally more academically respectable measure of labor market regulation (making it more suitable for econometric analysis over time), is provided by the Fraser Institute in its study of *Economic Freedom of the World*. It provides a multi-item index, described (Gwartney, Lawson, and Norton, 2008:7) in these terms:

Many types of labor-market regulations infringe on the economic freedom of employees and employers. Among the more prominent are minimum wages, dismissal regulations, centralized wage setting, extension of union contracts to nonparticipating parties, and conscription. The labor-market component...is designed to measure the extent to which these restraints upon economic freedom are present.

I utilize this measure – its labor market component – as my empirical index in the statistical analysis that follows (for details, see the 2008 appendix I: 192–3). Higher scores are obtained when countries "must allow market forces to determine wages and establish the conditions of hiring and firing," representing more "freedom" and thus less regulation; thus, we expect this variable to have a negative relationship with happiness, i.e., less regulation implies less happiness.[3] Of course, it is entirely possible that in the longer term, such rules actually have more negative than positive consequences, either by stifling economic growth or even by unintentionally reducing the individual's liberty by making them subject to state rules and bureaucracy. This is the empirical proposition to which this chapter is devoted.

I do not rely upon a single way of measuring labor market regulation; I also consider the index of the overall level of Employment Protection Legislation (EPL) developed by the OECD (2004). It consists of three components: "regulations governing the terms and conditions of permanent contracts in case of individual dismissals; additional provisions in the face of mass layoffs; and regulations governing the possibility of hiring on temporary contracts" (2004: 2). The index was designed by the OECD as part of a strategy for determining "how to reconcile the demand for flexibility in the labour market expressed by firms with the demand for job security expressed by workers" (2004: 1). We see again, in more bureaucratically neutral language, the same fundamental divergence of interest between worker and employer found in the more colorful Heritage and Fraser Institute phrasing. In the argot of the economist, the labor market requires "flexibility," meaning the ability of employers to hire and dismiss workers at will, with minimal or nonexistent severance packages, notice periods, or other regulations to achieve maximum "efficiency."

---

[2] Conspicuously absent from the list are workplace regulations of particular relevance to women (e.g., family leave, sexual harassment, legally mandated equal pay), which are generally (though it must be admitted, not consistently) advocated by labor unions and left-liberal political parties and (with more consistency) opposed by business and conservatives.

[3] The variable has a mean of 5.17 (with a standard deviation of 1.64) and range of 2.83 to 8.11.

At the same time, workers clearly prefer the job security that EPL provides. The index measures each country's attempt at accommodating these opposed interests. Higher scores indicate greater worker protection, such that a positive coefficient on this variable would suggest that greater employment protection promotes greater levels of subjective well-being.[4]

LABOR ORGANIZATION

Unionization has been argued to contribute to subjective well-being through a variety of mechanisms discussed above and in prior chapters. I will not rehearse these arguments in any depth, but instead offer only a brief summary, embellished with some specific insights from the literature on job satisfaction not previously reviewed.

Work is one of the central focuses of most people's lives. Labor market participants certainly spend a large portion of their working lives in the workplace. To the extent that the work experience is an agreeable one, people surely ought to be more satisfied over all. Empirical evidence confirms that intuition: job satisfaction is one of the most important determinants of overall life satisfaction (Argyle, 2001; Sousa-Poza, 2000). Belonging to a labor union may tend, in turn, to increase job satisfaction (Pfeffer and Davis-Blake, 1990).[5] The mechanisms are many, but the core relationships are clear enough: job security and a good work environment nurture satisfaction with one's job (Sousa-Poza, 2000). Unions, it is argued, tend to increase the production of those goods. If unions contribute to job satisfaction, and if job satisfaction contributes to life satisfaction, then union members should demonstrate higher life satisfaction.

A closely related argument states that unions may help reduce alienation by giving individuals a collective say in how the enterprise at which they work is managed. Individuals who are less alienated are, in turn, more likely to be more satisfied with their jobs, and thus, with their lives. Alienating work imposes psychological costs on individuals that contribute to depression (Erikson, 1986), job dissatisfaction (Greenberg and Grunberg, 1995), and a general decline in

---

[4] The variable has a mean of 2.04 (with a standard deviation of 1.05) and a range of .21 to 4.1.

[5] An interesting paradox in the earlier literature arose from evidence suggesting that union members are more dissatisfied than nonmembers, but also that they are much less likely to quit than are nonmembers (Freeman and Medoff 1984). This seeming contradiction was resolved by applying the "voice hypothesis," such that unionization allows members to complain about their working conditions precisely because they are in a position to ameliorate them through collective action. Workers thus sought to improve their working conditions rather than "exit" because they could, and presumably, because they valued the job enough to try. There is also an endogeneity problem that Pfeffer and Davis-Blake (1990) successfully explain. The issue is nicely expressed by Clark (1996: 202): "if unions address worker dissatisfaction, the more dissatisfied workers will be the most attracted by union membership," so that union shops will emerge in those industries, and under those employers, that create the most initial dissatisfaction. When controlling for this effect, Pfeffer and Davis-Blake demonstrate that "unionization has a significant positive effect on [job] satisfaction." Similar evidence is provided by Bender and Sloane (1998).

life satisfaction (Loscocco and Spitze, 1990). Similarly, it is widely agreed that autonomy on the job is vital for well-being. As Kohn and Slomczynski (1990: 964) put it, "occupational self-direction...affects values, orientations, and cognitive functioning" in exactly the way one would imagine: those who lack self-direction are more prone to psychological "distress" (anxiety and a lack of self-confidence). To be sure, alienation, and especially autonomy, are largely determined by occupation, but there are reasons to expect those represented by unions to evidence these pathologies to a lesser degree for any given type of occupation.

Although the union workplace may, of course, actually reduce autonomy in the abstract – given that union rules are indeed more rules that must be adhered to – unions are also contextually more supportive of self determination in two respects. First, they establish a degree of autonomy for their members though collective bargaining at a level that is almost by definition higher than in non-union workplaces. Workers thus rightly interpret autonomy as something collectively achieved, i.e. as a benefit of organization (Edwards, 1979). Further, as Fenwick and Olson (1986) observe, the experience of union membership fosters cognitive changes that encourage exactly the workplace participation that unionization allows, which may, in turn, foster more self-direction. To the extent that unions lessen alienation, it follows that we should again see a positive relationship between membership and well-being, net of other factors.

Unions may also contribute to well-being through their effect on another variant of connectedness. A large literature in social psychology has demonstrated that individuals are afforded some protection against the deleterious consequences of stress, and especially job related stress, through social support networks (Cohen and Wills, 1985). Work, even enjoyable work, can be a major source of stress, particularly when performance affects one's livelihood. Although support from all quarters is surely helpful, evidence suggests that buffering is most effective when the source of support is from the same domain as the source of stress. Work-related stress, then, is best buffered by having sources of emotional support at work (Jackson, 1992). Common sense would suggest that unions may facilitate such support, in that they help build not only connections but also a sense of solidarity among coworkers. Indeed, Uehara (1990) goes so far as to specify "solidarity" as a critical agent in effective social support networks. By nurturing solidarity, unions may thus provide an ideal context in which to find the type of social support that helps insulate against work-related stress.

There are few rigorous empirical studies of the general role of unions, social connection and stress, but the extant literature does offer some evidence suggesting that unions facilitate both general social support (Lowe and Northcott, 1988) and protection against job related stress per se (Brenner, 1987). The evidence in regard to the effect of job stress on life satisfaction is clearer still. Loscocco and Spitze (1990) demonstrate that precisely the negative consequences for satisfaction that one would expect do in fact occur. Unions may thus again contribute to higher quality of life among their members.

The preceding arguments bring us to social capital (Putnam, 2000a). At its core, "social capital refers to connections among individuals – social networks and the norms of reciprocity and trustworthiness that arise from them" (Putnam 2000a: 19). Generalizing slightly, the implicit idea at its most basic is that social networks facilitate positive psychological and cognitive changes in individuals that are not only politically desirable, but that are also conducive to greater personal well-being (Putnam 2000a: 333–4). The literature, indeed, is unanimous in suggesting that social connectedness fosters greater subjective well-being. This argument is made most persuasively by Robert Lane (1978a, 1978b, 2000), who places the blame for declining levels of subjective well-being in the United States and Western Europe on a growing "famine" of "interpersonal relationships" (2000: 9). That unions as organizations facilitate the building of social networks requires no elaboration. That they are as likely as fraternal organizations to foster norms of reciprocity and solidarity is equally clear. We have already noted the positive effect of union membership on social connections in the workplace. We thus have reasons to hypothesize further that union members, given that they tend to enjoy their jobs more and to suffer from less work-related stress, to say nothing of having more social connections (and indeed more social capital), are likely to be better able to build and maintain intimate and rewarding relationships. Labor organization can thus affect the quantity and quality of personal connections between human beings, which in turn surely contributes to subjective well-being (Lane, 2000). To the extent that social capital and social connectedness contribute to a better quality of life, we consequently return again to the hypothesis that labor organization promotes well-being.

The social level of unionization should also contribute to people in general – rather than just union members – enjoying better lives. There are two mechanisms, neither of which requires extensive elaboration. One is a simple contagion effect: if one's own subjective well-being is to some extent determined by interactions with others – such that we are likely to be more satisfied ourselves the more we interact with other satisfied people – then those in countries with a higher proportion of more-satisfied-than-otherwise union members are likely to be more satisfied, on average, than those in countries with fewer proportional union members. This effect will be most apparent in the intimate relationships discussed earlier, but the logic extends to all forms of social interaction (for a discussion of the powerful role of contagion in affecting levels of happiness, see Fowler and Christakis, 2008).

Unions may also contribute to the well-being of their members, and perhaps to society at large, through their capacity (in varying degrees) as participatory institutions. It is often argued that participating in organizations such as unions tends to teach individuals cognitive and social skills. People learn how to communicate with each other as well as to analyze and solve problems better. Evidence also suggests that belonging to an organization helps individuals understand their preferences and interests more clearly. The participatory or developmental strand of democratic theory encourages worker participation and involvement in decision making in the workplace because such participation is believed capable of creating better citizens – citizens who are more sophisticated, more knowledgeable, more tolerant, and more civic minded (Pateman, 1970). An extensive body of analysis generally supports the empirical veracity of this presumption (for a discussion, see Radcliff and Wingenbach, 2000). Thus, if participation in organizations contributes to human development, and if being a union member implies at least some degree of participation in the organization, then more union membership should mean more-developed citizens. If we are willing to accept that more-developed humans will tend to be more satisfied humans, then union membership should contribute to satisfaction in this way. Further, although they do not frame their argument in a developmental framework, Frey and Stutzer (2002) do demonstrate that institutional settings that foster greater democratic participation produce greater levels of subjective well being. If so, then unions should similarly contribute, at least to the extent that they offer participatory opportunities.

A more immediate argument relates to the political consequences of having a strong labor movement. One of the best-documented relationships in social science is that between the strength of organized labor and the success of Left and progressive political parties, which have traditionally championed the panoply of social rights associated with the social democratic project of a more egalitarian society, including universal health care, full employment policies, and, of course, a generous and decommodifying welfare state. Decommodification, as we have seen, promotes greater subjective well-being, such that labor unions, as agents in the creation and maintenance of the welfare state, should positively affect well-being through this indirect pathway.

As a final observation, it may be worth reiterating that while some of the presumed effects of unionization are direct, in the sense that they affect organized workers as individuals (or families) per se, others are indirect, and affect both the organized and the unorganized alike. Both mechanisms should increase mean levels of happiness. In the first, society must have a greater average satisfaction as union density increases because the benefits of organization apply to a larger share of society's members. In the other, aggregate levels of well-being increase with density because greater organization alters social arrangements so that they better contribute to a generalized improvement in living conditions. This suggests two arguments: that individual members of unions show greater satisfaction and that the overall level of organization – the level of union density – should positively affect the satisfaction of everyone, union members or otherwise. These, at least, are the contentions that we will now proceed to test empirically.

ANALYSIS

I adopt the same estimation strategy, data, and methods introduced in Chapter 5. The data are again from World Values Study from 1981 to 2007 for the OECD countries. As before, they are analyzed in two basic fashions: first using individuals as the units of analysis and then aggregating to the level of national means for the given country-year. In the first, I focus on the simple survey question on life satisfaction, treating the given individual's level of satisfaction as the dependent variable. In the second, attention is moved to the average level of satisfaction within the given country at the particular year in question.

Labor Market Regulation

Table 6.1 presents the individual-level results for the labor market regulation variables, using the base model introduced in the prior chapter.[6] As reported in column (a), for the Fraser Institute measure of economic "freedom" (meaning, the lack of regulation), the coefficient is negative and significant, as predicted. This implies that as the amount of regulation in the economy declines (or its level of economic "freedom" increases) satisfaction also declines. The same substantive conclusion obtains for the OECD measure of Employment Protection Legislation. Here, higher values of the index indicate greater protection, so that we expect a positive relationship with satisfaction; that is, as protection from the market increases, satisfaction increases. This is apparent in column (b), where the EPL coefficient is positive and significant, pursuant with expectations. Note that the interactions with income remain insignificant.

To interpret the substantive rather than purely statistical impact of these variables on satisfaction, I again compare the estimated impact on satisfaction of moving from the highest to the lowest observed value of market regulation to the estimated impact of being unemployed. For both the Fraser Institute index and the EPL measure the estimated impact on satisfaction is more than three times the boost in satisfaction an unemployed person receives when finding a job. As with the size of government variables discussed in the prior chapter, the practical consequences of the cross-national differences in how well states protect workers in the labor market has profound implications for human well-being.

Table 6.2 reports the results when considering mean levels of satisfaction across nations. Results are much as before, with each of the coefficients of interest being significant and of the predicted sign. This confirms, of course, the conclusions noted earlier: more regulation and more protection suggest happier citizens.

Labor Unions

Recall that there are two basic hypotheses: individual members of labor unions show greater satisfaction and that the overall level of organization – union

---

[6] Results are similar when using the expanded models including additional variables as reported in the prior tables. The individual-level models reported in Tables 6.1 and 6.3 also give similar results if estimated using HLM.

TABLE 6.1. *Life Satisfaction and Labor Market Regulation: Individual-Level Data OECD Countries (1981–2007)*

	(a) Economic "Freedom"	(b) EPL
Economic "Freedom"	−.218***	n/a
	(.035)	
Economic "Freedom" Interaction	.002	n/a
Term with Income	(.004)	
Employment Protection Legislation	n/a	.337***
		(.055)
Employment Protection Legislation	n/a	.003
Interaction Term with Income		(.005)
Financial Satisfaction	.341***	.359***
	(.020)	(.022)
Social Capital	.255***	.259***
	(.026)	(.032)
Gender	−.042*	−.051*
	(.030)	(.033)
Age	−.033***	−.033***
	(.005)	(.004)
Age-squared	.000***	.000***
	(.000)	(.000)
Married	.447***	.444***
	(.027)	(.026)
Personal Health	1.280***	1.518***
	(.144)	(.166)
Unemployed	−.332***	−.321***
	(.077)	(.072)
Income	−.022	−.023**
	(.022)	(.013)
Church Attendance	.036***	.031***
	(.006)	(.004)
Constant	7.079***	5.126***
	(.300)	(.223)
Observations	58,270	35,083
R-squared	0.2621	0.2743

*significant at .10. **significant at .05 level. ***significant at .01 level.

Note: Dependent variable is life satisfaction. Table omits country and year dummy variables. Entries are unstandardized regression coefficients (country-clustered robust standard errors).

density – affects the overall, national level of happiness. The initial test of both contentions is provided in the first column of Table 6.3. Members of unions are indeed happier than are others, as suggested by the positive and significant coefficient for this variable. Density is also positive and significant, implying that density does indeed affect satisfaction generally.

TABLE 6.2. *Life Satisfaction and Labor Market Regulations: Aggregate-Level Data OECD Countries (1981–2007)*

	(a) Economic "Freedom"	(b) EPL
Economic "Freedom"	−.041*	n/a
	(.027)	
Employment Protection Legislation	n/a	.169***
		(.064)
Social Capital	.858**	.813**
	(.424)	(.404)
Unemployment	−.022**	−.028**
	(.012)	(.013)
Real GDP	−.000	−.000
	(.000)	(.000)
Individualism	.538***	.682***
	(.086)	(.136)
Catholic	.250*	.405**
	(.163)	(.225)
Economic Growth	.014	.005
	(.016)	(.013)
Constant	9.619***	8.537***
	(.833)	(.770)
Observations	72	45
R-squared	0.7563	0.7700

*significant at .10. **significant at .05 level. ***significant at .01 level.

Note: Dependent variable is life satisfaction. Entries are unstandardized regression coefficients (standard errors). Table omits year dummy variables (GLS random-effects model).

Of course, it seems likely that the effects of unionization might become less pronounced as one moves up the status hierarchy of work. Using education as a convenient and appealing proxy for this difficult concept, we find some evidence of this for individual-level membership but not for aggregate union density, as reported in column (b) of Table 6.3. Here we find that while the interaction between education and density is totally insignificant (with the main effect remaining significant), the interaction of education and individual membership is significant and negative, implying that the benefits of unionization do indeed decline as one's level of education increases. These results are entirely sensible, confirming our intuition that those with the highest levels of education benefit less from belonging to a union per se, while everyone (whatever their level of education) benefits from the generalized effects of higher union density. It is important to note, too, that the rate of decline in the positive effect of individual membership as one moves up the education ladder is very modest. Recall that education is measured in ten categories; it is only at the very highest categories that the effect of being a member of a union is reduced

TABLE 6.3. *Life Satisfaction and Labor Unions: Individual-Level Data OECD Countries (1981–2007)*

	(a) Base Model (main effects only)	(b) Add Interactions with Education
Union Membership	.038**	.168***
	(.022)	(.049)
Union Density	.011**	.011**
	(.005)	(.005)
Union Membership Interaction Term with Education	n/a	−.019***
		(.006)
Union Density Interaction Term with Education	n/a	−.000
		(.000)
Education	n/a	−.005
		(.007)
Financial Satisfaction	.342***	.339***
	(.020)	(.020)
Social Capital	.260***	.266***
	(.025)	(.024)
Gender	−.040	−.043
	(.031)	(.033)
Age	−.032***	−.033***
	(.004)	(.004)
Age-squared	.000***	.000***
	(.000)	(.000)
Married	.458***	.450***
	(.028)	(.028)
Personal Health	1.281***	1.295***
	(.142)	(.147)
Unemployed	−.321***	−.326***
	(.076)	(.088)
Income	−.015**	−.013*
	(.008)	(.008)
Church Attendance	.037***	.036***
	(.006)	(.006)
Constant	4.752***	4.895***
	(.516)	(.186)
Observations	57,126	52,676
R-squared	0.2626	0.2603

*significant at .10. **significant at .05 level. ***significant at .01 level.

Note: Dependent variable is life satisfaction. Table omits country and year dummy variables. Entries are unstandardized regression coefficients (country-clustered robust standard errors).

to zero. For everyone else the effect remains positive, diminishing slowly as education increases.

A general appraisal of the magnitude of the effect of union membership and union density suggests the following. For individual membership, the effect for those with the lowest level of education is – controlling for all the other factors in the equation – equal to about one-half that of the benchmark effect of unemployment. As noted, this slowly declines to zero for those with the highest level of education. Aggregate union density shows a much stronger effect (which is essentially invariant over education), such that moving from a high–union density country (density of 80 percent) to a low–union density country (10 percent) would suggest an increase in satisfaction equal to more than two times the increase in happiness an unemployed person receives when finding a job. These are, once again, extremely powerful effects on the quality of people's lives.

Turning to the aggregate analysis in Table 6.4, in which our focus is, of course, now entirely on density, we find the expected positive and significant coefficient for the base model reported in column (a). The obvious conclusion is that the average level of happiness in a country is positively affected by the strength of the labor movement within the country, as measured by the percentage of workers belonging to a union.

A potential complication in interpreting the results is the connection between labor union density and the size of the welfare state. Given that unions promote a more generous welfare state, and the welfare state, as we have seen, appears to generate greater levels of satisfaction, it is possible that the positive effects of unionization are entirely or mostly through this indirect effect. It is possible, thus, that unions might have positive consequences for subjective well-being only through this mechanism – meaning that it is ultimately the welfare state rather than unionization per se that is important in the immediate sense. Similarly, it is possible that the findings on social democracy reported earlier are artifacts of failing to consider labor organization. Column (b) of Table 6.4 addresses this possibility by adding a variable for the welfare state (the social wage, discussed in the prior chapter). If the positive role of unionization is due to its positive effect on the welfare state, the density variable should be reduced to insignificance when considering both simultaneously. Instead, we find that each are significant and of the expected sign, suggesting that the generosity of the welfare state and the strength of organized labor have independent and separable effects on life satisfaction. Simply put, the positive consequences of unionization for satisfaction cannot be attributed to the indirect effect of labor organization on the welfare state.

Before concluding this section, it is instructive to return to the question of whether union density benefits society in general, rather than members per se. This can be easily tested with the aggregate data by considering the effect of density on the mean level of satisfaction of members and nonmembers separately. This provides the most direct test possible of the contention that both

TABLE 6.4. *Life Satisfaction and Labor Union Density: Aggregate-Level Data OECD Countries (1981–2007)*

	(a) Union Density	(b) Union Density Controlling for Welfare State
Union Density	.006*	.005*
	(.004)	(.003)
Social Wage	n/a	.005*
		(.003)
Social Capital	.330	.247
	(.517)	(.507)
Unemployment	−.016	−.020*
	(.013)	(.012)
Real GDP	−.000	−.000
	(.000)	(.000)
Individualism	.478***	.485***
	(.148)	(.116)
Catholic	.181	.178
	(.244)	(.200)
Economic Growth	.016	.018
	(.015)	(.015)
Constant	7.641***	7.400***
	(1.172)	(1.131)
Observations	71	71
R-squared	0.7452	0.7915

*significant at .10. **significant at .05 level. ***significant at .01 level.

Note: Dependent variable is life satisfaction. Entries are unstandardized regression coefficients (standard errors). Table omits year dummy variables (GLS random-effects model).

members and nonmembers lead better lives, on average, when more workers are organized. Of course, it would be odd if union members did not benefit more than others, in that they receive both the particular benefits that come from belonging to a union as well as the more generalized benefits that accrue to everyone through the indirect effects of organization (e.g., via the public policy agendas that unions have historically supported), so the expectation, if the arguments about labor organization advanced previously are correct, is that the density coefficient will be larger for union members, but significant for both, and nontrivial in magnitude for nonmembers.

Table 6.5 presents the results. As is apparent, the density coefficient is indeed positive and significant for both members (column a) and nonmembers (column b). The coefficient is also larger for members than non-members, but (again as expected) the value for the latter remains about the same magnitude as the result for the general population reported earlier.

TABLE 6.5. *Life Satisfaction and Labor Density by Social Groups: Aggregate-Level Data OECD Countries (1981–2007)*

	(a) Union Members	(b) Nonunion Members	(c) High Income	(d) Low Income
Union Density	.014**	.005*	.006**	.007*
	(.006)	(.003)	(.003)	(.004)
Social Capital	−.065	.158	.597	.177
	(.900)	(.550)	(.587)	(.593)
Unemployment	.011	−.015	.006	−.013
	(.022)	(.013)	(.015)	(.015)
Real GDP	.000	.000	.000	.000
	(.000)	(.000)	(.000)	(.000)
Individualism	.287*	.476***	.361***	.452
	(.207)	(.133)	(.113)	(.142)
Catholic	.333	.129	.170	.188
	(.358)	(.229)	(.202)	(.244)
Economic Growth	−.006	.014	.023	.005
	(.027)	(.016)	(.019)	(.018)
Constant	6.366***	7.216***	8.095***	7.049***
	(2.018)	(1.238)	(1.310)	(1.334)
Observations	67	67	67	67
R-squared	0.5602	0.7555	0.6939	0.7420

*significant at .10. **significant at .05 level. ***significant at .01 level.

Note: Dependent variable is life-satisfaction. Entries are unstandardized regression coefficients (standard errors). Table omits year dummy variables (GLS random-effects model).

In addition to confirming that unions benefit both members and nonmembers, it would clearly also be helpful to know that unions also contributed to the well-being of high- and low-income groups, as done in the prior chapters, if attempting to make the argument that strong labor unions contribute to the general betterment of society. When doing so, we find that both the relatively affluent (column c) and the relatively impoverished (column d) do indeed enjoy higher levels of satisfaction as the percentage of workers organized increases.[7]

In sum, it does indeed seem entirely reasonable to conclude that labor unions benefit society.

---

[7] Note too that the same results also obtain when considering men versus women; that is, the unionization variable remains significant for both groups. More interestingly, the density coefficient remains significant and virtually identical in magnitude for both left-wing ($b = .008$, $p < .05$) and right-wing individuals ($b = .007$, $p < .05$), implying of course that the strength of the labor movement benefits those on the left and the right equally, as we would expect if the impact of labor organization manifests itself (as its defenders maintain) through policies that nurture a broad middle class that in turn ultimately benefits all. Just as the welfare state did, labor unions benefit rich and poor, men and women, and those on both the left and right of the political spectrum.

CONCLUSION

The market economy has much to recommend it. Indeed, few people, whatever their ideological commitments, deny that the market as a central organizing principle provides advantages in both material prosperity and human liberty unrealized by any prior mode of economic production. Still, any form of social organization involves inevitable conflicts of interest that arise spontaneously from the structure of that organization. As both Adam Smith and Karl Marx were perceptive enough to see, the principal conflict in capitalist societies is in the asymmetry of power between workers who must as a matter of necessity sell their labor power as a commodity in order to survive, and those who buy that commodity in pursuit of their own private interests. Without this asymmetry, as discussed in Chapters 2 and 3, workers would not agree to the sale of their labor power at a rate that allowed employers to profit by its purchase, and the system of capitalism as we understand it could not exist. The natural conflict between employer and the employed thus finds expression in the attempts of each to either reduce or expand the degree of this asymmetry. The smaller the asymmetry, the greater is the relative bargaining power of workers, and thus the greater their share in the wealth that their labor helps bring into being. Conversely, of course, the larger the disparity in bargaining position, the greater is the ability of employers to use that position to strike more advantageous compromises with workers.

This conflict over negotiating position, while also at the heart of the political debate over how generous the welfare state should be, is even more transparently obvious when considering the actual conditions and terms of employment that the ordinary worker, and the typical firm that employs them, face in their day-to-day lives. This conflict manifests itself at several levels, from wages and related benefits, the security with which employment is held, and the rules that govern employment, from safety regulations to maximum hours to all the minute details of the rules that govern the workplace. The labor market regulations and worker protection laws we have considered earlier involve the most obvious and important of such rules. To the extent that the law establishes relatively strong protections for workers, the quality of life for most citizens is improved.

Labor unions are, from the point of view of employees, a further "escalation" in their relative bargaining position, in that the union represents a nominally democratic political entity that represents them against their employer, in the same way that representative institutions protect the individual against an arbitrary government. This is the essential value of the labor union: in the end, it is in its own limited way a democratic institution whose purpose is to help those it represents to "secure" their "inalienable rights" including "Life, Liberty, and the pursuit of Happiness." As we have seen, unions not only appear to do this – to support the happiness of their members per se – but they also appear to contribute to the happiness of all, members and nonmembers, rich and poor. They do so not so much out of any extraordinary (and thus empirically dubious) altruism but because it has generally been in their material interests to pursue policies that extend prosperity and security to larger segments of the population. Unions have consistently supported higher minimum wages for all, social security and health care for all, and so on, because it is in the interests of organized workers to do so. If the large and relatively prosperous "middle class" that unions have been instrumental in creating can be thought of as a positive "externality" attributable to their own rational pursuit of self-interest, it actually provides one of the best testaments to the truth of Smith's dictum that what serves the individual serves society: workers who organize themselves so as to collectively press their interests have succeeded, to the extent of their success in organizing, in adapting social policies to be more consistent with the interests of a progressively larger share of the general population.

The theoretical basis for such an understanding of both big government in general, and labor unions in particular, was developed in Chapters 1 through 3. It has been substantiated empirically at some length in this and the prior chapter when considering the universe of the industrial democracies of Western Europe, North America, and the Pacific – that is, by considering how different levels of welfare-state development, the size of government, market regulation, and labor organization are associated with different levels of life satisfaction across that large and diverse range of countries. The chapter that follows is an attempt to substantiate these claims in a rather different way: instead of looking across countries, I follow the tradition of looking across the states of the American federal system, which have long been argued to be the world's most important "laboratories of democracy."

7

The American States

This chapter completes the empirical analysis of the political determinants of life satisfaction by shifting geographical focus from the universe of industrial democracies to domestic politics in the United States. Whereas I previously attempted to deduce the consequences of different public policy regimes for quality of life by searching for statistical relationships between these phenomena over countries, I here attempt to find similar evidence when considering only variation across the states of the American federal system. The initial rationale for this strategy is simple enough: this approach allows tests of my basic propositions about the effects of the welfare state, economic regulation, and organized labor using data of an entirely different sort. If these data confirm prior results, this can only improve our confidence in them.

There are, however, particulars that make this extension of the analysis an especially fruitful one. First, by concentrating entirely on a single country, we hold literally constant various cultural, social, and historical aspects of a nation that we controlled for only econometrically in the cross-national study. Although those controls should be more than sufficient for isolating the relationships in question, any refinement in the method of control can, again, only further confirm and extend the earlier findings. While there are certainly cultural variations across regions of the United States, these fade into triviality compared to the differences one observes across countries as disparate as France, Sweden, Ireland, New Zealand, and Japan. This is doubly so since the Second World War, where the sometimes lamented "nationalization" (or "homogenization") of culture has further eroded what vestigial regional differences in sociocultural patterns existed in a country that has been since the Civil War undeniably a single country, with a single history and culture, at least in comparison to the differences between countries that have previously concerned us.

A second advantage of considering the states is our ability to make a virtue of what is normally a disadvantage in empirical research: that the independent variables – the political factors that I postulate affect satisfaction – show vastly less variation across states than they do across nations. When scanning the land-scape of American politics, one finds substantial differences in the generosity of the welfare state, the amount of pro-worker regulation of the market, and the strength of labor unions, but these are extremely modest in comparison with the cross-national pattern. It is one thing to find that the vast differences in public policy between, say, social democratic countries like Sweden or Denmark and liberal democracies such as the United States or Australia are sufficient to pro-duce differences in quality of life. It would be quite another thing to show that life satisfaction varies in much the same way when considering only the compar-atively modest differences we find between, say, relatively progressive states like California or Vermont and relatively conservative ones like Kansas or Texas. Further, variation among U.S. states is confined to what is, by international standards, the right of the ideological perspective, given that even the most liberal U.S. states remain paradigms of the minimalist welfare state. In sum, it would be no small thing to demonstrate that even policy moves within the confined space of the right-hand side of the ideological spectrum can produce meaningful changes in the extent to which people find their lives rewarding.

The states are appealing for a third reason, not unrelated to those just men-tioned: they provide an ideal venue for a case study of the power or authority of subnational governments to make changes in policy sufficient to materially and systematically alter quality of life. There has been a general movement, both political and scholarly, in support of the idea that federalism or similar "devo-lutions" of centralized national authority to local or regional governments produces "better" government in terms of both democratic and economic per-formance (for an extensive and critical review, see Gerring and Thacker, 2008). Even nominally unitary states of necessity rely on subnational authorities for the administration of law, which invariably implies at least some degree of autonomy in that administration. While we must be careful not to generalize too much from the U.S., the states do seem to provide a model – and thus much studied – environment in which to investigate the efficacy of provincial governments as they affect the ability of citizens to succeed in the "pursuit of happiness."

HAPPINESS AND THE STUDY OF POLITICS IN THE AMERICAN STATES

Within the literature on American politics, virtually no attention has been devoted to the political determinants of life satisfaction. There was a brief surge of interest in the subject in the 1970s, when no less icons of the field than Angus Campbell and Philip Converse (Campbell, Converse, and Rodgers, 1976) devoted an exploratory book to the subject. Their analysis focuses almost entirely, though, on a descriptive account of quality of life in the United States, along with an examination of group differences; they do not address explic-itly how the political system per se affects well-being. More recently, Putnam (2000a) has come closer to that mark by focusing our attention on how social capital (which we can conceive of as a collective property of society partially determined by political institutions) can have important consequences for psychological well-being.

Still, to my knowledge, there has thus far been no rigorous, econometric study of how electoral and policy outcomes affect life satisfaction in the United States.[1] I attempt such an appraisal by examining how differences in public policy regimes and partisan politics across the U.S. states affect subjective well-being. As political scientists we thus return to the issues central to the discipline: Do the results of democratic competition, as manifest in the ideological characteristics of elected governments and the policies they pursue, have important, consistent, and predictable implications for quality of life?

As we have seen, quality of life is largely determined by the extent to which a given sociopolitical order succeeds in satisfying human needs for the largest share of the population at the highest possible level. Thus, as Veenhoven put it, we are adopting (and, in so doing, testing empirically) the "commonsense" view that "subjective appreciation of life depends in the first place on the objective quality of life," such that "the better the living-conditions in a country [or region], the happier its inhabitants will be" (1995: 3). The basis of this interpretation is the intuitively appealing one "that there are universal human needs" – material, psychological, and social – which emerge from our common biological constitution. Human societies, in turn, can be understood as the institutionalization of "collective arrangements to gratify these needs," with variation in actual subjective quality of life across countries or regions reflecting nothing more than differences in how effective societies are in this endeavor. In sum, the more people have their needs gratified, the happier they tend to be.

The issue at hand is thus the familiar one of which approach to public policy best meets human needs: the political program of the Right, which focuses on an unfettered market, or the traditional Left, which stresses, first, an activist state attempting to supplement the cold efficiency of market outcomes with redistributive policies and, secondarily, the organization of workers into the labor unions that promote the interests of the ordinary citizen in both the workplace and in politics. Put in the terms of American politics, these abstract arguments reduce to a tangible question: Do liberal governments, and thus, presumably, liberal public policies, tend to produce greater or lesser amounts of well-being than their conservative equivalents?

The reality and importance of this perennial ideological conflict has given rise to a long tradition of attempting to model the degree of the "liberalism" of state governments. While it has not before been explicitly tied to the issue of life

---

[1] There certainly have been attempts to study subjective well-being in the United States, more generally, and even at the state-level, but such studies have not addressed the policy or labor organization questions at hand (see especially Oswald and Wu, 2010; Blanchflower and Oswald, 2002).

satisfaction, scholars have long acknowledged this concept as one of the central ideas for understanding state politics. Indeed, this literature has informed some of the most familiar and important work in American politics (e.g., Key, 1949; R. Erikson, Wright, and McIver, 1993; Hill, Leighley, and Hinton-Andersson, 1995; Hero, 1998). The task before us is to see if this familiar "workhorse" idea of state policy liberalism (and its cousin, labor union density) proves to have the tangible consequences for the quality of human life that the scholarship devoted to the subject has always implicitly presumed.

DATA AND METHOD

To address the questions posed above requires survey data that meet two substantive criteria: it has enough cases to examine the effects of state-level political factors, and it includes an appropriate measure of satisfaction with life. The DDB Life Style Survey, the use of which in social science was popularized by Putnam (2000a), meets those criteria. It contains a total of more than 45,000 respondents distributed over the forty-eight continental states, polled in yearly intervals from 1985 to 1998. It also contains a life satisfaction item that matches closely that used in the World Values Surveys, the Eurobarometer, and other data sets conventionally used in the literature: the respondent is asked to what extent he or she agrees that "I am very satisfied with the way things are going in my life these days" (with six response categories representing increasing levels of agreement).

I analyze these data in two ways. The first is introduced as yet another methodological variation whose purpose is to illustrate that the same fundamental results we have encountered elsewhere also obtain when using this alternative method. This approach is based upon creating a state-level metric that is the equivalent of what in the comparative literature on satisfaction is referred to as the "pure" or truly "national" level of satisfaction, that is, that portion of satisfaction that cannot be attributed to individual-level characteristics (e.g., Di Tella, MacCulloch, and Oswald, 1997; Radcliff, 2001). This is accomplished by regressing satisfaction on a set of individual-level characteristics and then by using the mean of the residuals from this model, by state, as the dependent variable. It should be noted this approach is highly conservative, in that the political variables that are the main focus of interest can influence some of the individual-level variables (e.g., income). It is, of course, precisely this conservatism that endorses the procedure, given that it assigns as much variance as possible to individual-level factors that are assumed to be apolitical, thus "raising the bar for showing that politics indeed affects average levels of satisfaction" (Radcliff, 2001).

In the second approach, I simply take the reported or nominal satisfaction of the individual – the original survey item itself – as the dependent variable, modeling it as a function of both individual- and state-level factors, as I have done before. In the first method, the unit of analysis is the state; here it is the individual.

Control Variables

Before discussing the political variables that are our principal interest, I first describe the control variables I utilize so as to be able to isolate political determinants. These follow the same battery of demographic and attitudinal items used earlier, modified slightly by the structure of the new data set and the application to a specifically U.S. context (Álvarez-Díaz, Gonzalez, and Radcliff, 2010): respondent's education; employment status; income and satisfaction with income; gender; dummy variables for African Americans and those of other races (leaving non-Hispanic whites as the reference category); age and age-squared (to account for the curvilinear relationship between age and satisfaction); dummies for those widowed, divorced, or married (leaving the single as the reference category); a dummy variable for those with children living at home; and church attendance. I also add, as before, measures of the respondent's self-reported health, given the strong correlation between it and subjective well-being (e.g., Frey and Stutzer, 2002), and the individual's level of generalized interpersonal trust, given the recognized connection between this aspect of social capital and satisfaction (e.g., Helliwell, 2003; Helliwell and Huang, 2008).[2]

The preceding variables account for the individual-level factors. They form the items used to estimate the "pure" state level of satisfaction (i.e., mean residual satisfaction) as well as the individual-level control variables for the analysis of the "raw" satisfaction data. For both sets of analyses, I also utilize a set of state-level variables that are (per Álvarez-Díaz, Gonzalez, and Radcliff, 2010) likely to affect quality of life in this context: per-capita personal income, the overall state level of social capital (Putnam's [2000b] "Comprehensive Social Capital Index"), racial diversity (the ratio of minority to white population as suggested by Hero and Tolbert [1996]), and state population (in thousands of persons).[3]

A last control, for culture, requires a brief comment. There are two fundamental approaches to understanding the role of culture in affecting subjective well-being, which we have encountered in the prior analyses. One focuses on

[2] Income is measured in fifteen categories in ascending order; education is highest level of education completed in six categories with higher values representing higher attainment; employment status is a dummy coded one if respondent is unemployed and zero otherwise; gender is coded one for females, two for males; church attendance is the frequency with which respondent attends "a church or other place of worship" in seven ascending categories; income satisfaction is from the survey question ascertaining level of agreement with the statement "Our family income is high enough to satisfy nearly all our important desires"; personal health is the survey item "I am in very good physical condition" with six response categories with higher values indicating greater agreement. Trust is measured by the degree to which individuals agree with the statement "Most people are honest" in six categories with greater values indicating more agreement.

[3] Putnam's (2000b) "Comprehensive Social Capital Index" taken from the "Bowling Alone" website, http://www.bowlingalone.com/data.php3 (accessed on 15 January 2006). Personal income from, Bureau of Economic Analysis, State Annual Personal Income (n.d, http://www.bea.gov/bea/regional/spi), accessed April 15, 2006.

ideographic national differences, such that there is something about being, say, Danish versus American, that affects one's level of happiness. This strand of the literature is perhaps best exemplified by Inglehart (1991), who conceives of variation across nations in levels of satisfaction with life as reflecting accumulated national experiences, absorbed in pre-adult socialization, that form a "national character." Thus, in the comparative context, culture can be controlled for in the obvious fashion: by fitting dummy variables for sets of nations thought to share similar cultures (e.g., Scandinavia, the Anglo-Saxon countries). Although it is unlikely that the modest level of variation in culture across the states can play the same role, I control for this possibility by including dummy variables for each of the nine regions of the country (as defined by the Census Bureau), except for a reference category.[4]

The other approach to culture has sought to connect international differences in satisfaction with variation not in ideographic national cultures, but with particular cultural characteristics. By far, the most successful of the latter, as we have seen, is the effort to show that the fundamental dimension of importance is that between "individualistic" as opposed to "collectivist" cultures. Of course, the amount of "collectivism" of culture is surely not likely to show great variation across the American states in the way it does across countries. In any event, I am aware of no subnational measure of this concept, and it would, in any event, be adequately captured by the region dummies.

Finally, in the individual-level analysis in which there is modest longitudinal variation in the data, I also as before include dummies for years (excepting a reference category), to account for pooling as well as possible secular trends in satisfaction over time. This not only relaxes any assumption about a linear trend over time (that including only the year as a variable would imply) but again also raises the econometric bar, given that still more of the variation in the dependent variable is absorbed into the fixed effects.

Political Variables

Our task is to provide variables that measure where a state's policy regime falls in the conflict between Left and Right. I attempt to do so by using a series of different plausible operationalizations, enumerated thus:

Welfare Spending: As the preferred decommodification data do not exist for the states, I of necessity utilize total per capita transfer payments from governments (local, state, federal) in real thousands of dollars, divided by state per capita income to account for differences in relative purchasing power across states.[5]

---

4 The regions (using the standard Census Bureau classification) are New England, the Mid Atlantic, the East North-Central, the West North-Central, the South Atlantic, the East South-Central, the West South-Central, Mountain, and Pacific.

5 Data are from the Bureau of Economic Analysis, http://www.bea.gov/bea/regional/spi/ (accessed on 15 April 2006).

The Regulation of Markets: Byars, McCormick, and Yandle (1999) have created several indices of "economic freedom" based upon an analysis of state policies. I utilize their recommended, overall summary index, which assesses how conservative state policies are in five categories: taxation (which "represents a government confiscation of private resources and is therefore a violation of economic freedom"), economic regulations (especially those which "set standards for employment and worker safety"), litigation procedures (i.e., how much the state "encourages frivolous law suits" against business), the size of government (given that "the portion of a state's consumption and production that is publicly – democratically – allocated" is inversely proportional to "economic freedom"), and, of course, welfare spending. It is essential to note that this measure, like similar indices regularly offered by the Fraser Institute or the Heritage Foundation for nation-states are, as one labor economist observes, transparent measures of how much "private businesses and investors are relatively unfettered by government policies, rules, or practices" (Stanford, 1999). Put differently, they are measures of economic "freedom" as seen from the ideological vantage point of business, i.e., from the market, and are perhaps more accurately described as measures of the degree of governmental intervention in, and regulation of, the economy. As such, this variable makes an ideal summary measurement of the main theoretical variable interest. Higher values indicate a greater level of political intrusion into markets (i.e., more governmental regulation).

Government Ideology: I use the cumulative average (up to the year of the observation) of the state governments' ideology index using updated data developed by Berry et al. (1998). Higher values indicate more liberal governments. We use the cumulative value as this best represents the general, long-term pattern of governmental ideology. In this, we follow Radcliff (2001), who argues that a similar measure (the cumulative share of cabinet seats held by left parties) shows a strong relationship with satisfaction across countries.

Party Control of Government: I utilize the cumulative percentage of the state legislature controlled by the Democratic Party (Klarner, n.d.). As the Democratic Party is at least nominally more disposed toward liberal policies than the Republican alternative, the greater their share of time in government, the less conservative may we expect the state's policy regime to be. I again use the cumulative value to the year of the observation, as with state government ideology.[6]

RESULTS

I first discuss the results for measures of political restraint of the market, paralleling the cross-national results presented in Chapter 5. I then turn to

---

[6] Both cumulative variables are scaled by dividing by 100 for ease in reporting coefficients.

TABLE 7.1. *Political Outcomes and Life Satisfaction: Aggregate-Level Analysis The American States*

	(a)	(b)	(d)	(c)
Transfer Payments	.140*** (.056)	n/a	n/a	n/a
Economic Regulation	n/a	.042** (.019)	n/a	n/a
Government Ideology	n/a	n/a	.015** (.006)	n/a
Democratic Party Control	n/a	n/a	n/a	.017** (.009)
Social Capital	.043** (.024)	.023 (.023)	.029 (.023)	.043* (.026)
Racial Diversity	.258** (.119)	.207** (.118)	.198** (.117)	.133 (.122)
State Income	−.000 (.000)	−.000* (.000)	−.000** (.000)	−.000 (.000)
State Population	−.000* (.000)	−.000 (.000)	−.000 (.000)	−.000 (.000)
Constant	−.110 (.148)	−.078 (.151)	.119 (.104)	.040 (.123)
Observations	48	48	48	47
R-squared	.3879	.3621	.3723	.3130

*significant at .10. **significant at .05 level. ***significant at .01 level.
Note: Dependent variable is life-satisfaction. Table omits regional dummy variables. Entries are unstandardized regression coefficients (standard errors).

the results for labor union organization, replicating to the extent possible the results for nations from Chapter 6.

Public Policy

Table 7.1 presents the aggregate-level results.[7] As is apparent from column (a), the coefficient for transfer payments is significant and positive, suggesting that higher levels of spending are associated with greater levels of life satisfaction. The greater the state's effort at income maintenance, the better quality of life is. An inspection of the outcome for the summary index of the amount of regulation of labor markets and the economy more generally tells a similar story (column b). The coefficient of interest is positive and significant, suggesting that the less friendly policies are to the free-market ideal (i.e., the greater the amount of regulation), the more satisfied citizens are with the quality of their lives. Thus, the more the state intervenes in the economy through the

---

[7] The simple OLS results are reported, but the same results obtain using robust standard errors to protect against any potential heteroscedasticity.

mechanisms specified in the index (regulation, taxation, spending, and law), the more people evaluate their lives positively. The coefficient for the liberalism of state governments (column c) shows the same positive and significant relationship as with prior results, implying that the more liberal are state governments, the higher are levels of satisfaction with life. Results are equally clear for party control of government, as seen in column (d): the coefficient for the long-term extent of Democratic control of the state legislature is significant and correctly signed.

Perhaps the most instructive way to interpret the substantive, rather than merely the statistical, significance of these results is to compute the predicted change in the dependent variable when moving across the observed range of the independent variables across the states (i.e., between the largest and smallest observed values). For ease of interpretation, I express the predicted change in terms of the number of standard deviations of the dependent variable. The strongest effect is for transfer payments, which suggests that moving from the lowest to the highest level of spending increases the state level of satisfaction by fully 2.6 standard deviations. The other variables show smaller but still very substantial impacts: economic regulation, 1.9 standard deviations; state government ideology, 1.5 standard deviations; and Democratic Party control, 1.7 standard deviations. Clearly, then, the public policies that state governments pursue have dramatic effects on the quality of life citizens experience, as does the ideological and partisan composition of government. The measures of policy show marginally stronger effects, which is sensible, given that they represent actual, tangible outputs of government, whereas ideology and partisanship reflect only the latent or generalized disposition of governments.

I also estimated the same models using robust regression, a technique which allows us to confirm that the results are not dependent upon a few atypical or otherwise overly influential cases.[8] The results are substantively identical to those reported in Table 7.2. The only appreciable difference is that three of the four coefficients of interest become both marginally more significant and slightly larger in magnitude. One may also note, incidentally, that the same results obtain if using only the mean of the original satisfaction variable, rather than the "pure" state level that the residual method relies on.

Turning to the second estimation approach discussed earlier, I regress satisfaction on the individual- and state-level controls, plus the political variables used previously. Where the unit of analysis was before the state, it is now the individual. Estimation is done with Huber-White robust standard errors, correcting for the pooled structure of the data (i.e., state clustered). This procedure yields estimates that are robust to both between-state heteroscedasticity and

---

[8] I relied upon the rreg procedure from Stata 11, which begins by removing cases with large values on Cook's D (i.e., extreme outliers, of which there were actually none with the present data), and then iteratively uses two complimentary methods of weighting cases to find an estimate that is robust.

TABLE 7.2. *Political Outcomes and Life Satisfaction: Aggregate-Level Analysis The American States Robust Regression*

	(a)	(b)	(c)	(d)
Transfer Payments	.185***	n/a	n/a	n/a
	(.048)			
Economic Regulation	n/a	.036*	n/a	n/a
		(.021)		
Government Ideology	n/a	n/a	.018***	n/a
			(.004)	
Democratic Party Control	n/a	n/a	n/a	.024***
				(.007)
Social Capital	.038**	.016	.032**	.062***
	(.021)	(.025)	(.016)	(.019)
Racial Diversity	.249**	.159	.276***	.240***
	(.103)	(.129)	(.080)	(.089)
State Income	.000	−.000*	.000	.000**
	(.000)	(.000)	(.000)	(.000)
State Population	−.000**	−.000	−.000**	−.000**
	(.000)	(.000)	(.000)	(.000)
Constant	−.338***	−.029	−.097	−.248***
	(.127)	(.165)	(.072)	(.089)
Observations	48	48	48	47
R-squared	n/a	n/a	n/a	n/a

*significant at .10. **significant at .05 level. ***significant at .01 level.
Note: Dependent variable is life-satisfaction. Table omits regional dummy variables. Entries are unstandardized regression coefficients (standard errors).

within-state correlation (i.e., robust to error terms being neither identically distributed nor independent).[9] I take advantage of this aspect of the data, which is the principal purpose of turning to them, by considering the possibility that the positive effects on well-being of the political factors noted earlier might vary by social class, such that lower-income individuals would benefit more than the affluent. I do so by including, in addition to the main effects of the political variables, interactions between them and the respondent's income.

Table 7.3 presents the results. As is apparent, in each model both the main effects and the interaction terms are significant and of the expected signs. The coefficients of welfare spending, the extent of economic regulation, the general ideological orientation of government, and the extent of Democratic Party control are all positive, while the interaction terms are negative, confirming that the positive effects of the political variables on satisfaction decline with greater income.

[9] The reported results are substantively unchanged when using a GLS random effects model as an alternative estimator.

TABLE 7.3. *Political Outcomes and Life Satisfaction: The American States Individual-Level Analysis*

	(a)	(b)	(c)	(d)
Political Variables				
Transfer Payments	.149***	n/a	n/a	n/a
	(.040)			
Economic Regulation	n/a	.050***	n/a	n/a
		(.016)		
Government Ideology	n/a	n/a	.022***	n/a
			(.006)	
Democratic Party Control	n/a	n/a	n/a	.015**
				(.007)
Interaction Terms with Income				
Transfer Payments	−.008**	n/a	n/a	n/a
	(.004)			
Economic Regulation	n/a	−.004***	n/a	n/a
		(.001)		
Government Ideology	n/a	n/a	−.002***	n/a
			(.000)	
Democratic Party Control	n/a	n/a	n/a	−.001**
				(.000)
Individual-Level Factors				
Income	.019**	.024***	.014***	.011***
	(.009)	(.008)	(.004)	(.004)
Financial Satisfaction	.394***	.394***	.394***	.394***
	(.005)	(.005)	(.005)	(.005)
Education	−.019***	−.019***	−.019***	−.018***
	(.005)	(.005)	(.005)	(.005)
Respondent Unemployed	−.311***	−.311***	−.311***	−.310***
	(.043)	(.043)	(.043)	(.043)
Gender	.087***	.087***	.088***	.088***
	(.013)	(.013)	(.013)	(.014)
Children	−.109***	−.109***	−.109***	−.111
	(.015)	(.015)	(.015)	(.015)
African American	−.198***	−.197***	−.199***	−.203***
	(.031)	(.031)	(.031)	(.031)
Other-nonwhite	.002	.002	.000	.001
	(.015)	(.016)	(.015)	(.015)
Age	−.042***	−.042***	−.042***	−.043***
	(.003)	(.003)	(.003)	(.003)
Age squared	.000***	.000***	.000***	.000***
	(.000)	(.000)	(.000)	(.000)
Widowed	.216***	.216***	.218***	.218***
	(.038)	(.038)	(.038)	(.038)
Divorced	.049	.048	.049	.052
	(.040)	(.040)	(.040)	(.041)

(*continued*)

TABLE 7.3 (*continued*)

	(a)	(b)	(c)	(d)
Married	.292***	.292***	.293***	.296***
	(.029)	(.029)	(.029)	(.029)
Church attendance	.031***	.030***	.030***	.030***
	(.003)	(.003)	(.003)	(.003)
Trust	.105***	.105***	.105***	.106***
	(.004)	(.004)	(.004)	(.004)
Health of	.148***	.148***	.148***	.148***
respondent	(.005)	(.005)	(.005)	(.005)
State-Level Factors				
State Population	−.000***	−.000***	−.000***	−.000**
	(.000)	(.000)	(.000)	(.000)
State Income	.000	.000	.000	.000
	(.000)	(.000)	(.000)	(.000)
Racial Diversity	.261***	.200**	.221**	.177*
	(.088)	(.100)	(.101)	(.117)
Social Capital	.045***	.024	.031*	.043**
	(.018)	(.024)	(.022)	(.022)
Constant	1.934***	1.983***	2.141***	2.125***
	(.143)	(.114)	(.110)	(.117)
Observations	47,636	47,636	47,636	47,228
R-squared	.3000	.3000	.3000	.2994

*significant at .10. **significant at .05 level. ***significant at .01 level.
Note: Dependent variable is life-satisfaction. Table omits regional and year dummy variables. Entries are unstandardized regression coefficients (state-clustered robust standard errors).

It is essential to note, however, that an interpretation of the magnitude of the coefficients shows that the fall-off across income categories is very modest. This is most easily seen by noting that the effective slopes for the policy variables actually remain positive for even the highest-income category (except for economic regulation, which becomes zero near the very top of the income distribution). Thus, while the effect of liberal policies does seem to decline somewhat with income, even those at the top of the income distribution still benefit from such policies.[10]

---

[10] I also considered the possibility suggested by some economists, as discussed in prior chapters, that individual ideology conditions the effect of political variables on satisfaction – so that liberals are happier when policies are more liberal – by substituting an interaction between ideology and the political variables for their interactions with income. In three of the four models, the political variables remain correctly signed and significant (and in the fourth, correctly signed), while the interaction is in each case both totally lacking in statistical significance and of the wrong sign. This suggests, at least, that the fulfillment of mere political *preferences* does not affect satisfaction with life in the same way that the provision of actual human *needs* (through political regulation of the economy, the welfare state, etc.) do. A conservative whose life is made better by liberal public policies he does not abstractly endorse may still have a better life because

Labor Unions

One failing of the DDB data is the absence of an individual-level union membership variable. We are thus not able to assess the effect of belonging to a union per se, but we can certainly examine the more important results for general labor-union density. Our basic hypothesis is, of course, that life satisfaction should vary directly with the level of labor-union density. Our principal independent variable is thus the percentage of the workforce organized in each state, using the standard data collection maintained by Hirsch and Macpherson (n.d.).[11]

Table 7.4 provides the results when using individuals as the units of analysis (and thus maintaining the reported or "raw" level of satisfaction as our dependent variable). The base model in column (a) confirms that union density follows the expected pattern: a positive and significant coefficient, suggesting that satisfaction increases as the share of workers organized into unions increases, other factors being equal. This result does not appear to be sensitive to income, as demonstrated in column (b), wherein the interaction term between density and the respondent's income is totally lacking in statistical significance. The implication is, of course, that the positive impact of unionization on satisfaction does not depend upon one's place in the income hierarchy: as with the cross-national data, unionization appears to spread its benefits across rich and poor alike. Finally, these results cannot be attributed to a failure to consider the connection between unions and the welfare state, as confirmed in column (c), which shows that the results from the prior model are unchanged when including the state's spending on transfer payments. Interestingly – and again confirming the cross-national pattern – this procedure shows that *both* unions and transfer payments contribute to higher levels of satisfaction when considering each simultaneously.

Returning to the aggregate analysis of the state mean level of residual ("pure") satisfaction, results are again consistent with expectations. Table 7.5 column (a) shows that the union density variable is significant and of the expected sign: higher density implies, again, higher average satisfaction. This is confirmed by the robust regression model in column (b).

Interpreting the magnitude of the results, using the base result from column (a), and using the same procedure as earlier in the chapter for comparing the predicted difference in satisfaction when moving from the state with the lowest to that of the highest level of labor organization, suggests a change in satisfaction equal to fully three standard deviations in mean satisfaction. This is, again, a huge effect in substantive terms. Roughly stated, this is the equivalent of moving to the 99th percentile in the distribution of average satisfaction across states.

of those policies. For a discussion of the importance of *policy delivery* instead of satisfaction of abstract preferences over policies, see Whiteley, Clarke, Sanders, and Stewart (2010).

[11] The data come from their comprehensive collection, http://www.unionstats.com (accessed on May 2, 2009).

TABLE 7.4. *Labor Union Density and Life Satisfaction: The American States Individual-Level Analysis*

	(a) Main Effects	(b) Add Interaction with Income	(c) Add Transfer Payments and Income Interactions
Political Variables			
Union Density	.006***	.007***	.004**
	(.002)	(.002)	(.002)
Union Density Interaction w/ Income	n/a	–.000 (.000)	.000 (.000)
Transfer Payments	n/a	n/a	.119*** (.046)
Transfer Payments Interaction w/ Income	n/a	n/a	–.008* (.005)
Individual-Level Factors			
Income	.004**	.006**	.019**
	(.002)	(.004)	(.009)
Financial Satisfaction	.394***	.394***	.394***
	(.005)	(.005)	(.005)
Education	–.019***	–.019***	–.019***
	(.005)	(.005)	(.005)
Respondent Unemployed	–.312***	–.312***	–.312***
	(.043)	(.043)	(.043)
Gender	.087	.087***	.087***
	(.013)	(.013)	(.013)
Children	–.109***	–.109***	–.109***
	(.015)	(.015)	(.015)
African American	–.199***	–.199***	–.198***
	(.031)	(.031)	(.031)
Other-nonwhite	.000	.001	.001
	(.016)	(.016)	(.015)
Age	–.042***	–.042***	–.042***
	(.003)	(.003)	(.003)
Age squared	.000***	.000***	.000***
	(.000)	(.000)	(.000)
Widowed	.215***	.215***	.215***
	(.038)	(.038)	(.038)
Divorced	.048	.048	.048
	(.040)	(.040)	(.040)

	(a) Main Effects	(b) Add Interaction with Income	(c) Add Transfer Payments and Income Interactions
Married	.291***	.291***	.292***
	(.029)	(.029)	(.029)
Church attendance	.030***	.030***	.031***
	(.003)	(.003)	(.003)
Trust	.105***	.105***	.105***
	(.004)	(.004)	(.004)
Health of Respondent	.148***	.148***	.148***
	(.005)	(.005)	(.005)
State-Level Factors			
State Population	−.000***	−.000***	−.000***
	(.000)	(.000)	(.000)
State Income	.000	.000	.000
	(.000)	(.000)	(.000)
Racial Diversity	.260***	.262***	.290***
	(.080)	(.080)	(.077)
Social Capital	.039**	.039**	.046***
	(.018)	(.018)	(.017)
Constant	2.247***	2.230***	2.002***
	(.108)	(.110)	(.170)
Observations	47,636	47,636	47,636
R-squared	.3000	.3000	.3000

*significant at .10. **significant at .05 level. ***significant at .01 level.

Note: Dependent variable is life-satisfaction. Table omits regional and year dummy variables. Entries are unstandardized regression coefficients (state clustered robust standard errors).

Although we cannot demonstrate that the results obtain for both union members and nonmembers, given the absence of the appropriate variable in the data, we can confirm that they obtain for two other basic divisions of the population: those of relatively high versus relatively low education (having already seen, with the individual-level data, that the effect of income is negligible) and women versus men. These models are reported in Table 7.6. As can be seen by inspection, for each subgroup, the coefficient of density is positive and significant, implying that those of high and low education, as well as both men and women, benefit from higher levels of labor organization. To be sure, the magnitude of the density coefficient is somewhat smaller for the higher income group, as the benefits of unionization are likely (as we again saw in Chapter 6) to be marginally – but only marginally – less for those of higher socioeconomic status. For men and women, the difference between the coefficients is negligible. For the sake of brevity, I have not reported the robust regression results for

TABLE 7.5. *Labor Union Density and Life Satisfaction: The American States Aggregate-Level Analysis*

	(a) OLS	(b) Robust Regression
Union Density	.009***	.008***
	(.003)	(.003)
Social Capital	.045**	.034*
	(.023)	(.025)
Racial Diversity	.380***	.276**
	(.128)	(.136)
State Income	−.000***	−.000***
	(.000)	(.000)
State Population	−.000	−.000
	(.000)	(.000)
Constant	.070	.109
	(.101)	(.108)
Observations	48	48
R-squared	.2181	n/a

*significant at .10. **significant at .05 level. ***significant at .01 level.

Note: Dependent variable is life satisfaction. Table omits regional dummy variables. Entries are unstandardized regression coefficients (standard errors).

the last models, but they can be summarized simply enough: they confirm the prior results. Indeed, the only appreciable difference is that the magnitude (and the significance) of the unionization variable for the higher education group is larger, diminishing the difference between educational groups to essentially nothing at all.

CONCLUSION

The principal implications of the analyses offered in this chapter are easily summarized: life satisfaction varies directly with a state's commitment to income maintenance, to its degree of economic regulation, and, overall, its ideological and partisan composition. The organization of wage and salary earners into labor unions has a similar but independent effect. In all instances, we see only a modest attenuation of these relationships when considering how they are mediated by socioeconomic status (or other demographic characteristics, such as gender). Liberal public policies and liberal governments, as well as strong labor movements, appear to contribute to a better life for everyone, rich and poor alike. Overall, the results are thus entirely consistent with the cross-national patterns that emerged in previous chapters. To belabor the general importance of these particular results, or to ruminate on either their theoretical basis or their theoretical implications, seems

TABLE 7.6. *Labor Union Density and Life Satisfaction: The American States Aggregate-Level Analysis for Subgroups*

	(a) Men	(b) Women	(c) Low Education	(d) High Education
Union Membership	.010**	.009**	.011***	.007*
	(.005)	(.004)	(.004)	(.005)
Social Capital	−.038	.113***	.057**	.040
	(.040)	(.032)	(.029)	(.039)
Racial Diversity	.157	.586***	.559***	.257
	(.220)	(.174)	(.160)	(.215)
State Income	.000	.000***	.000***	.000
	(.000)	(.000)	(.000)	(.000)
State Population	−.000	−.000	−.000	−.000
	(.000)	(.000)	(.000)	(.000)
Constant	−.108	.204	.072	.119
	(.175)	(.138)	(.128)	(.171)
Observations	48	48	48	48
R-squared	.2789	.4591	.4245	.2753

*significant at .10; **significant at .05 level; ***significant at .01 level.

Note: Dependent variable is life-satisfaction. Table omits regional dummy variables. Entries are unstandardized regression coefficients (state clustered robust standard errors in parentheses).

unnecessary, both because we have already had ample occasion to consider such matters and because, in any case, I return to such concerns in the final chapter that follows.

Before proceeding to that discussion, however, it may be worthwhile to briefly comment on what the results for the states say for the secondary factors which motivated this case study. Chief among those was the highly limited, and right-skewed, variation in political conditions that we find in the states, compared to that which we see across OECD countries. As we have seen, the decidedly modest disparities in the generosity of the social safety net that we see across parts of the United States are themselves large enough to create substantial differences in the quality of life that people experience. It is not necessary, in other words, to move from welfare "laggards" like the United States to social democratic exemplars like Denmark or Sweden to see how a more generous welfare state contributes to a better quality of life: it is necessary only to consider the relatively trivial differences between places like Kansas or Arizona and Oregon or Vermont. Similarly, for labor unions to have a profound effect on how agreeable people on average find life to be, one need not reach Scandinavian levels of organization: the states with the strongest labor movements, such as Michigan or Illinois, manage to reach only the lower range of the OECD norm, exemplified by countries such as Australia, Japan, or Switzerland. Thus, whether considering public policies or labor union density, modest changes in these factors – modest improvements from the point of view of their ideological and intellectual defenders – are sufficient to dramatically improve quality of life for the typical person.

This fact further confirms what we have already had occasion to see in other ways: human happiness appears to be highly elastic in response to the political conditions of life. We need not entirely restructure society to make significant improvements in the levels of subjective well-being: quality of life can be affected by changes modest enough to be realistically hoped for without the massive political revolutions in social policy that first gave rise to the modern welfare state. One needs neither the political vision nor the supporting mass movements that helped Roosevelt and Attlee jump-start their welfare states to make policy changes important enough to dramatically affect the extent to which people find life rewarding.

That is good news for anyone – democratic theorist or political partisan – who hopes that subnational governments can indeed serve as meaningful arenas in which to press important political agendas. That differences across states matter is encouraging because the independence of state governments is highly limited not only constitutionally, but even more by their competition with each other for the beneficence of the business community that provides the jobs and investment their economies depend upon. If the states can dramatically affect quality of life despite their limited ability (legally and practically) to tax, spend, and regulate, this offers reasons to suspect that the policies pursued by subnational governments in many other countries may have similar consequences for quality of life.

8

Between Market and Morality

The empirical findings and theoretical arguments advanced in prior chapters do not by this point require further rehearsal. They can be summarized most succinctly. In the debate between Left and Right over the scope or size of the state, it is eminently clear that "big government" is more conducive to human well-being. As we have seen, the surest way to maximize the degree to which people positively evaluate the quality of their lives is to create generous, universalistic, and truly decommodifying welfare states. The greater the "social wage" that society pays its members, the happier people tend to be. Similarly, satisfying lives are best nurtured by larger state sectors, wherein a larger share of the economy is "consumed" by government in furtherance of the goal of providing public services beyond the immediate subsidies provided through cash subsidies ("transfer payments") to individuals and families. Overall, it is clear that the quality of human life improves as more of the productive capacity of society comes under political – which is to say, *democratic* – control. This subjection of the market to democracy thus appears to promote human happiness in precisely the way that advocates of social democracy have always argued.

Similar conclusions emerge when considering political regulation of the economy. Labor market regulations that establish comparatively strong protections for workers appear to achieve their end of making life a more agreeable experience. The empirical evidence is unambiguous: the more we rely on the law to protect employees rather than trust in the market to do so, the more satisfied people tend to be.

The effect of applying democratic principles to the economy is also evident when considering the consequences of labor organization. At least for their proponents, labor unions are democratic entities that represent employees against a potentially arbitrary employer in the same way that parties and elections protect citizens against a potentially arbitrary government. Empirically, unions seem to fulfill that democratic ambition, in that, simply stated, being represented by a labor union makes people happier. Further, the evidence clearly indicates that a strong labor movement – in the sense of a larger share of workers being organized – has strongly positive effects for society in general, not merely for organized workers themselves.

Finally, all the relationships just noted also obtain regardless of one's income or social status. At the individual level, the data show that the positive consequences for well-being of all the variables studied do not disappear as one becomes more prosperous. Everyone profits from a more generous welfare state, from labor laws that protect workers, and by strong labor unions, whatever their income. The data are consistent in documenting that everyone benefits from policies traditionally favored by the Left. The welfare state, labor unions, and political regulation of the economy thus contribute to creating a world that offers the promise of a satisfying life to all.

IMPLICATIONS FOR THE STUDY OF LIFE SATISFACTION

Before turning to the practical implications of these factors for public policy and the general debate between Left and Right over the direction of public life, it may be instructive to consider first their theoretical implications for the academic study of life satisfaction. The lessons to be gained from the present analysis are not merely about the welfare state, unions, and labor market regulations as agents of well-being. They also serve to focus our attention on the theoretical debates within the literature on subjective well-being. Chief among these, and the source of many smaller controversies, is which of the basic theoretical approaches to the subject commends itself as the most scientifically useful "paradigm" (Kuhn, 1957) or "research program" (Lakatos, 1970). As we have previously had occasion to discuss, there are three such paradigms competing, as Kuhn might put it, for the "allegiance" of scholars.

One is the idea that happiness is relative, in the sense of being based on a comparison of one's own life to that of others, particularly but perhaps not exclusively as it relates to income (and thus all that money buys). A second is "trait" theory, which conceives of happiness as a relatively fixed and immutable aspect of the person, which responds only moderately, and then only temporarily, to changes in the circumstances of one's life. The final paradigmatic approach to subjective well-being depends on a simple presumption: that we are happy to the extent that our needs as *human* animals are met. We have reviewed the nature of such needs, which, following Maslow (1970), we can think of as a hierarchy whose base is formed of essentials such as food, clothing, and shelter, proceeding upward progressively to physical and financial security, love and friendship, self-esteem, and so on. As I argued in Chapter 4, social comparison and set-point theories, however compelling, are not incompatible with a needs-based paradigm, such that a synthesis of their internal logics suggested that observable differences across societies should be theorized as being driven primarily by differences in success in meeting human needs.[1]

---

[1] Indeed, social comparison theory, given that it directs our attention away from the narrow pursuit of economic growth and toward the production of other goods that are not strongly

That the welfare state and similar political "intrusions" into the market designed to improve the level of need fulfillment do in fact make people more satisfied with their lives is itself strong evidence in favor of a needs-based "livability" theory (e.g., Veenhoven, 2009). If the provision of human needs does not at least in large part drive human happiness, we could not possibly see the results obtained here. That we do is, again, compelling evidence in favor of a needs-based approach to studying well-being, while by no means denying the relevance of genetics, adaptation, personality, or social comparison.

Two implications follow. First, focusing on needs should direct our attention away from studying independent variables – the factors we hypothesize to affect satisfaction – that are not strongly and intimately related to need fulfillment. Thus, attention to mere political preference should be discouraged, such that we should not attempt to use, say, the extent of one's agreement with that government's ideological orientation to predict life satisfaction, as this correspondence is unlikely to qualify as an important human need. I may certainly prefer that the party I ideologically identify with wins elections, and, even more, proceeds to enact the kind of public policies I endorse, but neither of those things in and of themselves is likely to have a substantial or enduring effect on my overall satisfaction with life, in that what is being supplied is only the fulfillment of an abstract philosophical preference, rather than an actual human *need*. The election of Margaret Thatcher as prime minister of the United Kingdom in 1979, for instance, pleased some and frustrated others, but it was not the election result per se that went on to affect people's lives, but rather what she and her party did once in power. Recent empirical evidence on life satisfaction in the United Kingdom suggests precisely this reality: it is the quality of "policy delivery" to individuals, such as their experiences with the National Health Service, far more than abstract evaluations of the government or its policies, that affect how satisfied people are with their lives (Whiteley et al., 2010).

Thus, I might prefer, as a matter of political philosophy, that the welfare state be less generous, or that people not have automatic access to a health care provider as a social right, but if I benefit from such policies in ways that objectively improve my quality of life, then, obviously, I do in fact have a higher quality of life, and, thus, presumably, a higher level of satisfaction with life. What matters for my subjective well-being is what the government actually does to affect me, my friends, family, coworkers, and neighbors. If a policy improves life, it improves life. That I may abstractly disagree with the policy or dislike the party that supports it does not change the fact that it improved my life, either directly (by, say, providing me with access to medical care and prescription drug coverage that spared me much pain and suffering that I would otherwise have endured because of lack of such benefits) or indirectly (e.g., knowing that my aged parent receives a state pension that saves her from

affected by comparison – such as security, agency, and human dignity – dovetails nicely both with needs based theory and with the substantive conclusions in prior chapters about the welfare state and other social democratic institutions.

penury, or a home-care provider that would otherwise leave her in a nursing home).

Focusing on needs suggests the path by which research might proceed more profitably. Whether relying on Maslow's (1970) celebrated catalogue of needs or some other, we should proceed by clarifying the relationship between certain types of needs and happiness. One might, for instance, take Maslow's hierarchy of specific needs, operationalize how well a given society fulfills them, and then proceed to determine the existence, the strength, and, perhaps, the hierarchical structure of, the relationship between such factors and the observed levels of happiness across countries. Are there diminishing returns as one ascends the hierarchy of needs, such that reaching the highest level of "self-actualization" provides relatively little (or no) improvement in satisfaction? Or is the reverse true, such that the higher level needs provide the greatest improvement in satisfaction? In either event, which public policies prove most effective in meeting the needs in the hierarchy that prove to be the most vital for human flourishing? These are the kinds of questions that a focus on needs would call to our attention.

A PRESCRIPTION FOR THE HUMAN CONDITION: TREATING COMMODIFICATION AS A SOCIAL PATHOLOGY

In documenting the existence of a powerful relationship between political interventions in the market and human happiness, the empirical results reported in prior chapters also naturally focuses our attention on the market itself. It is not controversial to suggest that we are products of a market society, in which the market conditions many aspects of our lives, from the organization of the economy and the day-to-day environment in which we work, to our ways of thinking about and interpreting the world. In large measure, we are naturally inclined to think and behave in ways the market encourages. Whether friend or skeptic of the market, no one denies that capitalism is the central institution of modern life, so that it inevitably comes to affect most aspects of our lives. However much there is to be said in favor of the market, it is a system that also has costs. As we have seen, those costs manifest themselves in a currency more valuable than money: in the degree to which people actually enjoy being alive.

This fact in turn should draw our attention to the internal dynamics of the market as holding the keys to understanding how we might be capable of truly building a world in which more people lead positive and rewarding lives. In particular, the present analysis vindicates the utility of the basic model of society developed in Chapter 2, which focused on the inherent conflict of interest (and disparity in power) between worker and employer, which in turn are conceived of as setting the rules that determine how the "game of life" is played. It is a conspicuous failure of the existing literature on subjective well-being that it devotes so little consideration to the market society in general, and to the individual's particular position in the hierarchy of the market society in particular (see Lane, 1991, 2000). Surely if happiness is determined by need satisfaction, and if, as is certainly the case, the only realistic option for nearly everyone in modern society is to meet their basic needs by selling their labor power as a commodity, we should surely look to the market as *the* context in which to understand human happiness. This means beginning with the market, and the individual's place or role in the market, in approaching the question of how to make human life as satisfying as possible.

Such a model can be succinctly articulated. In the most basic sense, what is capitalism? It is, as just noted, a system of economic production in which the great mass of citizens depend for their survival upon the sale of their labor power as a commodity. Nearly all people lack the means necessary for an independent living and are thus forced to seek employment from another class of persons who own the means of production. While this situation might well produce outcomes that leave everyone better than they otherwise might be, it remains the case that the system leaves the broad "working class" of salary and wage earners in a subordinate position, given that they are allowed access to a livelihood only when it is in the interest of the "owning class" to grant them that access. It becomes necessary, to again invoke Esping-Andersen's (1990: 36) memorable phrase, "to behave as a commodity in order to survive." Thus, as he and others have observed, the market, however liberating it may be in some ways, is also a "prison."

It is telling that the metaphor of "market as prison" is common in the political economy literature, in that it speaks to the way that both the Left and the Right understand the market economy. The Left, conceiving of the market as a prison whose bricks are made of the commodification of labor, sees wisdom in a program of "emancipation" from the market through the welfare state and other social democratic measures, because these reduce the amount of commodification. From the ideological perspective of the Right, the metaphor is also interesting, but entirely misplaced. From their point of view, the entire moral point of the market system is that it *liberates* individuals, making nearly everything that happens in society the product of human choices – the freely made choices of self-interested utility maximizers who are at liberty to make different choices any time they please. To interfere with free choice, as the Left is charged with doing, is not liberation but rather *The Road to Serfdom* (von Hayek, 1944). Here again is the basis of the philosophical and normative disagreement over political interventions in the market: do they succeed in "emancipating" us from the "prison" of the market, making life better for us – or do they instead enslave us, making life decidedly worse? Is the market something to escape from, or is it itself the embodiment of freedom? The answer depends entirely on whether commodification has the negative effects a class theorist attributes to it. Given that *decommodifying* public policies (like the welfare state), institutions (like labor unions), and labor market regulations (like the minimum wage) all appear to contribute to greater levels of human happiness, the empirical evidence suggests that commodification is indeed a social ill. The empirical analyses in Chapters 5 through 7 demonstrate that societies enjoy greater quality of life to the degree they have successfully treated it.

MARKETS AND THE PURSUIT OF HAPPINESS

It would be peculiar for a monograph on happiness to eschew a practical discussion of what can be done to improve the human condition. Beyond recommending the particular policies stressed again and again throughout the book, summarized in the discussion of commodification above, I propose a general conclusion: when market principles conflict with democratic principles, we should genuflect toward democracy. Thus, when considering the individual's relationship to the market, our political system should be predicated upon the notion that the market is not an end in itself, but only a means that we adopt because it appears useful in ensuring the individual's right to the "pursuit of happiness." Tellingly, the document that provided this famous phrase did not enumerate among our "unalienable rights" a market economy, much less suggest that we had a right to be "free" from high taxes, redistributive policies, governmental regulation of the economy, or labor unions. Whether these institutions are good or bad, insofar as they promote or inhibit the production and equitable distribution of human well-being, is an empirical question this book has attempted to answer.

I have been repeatedly at pains to observe that it seems certain that the market economy does contribute to human well-being. The market as a basis of economic organization is doubtless a good thing – being, as I have noted, among the greatest achievements of the human race. But in the end, the market is not an absolute – we value it only because of its consequences. Unlike democracy, which is a foundational right necessary to ensure all other rights, the market is only instrumentally useful, and like any instrument, it is one we can modify and adapt to best suit our needs. If the "pursuit of happiness" is best served by a more generous welfare state, strong labor unions, and a regime of economic regulation designed to protect workers, such deviations from the pure market economy envisioned by "market fundamentalists" commend themselves to us without need of apology or further justification.

The idealization – if not deification – of the market is less pronounced within the academy and society in general than it is among the quasi-official political class that monopolizes political debate in the United States. Still, insofar as the economy is concerned, there is a pervasive tendency to avoid true ideological conflict in either public or academic debate, with argumentation predicated instead upon nuanced disagreements around either an imaginary "apolitical" standard of value neutrality or an equally mythical non-ideological "center" or "mainstream." Both include among their features not merely an unconscious reverence for the market but the presumption of its natural sovereignty over democracy – a process conveniently achieved by demoting the idea of democracy, perhaps the most noble of all human ambitions, to the base substance of mere "politics."

This manifests itself nowhere more clearly than in the study of life satisfaction. Nearly all of the nominally "political" research in the new "science of happiness" has consciously adopted such a non-ideological, non-partisan attitude that one would scarcely realize from this work that we live in capitalist economies. This is perhaps most easily seen in the recent United Nation's commissioned *World Happiness Report* (Sachs, Helliwell, and Layard, 2012), which while ostensibly devoted to offering advice to governments on "happiness as a goal of public policy," succeeds in avoiding any mention of income maintenance programs, minimum wage or workplace safety laws, workers' rights to organize, employee protection legislation, etc. It is also astonishing that while the report devotes much time and attention, as it should, to the enormous distress caused by unemployment, and to the importance to workers of nonmaterial issues such as job security and job satisfaction, it avoids any discussion whatsoever of unemployment insurance, or the labor unions and labor laws that are instrumental in providing security and satisfaction in the workplace.[2]

In his equally well-meaning and equally apolitical work, Putnam (e.g., 2000a) has focused our attention on improving human well-being by raising our stock of social capital, which is indeed a feasible strategy given the strong connection at both the individual and the social level between happiness and the conventional indicators of social capital (for compelling evidence, see in particular, Helliwell, 2003). Indeed, Putnam proposes a number of specific recommendations for ways in which the political system can foster greater social capital and thus greater happiness. In the same way, two recent books on politics and happiness, Layard (2005) and Bok (2010), are good examples of the general trend in scholarship on the subject, in that while they are willing to suggest using public policy to promote happiness – itself something some economists, such as Frey and Stutzer (2009) take a principled stand against – they limit themselves primarily to things like finding ways to encourage less materialism and less obsession with work and career, on the logic that such will create a better work-life balance and thus greater happiness. Both similarly argue that governments themselves focus too exclusively on maintaining economic growth, with Bok urging greater attention to the environment and education and Layard on stimulating less competition and greater cooperation among citizens.

---

[2] The same deference to the market over "politics" is also apparent in the literature on the "quality of governance" that we have previously encountered. Some economists, such as Helliwell and Huang (2008), wish to focus not on the size of government or the range of services or protections it provides, but only on its technocratic quality, in the sense of a non-corrupt, efficient bureaucracy. There is, again, doubtless much to be said for honest and efficient government, and such administration is unquestionably necessary for the successful delivery of services to citizens. That said, it strains credulity to believe that a tiny welfare state will provide as much well-being as a generous one, so long as both are equally efficient and professionally administered. It is inconceivable, for instance, that retirees or the unemployed are just as happy with small as large checks so long as the bureaucracy is equally efficient in providing them.

All of this work is both insightful and motivated by the highest ideals. Surely the world would be a better place if there were more social capital, if individuals could devote themselves more to family and personal life than to work, and if governments devoted more resources to saving the environment and educating children. But collectively these proposals all suffer from political caution and a studied ideological innocuousness. This is perhaps most obvious in the work of Putnam and other "social capitalists," whose focus on building social connections among people expands to a panacea for social ills that often only distracts our attention away from explicitly political agendas for social change that I would argue are needed to affect the structure of human society enough to make dramatic improvements in quality of life. Thus, while Putnam makes a series of perfectly reasonable suggestions for increasing social capital, he puts great emphasis on such matters as wishing to see more "participation and deliberation" in things like "team sports and choirs," wanting more people involved in voluntary community service programs, and seeing more participation in extracurricular activities in schools. His prescriptions for making the world a better place focus almost entirely on things like encouraging people to socialize more – especially by entertaining others in their homes – and finding more ways of tapping into the "crucial reservoir" of social capital that he believes exists in "faith-based communities." Thus, in the end he suggests we place our hope for a better world in a "Great Awakening" of a "spiritual community of meaning."

It seems improbable, first, that we can (or even would wish to) effectively legislate any of these suggestions. The only thing more unlikely than the state passing laws that encourage (through subsidies? or penalties?) more entertaining at home, or more participation (much less more "deliberation") in "team sports and choirs" is the likelihood that such things, if achieved, would profoundly affect the general level of human well-being. Like the strategies suggested by the students of positive psychology (such as "gratitude journals"), these activities doubtless do help many individuals, but is the overall quality of human life across the industrial world going to be dramatically improved by such measures? It is like trying to improve the world by having parliaments encouraging everyone to start practicing yoga or meditation: these are not viable political solutions to real political problems.

Carol Graham (2009) wisely reminds us that we should "tread carefully" in using public policy to promote happiness, particularly when using policy instruments that are novel. But the political institutions I have stressed throughout this book as the means to improving the human condition – the welfare state, labor market regulation, and labor unions – have a long and venerable history. Concentrating on these institutions is certain to provide greater leverage than hoping for an organic explosion of communal aspiration, if for no other reason than these are political arrangements that we are readily capable of enacting. We certainly know how to increase or decrease the spending on income maintenance programs. We know how to pass regulations that protect workers and consumers. We know how to fashion labor laws that facilitate rather than discourage workers organizing. It is far less obvious how we see to it that "Americans spend less leisure time sitting passively alone in front of glowing [computer and TV] screens and more time in active connection with our fellow citizens," to take another (and highly illustrative) of Putnam's (2000a) suggestions. Rather than awaiting another nebulous "Great Awakening" of the American spirit he envisions, focusing on the institutions I have emphasized points us toward tangible and readily achievable changes in macro-social institutions that are under our political control. If the welfare state and the labor union have profound consequences on well-being, then pursuing their realization is the surest route to social betterment.

Many of the proposals made by scholars like Bok and Layard are equally so small in scale as to promise, at best, only the most modest effects on overall levels of happiness (however much they might make for good public policy based on other criteria). Layard, for instance, urges that we ban commercial advertising directed at young children, which seems sensible enough, but this is not going to have any dramatic impact on how satisfying people find life. Although both authors do make some larger-scale proposals, these tend to suffer from much of the vagueness and unreality of Putnam's "spiritual awakening of meaning." For instance, both urge us to strengthen families and other interpersonal relationships by discouraging individuals from concentrating excessively on their jobs and finances, but this presumes that people have the genuine option of doing so.[3] While the secure and prosperous may be able to devote themselves less to their careers merely by electing to, the ordinary person, who may well have only a job rather than a career, generally lacks the resources simply to decide to de-emphasize that job, often precariously held, in that their financial survival depends upon it. Less still are people able to just decide to stop worrying so much about their family's financial health when they have good reasons for concern.

For the ordinary working- or middle-class person, what is required is not a government paternalistically teaching them how to be happy with what they have, but a government that is willing to provide them with the financial security and peace of mind that might allow them to be happier. It is such security and related human needs that "big government" and strong labor unions are precisely designed to provide. To be fair, none of the authors discussed above are oblivious to inequality or economic deprivation, and they frequently demonstrate sensitivity to the importance of such matters. But these are not their real concerns – indeed, they are generally opposed to the idea (as is Lane, 2000) that the key to making human life more satisfying is to be found in

---

[3] Tellingly, Layard's principal means of encouraging the behaviors he favors are negative sanctions, taking the form of unusual taxation policies, which are purposely designed to discourage people from working "harder and longer." Rather than provide more for people by strengthening unions, raising the minimum wage, or expanding the welfare state so that they can be free to concentrate on their personal lives, we have instead disincentives to hard work in pursuit of a better life.

the economy. While individual persons may do better to look for satisfaction outside of the market when they are empowered to do so, as social theorists we must keep our attention on the struggle to earn a living that is the basis of human life. My strategy, consequently, has been to focus on that most basic aspect of human life – our need to work in order to survive and to flourish – on the logic that the structure of this fundamental part of life will systematically affect its other aspects. Having a good marriage, for instance, doubtless contributes to greater life satisfaction, but good marriages are easier to maintain when the individuals involved suffer fewer of the negative consequences that come from "having to behave as a commodity in order to survive."

Ignoring the economic basis of human life when attempting to determine what makes people emotionally healthy is the equivalent of attempting to treat a patient's symptoms while ignoring their actual maladies. Prescriptions for making life better that ignore the market as the basis of our civilization, however well intentioned, admit of no cure for the pathologies introduced by the market system. Fortunately, such are readily at hand in the form of establishing the sovereignty of the person rather than the market through public policies that make the individual more a human being and less a commodity.

A CODA: HOW TO MAKE HUMAN LIFE AS SATISFYING AS POSSIBLE

I have returned many times throughout this book to the 1949 essay by Albert Einstein on "how the structure of society... should be changed in order to make human life as satisfying as possible." His own answer is apparent from the title of that paper: "*Why Socialism?*" In the end, he argued, it was obvious that it was socialism – by which he meant the West European social democratic project – that provided the best method for making "human life as satisfying as possible." Much has changed since he wrote, but I would argue that both his diagnosis of the world's maladies, what he called its "true sources of evil" – the exploitation, insecurity, and competitive individualism inherent in capitalism – and his prescribed cure in the form of social democracy – retain his characteristic insight. Having provided the empirical case for the social democratic solution, I would like to offer as a coda my own reflections on the normative basis for this assessment.

The modern world suffers from the inherent contradiction between two poles of human motivation: the way in which we materially organize our societies, and the way we order our moral world. The market does indeed commend itself as a method for organizing human behavior precisely because it does tend to promote greater levels of, and perhaps even a more equitable distribution of, material well-being. Given that the market does fulfill more basic human needs than other modes of production, and given that the gratification of such needs are essential for human happiness, the market certainly does, as its conservative proponents argue, warrant its status as the basis for any economic system devoted to "making human life as satisfying as possible." There is also much to be said for the contention that the market promotes human liberty: we can acknowledge both the practical and ideological limitations of market freedoms without dismissing them as being empty or without value. At the same time, the market demonstrably and of necessity operates in dialectical opposition to the most basic and universal of human moral codes, in that it demands that some individuals (employers or investors) use other human beings (employees) solely as means to making profits for themselves.

As we have seen, capitalism by definition depends upon the ability of one class of people to, using Einstein's word, "exploit" another through the institution of wage or salary labor. I employ others, as both Adam Smith and common sense suggest, precisely and only because I benefit by retaining for myself a portion (indeed, the largest possible portion I can compel them to surrender) of the value their labor creates. My purpose in employing others is for my own interest, that is, to use them for my ends. In using other persons in this way, I am violating what Kant called the Second Maxim of the Categorical Imperative: not to treat others as a means to one's own ends. Given that the market economy is predicated entirely upon the very idea of using others as a means to the ends of making profits, in the same way one uses tools, raw materials, or any other commodity, the market economy is the very institutionalization of a principle that most human beings would agree to be profoundly immoral.

This is no small thing. Given how closely and universally the precept not to use other persons as a means to our own ends does correspond to our moral intuitions, it would be difficult to argue that a practice based precisely upon using people in this way does not violate our collective sense of morality. Clearly, then, the central organizing institution of the market society is itself, in this admittedly limited sense, transparently immoral.

The contradiction, then, is clear: we rationally endorse the market because of its material consequences, but we simultaneously recognize its immorality. This is not to deny that one can make arguments in favor of the market – indeed, one might well reason that to forgo the market would itself be *more* immoral than embracing it, given that a nonmarket world would presumably produce less affluence, less freedom, and yet even more objectionable forms of exploitation. To say that our present system is justified because the obvious alternatives (say, feudalism or Communism) are even more immoral may commend the market as an expedient, but it does not make the market's injustices any less real to those who suffer them. Thus, the initial point is inescapable: the market enriches the human condition by increasing the aggregate level of prosperity (and perhaps liberty) but simultaneously impoverishes it by institutionalizing a system that, because of its exploitative nature, violates our collective intuitive understanding of justice.

The effects on the human condition are not difficult to discern. The typical person may enjoy the benefits of the market, yet she may also feel herself to be systematically victimized by it. Even if the same hypothetical worker were to be sophisticated enough to understand that in some sense this system is all for the best – that both she and the world in general might well be worse off without it – this would hardly change the lived conditions of her life.

To understand that all economic systems involve exploitation, and that one might indeed consider oneself lucky to be living in the prosperity- and liberty-producing kind of kleptocracy we know as market democracy, does not alter the fact that one *is* being exploited by that same system. Although perhaps unable to articulate her experience in such abstract terms, the typical working person certainly has no difficulty understanding her subordinate position in the class system. The secretary, the waiter, the high school teacher, the security guard, the factory worker, the salesperson, the nurse, and the accountant all contend on a daily basis with the abstractions discussed here: the reality that one is dependent on others for the job that a good life requires; that one is employed only for the purpose of enriching others, such that one's work life consists of following rules and orders designed by others for the benefit of themselves; and, above all, the explicit understanding that one's livelihood depends on successfully subordinating oneself to the interests, the demands, and the caprices of employers to whom one is nothing but a commodity. Further, these day-to-day pressures themselves take place within a more generalized context of subordination to the market system itself, in the form of the powerlessness and insignificance people feel when contending with a global economy dominated by giant corporations and faceless financial institutions, to whom individual human beings are, again, nothing but commodities with no more hope for fraternal treatment than tons of wheat or barrels of oil.

The solution is to use the other source of power besides the market available to us: democracy. We have it within our power to foster justice through the political institutions we elect to create. Welfare states, labor unions, and labor market regimes sympathetic to the needs of workers and their families are three such institutions. As I strove to demonstrate throughout this book, they contribute to people leading better lives because they promote mercy, justice, and human dignity amid a system that is otherwise driven by efficient but pitiless market forces. By providing mechanisms by which society can use the market for the betterment of life, rather than be used by the market in pursuit of the dubious "spontaneous order" that is the market's only promise, these institutions offer what is the best, and perhaps the only, method for resolving the tension between market and morality. We can embrace the market, but also devote ourselves to a political program that limits the extent to which the market reduces persons to commodities. The present study has demonstrated empirically that human life is more rewarding for everyone, rich and poor alike, to the extent that our politics are devoted to that end.

References

Achen, Christopher. 1982. *Interpreting and Using Regression*. New York: Sage Publications.

Adams, John. 1776. *Thoughts on Government*. Accessed 23 October 2012. http://press-pubs.uchicago.edu/founders/documents/v1ch4s5.html.

Álvarez-Díaz, Angel, Gonzalez, Lucas, and Radcliff, Benjamin 2010. "The Politics of Happiness: On the Political Determinants of Quality of Life in the American States." *The Journal of Politics* 72 (3): 894–905.

Appleby, Joyce. 1986. "Republicanism in Old and New Contexts." *William and Mary Quarterly*, 43 (January): 20–34.

Argyle, Michael. 2001. *The Psychology of Happiness*. 2nd ed. London: Methuen.

Atkinson, Anthony Barnes. 1999. *The Economic Consequences of Rolling Back the Welfare State*. Cambridge, MA: MIT Press.

Beckwith, Harry, and Christine Beckwith. 2007. *You, Inc.: The Art of Selling Yourself*. New York: Business Plus.

Bender, Keith, and Peter Sloane. 1998. "Job Satisfaction, Trade Unions, and Exit-Voice Revisited." *Industrial and Labor Relations Review* 51 (2): 222–240.

Berry, William, Evan Ringquist, Richard Fording, and Russell Hanson. 1998. "Measuring Citizen and Government Ideology in the American States." *American Journal of Political Science* 42 (1): 145–160.

Bjørnskov, Christian, Axel Dreher, and Justina A. V. Fischer. 2008. "Cross-Country Determinants of Life Satisfaction: Exploring Different Determinants Across Groups in Society." *Social Choice and Welfare* 30 (1): 119–173.

Blank, Rebecca. 1997. *It Takes a Nation: A New Agenda for Fighting Poverty*. Princeton, NJ: Princeton University Press.

Bok, Derek 2010. *The Politics of Happiness: What Government Can Learn from the New Research*. Princeton, NJ: Princeton University Press.

Bourdieu, Pierre. 1986. "The Forms of Social Capital." In *Handbook of Theory and Research for the Sociology of Education*, edited by J. Richardson, 241–258. New York: Greenwood.

Boyce, Christopher J., Alex M. Wood, and Nattuvudh Powdthavee. 2012. "Is Personality Fixed? Personality Changes as Much as "Variable" Economic Factors and More Strongly Predicts Changes to Life Satisfaction." *Social Indicators Research* 108: 1–13.

Blanchflower, David, and Andrew Oswald. 2002. "Well-being over Time in Britain and the USA." University of Warwick, working paper. Accessed March 18, 2009. http://www2.warwick.ac.uk/fac/soc/economics/staff/faculty/oswald/finaljpubecwellbeingjune2002.pdf.

Brenner, M. Harvey. 1977. "Personal Stability and Economic Security." *Social Policy* 9: 2–14.

Brenner, R. 1987. *Rivalry: In Business, Science, among Nations.* New York: Cambridge University Press.

Brickman, P., Coates, D., and Janoff-Bulman, R. 1976. "Lottery Winners and Accident Victims: Is Happiness Relative?" *Journal of Personality and Social Psychology* 36 (8): 917–927.

Buckingham, Alan. 2000. "Welfare Reform in Britain, Australia and the United States." In *Reforming the Australian Welfare State,* edited by Peter Saunders, 72–88. Melbourne: Australian Institute of Family Studies.

Byars, John, Robert McCormick, and Bruce Yandle. 1999. *Economic Freedom in America's 50 States.* Center for Policy and Legal Studies. Clemson, SC: Clemson University.

Campbell, Angus, Phil Converse, and Willard Rodgers. 1976. *The Quality of American Life.* New York: Russell Sage Foundation.

Clark, Andrew E. 1996. "Job Satisfaction in Britain." *British Journal of Industrial Relations* 34 (2): 189–217.

Cohen, Sheldon, and Thomas Ashby Wills. 1985. "Stress, Social Support, and the Buffering Hypothesis." *Psychological Bulletin* 98: 310–357.

Dasgupta, Partha. 1997. *Economics: A Very Short Introduction.* Oxford: Oxford University Press.

Di Tella, Rafael, Robert MacCulloch, and Andrew Oswald. 1997. "The Macroeconomics of Happiness." The Labour Market Consequences of Technical and Structural Change Discussion Paper Series, No. 19, Centre for Economic Performance, Oxford University.

Di Tella, Rafael, and Robert McCullough. 2006. "Some Uses of Happiness Data." *Journal of Economic Perspectives* 20: 25–46.

Diamond, Jared. 1999. *Guns, Germs, and Steel: The Fates of Human Societies.* New York: W. W. Norton & Company.

Diener, Ed, Marissa Diener, and Carol Diener. 1995. "Factors Predicting the Subjective Well-Being of Nations." *Journal of Personality and Social Psychology* 69 (55): 851–864.

Diener, Ed, John F. Helliwell, and Daniel Kahneman, eds. 2010. *International Differences in Well-Being.* Oxford: Oxford University Press.

Diener, Ed, Eunkook M. Suh, Richard E. Lucas, and Heidi L. Smith. 1999. "Subjective Well-Being: Three Decades of Progress." *Psychological Bulletin* 125 (2): 276–302.

Durkheim, Emile. 1893. *The Division of Labor in Society.* New York: Free Press.

Dutt, Amitava. 2009. "Happiness and the Relative Consumption Hypothesis." In *Happiness, Economics, and Politics,* edited by Amitava Dutt and Benjamin Radcliff, 45–69. Chelthenham, UK: Edward Elgar.

Dutt, Amitava Krishna, and Charles Wilber. 2010. *Economics and Ethics.* New York: Palgrave-MacMillan.

Easterlin, Richard. 1974. "Does Economic Growth Improve the Human Lot?" In *Nations and Households in Economic Growth,* edited by Paul David and Melvin Reder, 89–125. New York: Academic Press.

———. 1979. *Contested Terrain*. New York: Basic Books.

———. 1995. "Will Raising the Incomes of All Increase the Happiness of All?" *Journal of Economic Behavior and Organization* 27: 35–47.

———. 2005. "Feeding the Illusion of Growth and Happiness: A Reply to Hagerty and Veenhoven." *Social Indicators Research* 74: 429–443.

———. 2006. "Building a Better Theory of Well-Being." In *Economics & Happiness: Framing the Analysis*, edited by Luigino Bruni and Pier Luigi Porta, 29–64. New York: Oxford University Press.

Easterlin, Richard A., Laura Angelescu McVey, Malgorzata Switek, Onnicha Sawangfa, and Jacqueline Smith Zweig. 2011. "The Happiness–Income Paradox Revisited." Accessed May 22, 2010. http://www.pnas.org/cgi/doi/10.1073/pnas.1015962107.

Ehrenreich, Barbara. 1990. *The Worst Years of Our Lives: Irreverent Notes from a Decade of Greed*. New York: Harper Collins.

Einstein, Albert. (1949) 2002. "Why Socialism?" *Monthly Review* 52 (1): 36–44.

Emmons, R. A., E. Diener, and R. J. Larsen. 1986. "Choice and Avoidance of Everyday Situations and Affect Congruence: Two Models of Reciprocal Interactionism." *Journal of Personality and Social Psychology* 51: 815–826.

Erikson, Kai. 1986. "On Work and Alienation," *American Sociological Review* 51(1): 1–8.

Erikson, Robert S., Gerald C. Wright, and John P. McIver. 1993. *Statehouse Democracy*. New York: Cambridge University Press.

Esping-Andersen, Gøsta. 1988. "Decommodification and Work Absence in the Welfare State." European University Institute Working Paper 337. San Domenico, Italy.

———. 1990. *The Three Worlds of Welfare Capitalism*. Princeton, NJ: Princeton University Press.

Fenwick, Rudy, and Jon Olson. 1986. "Support for Worker Participation." *American Sociological Review* 41(4): 505–522.

Foner, Eric. 1976. *Tom Paine and Revolutionary America*. New York: Oxford University Press.

Fowler, James H., and Nicholas A. Christakis. 2008. "Dynamic Spread of Happiness in a Large Social Network: Longitudinal Analysis Over 20 Years in the Framingham Heart Study." *British Medical Journal* 337: 2338–2346.

Frank, Robert H. 2009. "The Easterlin Pardox Revisited." In *Happiness, Economics, and Politics*, edited by Amitava Dutt and Benjamin Radcliff, p. 151–157. Chelthenham, UK: Edward Elgar.

Freeman, Richard, and James Medoff. 1984. *What Do Unions Do?* New York: Basic Books.

Frey, Bruno S., and Alois Stutzer. 2002. *Happiness and Economics*. Princeton, NJ: Princeton University Press.

Fukuyama, F. 1992. *The End of History and the Last Man*. New York: Free Press.

Galea, Sandro, Jennifer Ahern, Arijit Nandi, Melissa Tracy, John Beard, and David Vlahov. 2007. "Urban Neighborhood Poverty and the Incidence of Depression in a Population-Based Cohort Study." *Annals of Epidemiology* 17(3): 171–179.

Garegnani, P. 1984. "Value and Distribution in the Classical Economists and Marx." *Oxford Economic Papers* 36: 291–325.

Gerring, J., and S. C. Thacker. 2008. *A Centripetal Theory of Democratic Governance*. Cambridge: Cambridge University Press.

Gibson, Alan. 2006. *Interpreting the Founding*. Lawrence: University of Kansas Press.

———. 2010. *Understanding the Founding.* 2nd ed. Lawrence: University of Kansas Press.

Gill, Anthony, and Erik Lundsgaarde. 2004. "State Welfare Spending and Religiosity: A Cross-National Analysis." *Rationality and Society* 16 (4): 399–436.

Gonzales de Olarte, E., and P. Gavilano Llosa. 1999. "Does Poverty Cause Domestic Violence? Some Answers from Lima," In *Too Close to Home: Domestic Violence in the Americas,* edited by A.R. Morrison and M.L. Biehl, 35–80. Washington, DC: John Hopkins University Press.

Graham, Carol. 2005. "The Economics of Happiness." *World Economics* 6 (3): 41–55.

———. 2009. *Happiness around the World.* Oxford: Oxford University Press.

Greenberg, Edward, and Leon Grunberg. 1995. "Work, Alienation, and Problem Alcohol Behavior." *Journal of Health and Social Behavior* 36: 83–102.

Greenwald, Bruce, and Joseph E. Stiglitz. 1986. "Externalities in Economies with Imperfect Information and Incomplete Markets." *Quarterly Journal of Economics* 101(2): 229–264.

Gwartney, J. and R. Lawson, with S. Norton. 2008. "Economic Freedom of the World: 2008 Annual Report." Vancouver, Canada: Economic Freedom Network. http://www.freetheworld.com/2008/EconomicFreedomoftheWorld2008.pdf, accessed July 13, 2012.

Haan, Mary, George A. Kaplan, and Terry Camacho. 1987. "Poverty and Health Prospective Evidence from the Alameda County Study." *American Journal of Epidemiology* 125 (6): 989–998.

Hagerty, M. R., and R. Veenhoven. 2003. "Wealth and Happiness Revisited: Growing National Income Does Go with Greater Happiness." *Social Indicators Research* 64: 1–27.

Hayek, F. A. 1944. *The Road to Serfdom.* London: Routledge.

——— 1960. *The Constitution of Liberty.* Chicago: University of Chicago Press.

———. 1988. *The Fatal Conceit: The Errors of Socialism.* London: Routledge.

Headey, Bruce. 2008. "The Set Point Theory of Well-Being." *Social Indicators Research* 85: 389–403.

Heilbroner, Robert. 1985. *The Nature and Logic of Capitalism.* New York: Norton.

Heise, L. 1998. "Violence against Women: An Integrated, Ecological Framework." *Violence against Women* 4 (3): 262–290.

Helliwell, John F. 2003. "How's Life? Combining Individual and National Variables to Explain Subjective Well-Being." *Economic Modeling* 20 (2): 331–360.

Helliwell, John F., and Haifain Huang. 2008. "How's Your Government? International Evidence Linking Good Government and Well-Being." *British Journal of Political Science* 38 (4): 595–619.

Helliwell, John, and Robert Putnam. 2004. *Social Context of Well-Being.* London: Philosophical Transactions of the Royal Society B: Biological Sciences.

Heritage Foundation. 2008. *Index of Economic Freedom* Washington, DC: Heritage Foundation.

———. 2007. *Social Capital: Equality and Community in America.* New York: Cambridge University Press.

Hero, Rodney. 1988. *Faces of Inequality: Social Diversity in American Politics.* Oxford: Oxford University Press.

Hero, Rodney, and Caroline Tolbert. 1996. "A Racial/Ethnic Diversity Interpretation of Politics and Policy in the States of the U.S." *American Journal of Political Science* 40 (3): 851–871.

Hill, Kim Quaile, Jan Leighely, and Angela Hinton-Andersson. 1995. "Lower-Class Mobilization and Policy Linkage in the U.S. States." *American Journal of Political Science* 39: 75–86.

Hirsch, B., and D. Macpherson, D. n.d. "Union Membership and Coverage Database from the CPS." Accessed May 2, 2009. http://www.unionstats.com.

Hirschman, Albert. 1991. *The Rhetoric of Reaction: Perversity, Futility, Jeopardy.* Cambridge, MA: Harvard University Press.

Hochschild, A. R. 1997. *The Time Bind: When Work Becomes Home and Home Becomes Work.* New York: Metropolitan Books.

Huber, Evelyne, and John D. Stephens. 2001. *Development and Crisis of the Welfare State.* Chicago: University of Chicago Press.

Inglehart, Ronald. 1990. *Culture Shift in Advanced Industrial Democracies.* Princeton, NJ: Princeton University Press.

———. 1990. *Culture Shift in Advanced Industrial Democracies.* Princeton, NJ: Princeton University Press.

———. 2010. "Faith and Freedom: Traditional and Modern Ways to Happiness." In *International Differences in Well-Being*, edited by E. Diener, J. Helliwell, and D. Kahneman, 351–397. Oxford: Oxford University Press.

———. 2009. "Democracy and Happiness: What Causes What?" In Amitava Dutt and Benjamin Radcliff, eds., *Happiness, Economics, and Politics.* Cheltenham, UK: Edward Elgar.

Inglehart, Ronald, and Hans-Dieter Klingemann. 2000. "Genes, Culture, Democracy, and Happiness," In *Culture and Subjective Well-Being*, edited by Ed Diener and Eunkook Suh, 165–183. Cambridge, MA: MIT Press.

Inglehart, Ronald, and C. Welzel. 2005. *Modernization, Culture Change, and Demcoracy.* New York: Cambridge University Press.

Jackson, Pamela. 1992. "Specifying the Buffering Hypothesis: Support, Strain, and Depression." *Social Psychology Quarterly* 55 (4): 363–378.

Kahneman, Daniel 1999. "Objective Happiness." In *Well-Being: The Foundations of Hedonic Psychology.* New York: Russell Sage Foundation.

———. 2008. "The Sad Tale of the Aspiration Treadmill." *The Edge.* Accessed October 5, 2009. http://www.edge.or g/q2008/q08_17.html#kahneman.

Kahneman, D., A. B. Krueger, D. A. Schkade, N. Schwarz, and A. A. Stone. 2004. "A Survey Method for Characterizing Daily Life Experience: The Day Reconstruction Method." *Science* 3 (306): 1776–1780.

Kaplan, Esther. 2009. "Can Labor Revive the American Dream?" *The Nation*, January 26, pp. 11–16.

Kaufmann, D., A. Kraay, and M. Mastruzzi. 2005. "Governance Matters IV: Governance Indicators for 1996–2004." World Bank Policy Research Working Paper Series No. 3630, World Bank, Washington, DC.

Kawachi, I., B. P. Kennedy, K. Lochner, and D. Prothrow-Stith. 1997. "Social Capital, Income Inequality, and Mortality." *American Journal of Public Health* 87 (9): 1491–1498.

Kenworthy, Lane. 1999. "Do Social-Welfare Policies Reduce Poverty? A Cross-National Assessment." *Social Forces* 77 (3): 1119–1139.

Key, V. O. 1959. *Southern Politics.* New York: Vintage Books.

Klarner, Carl. n.d. "State Partisan Balance 1959–2000." Accessed April 15, 2006. http://ww.unl.edu/SPPQ/journal_datasets/klarner_data/1959_2000Short.xls.

Kohn, Melvin L., and Kazimierz M. Slomczynski. 1990. *Work, Class and Stratification: A Comparative Analysis of Their Psychological Impact in Capitalist and Socialist Society*. Oxford: Blackwell.

Korpi, Walter. 1983. *The Democratic Class Struggle*. London: Routledge & Kegan Paul.

Kuhn, Thomas. 1957. *The Structure of Scientific Revolutions*. Chicago: University of Chicago Press.

Kurtz, Marcus, and Andrew Schrank. 2007. "Growth and Governance." *Journal of Politics* 69 (2): 538–554.

Kuttner, Robert. 1986. "Unions, Economic Power, and the State." *Dissent* 33: 33–44.

Lakatos, I. 1970. *Criticism and the Growth of Knowledge*. New York: Cambridge University Press.

Lane, Robert E. 1978a. "Markets and the Satisfaction of Human Wants." *Journal of Economic Issues* 12 (4): 799–827.

———. 1978b. "Autonomy, Felicity, Futility: The Effects of the Market Economy on Political Personality." *Journal of Politics* 40 (1): 2–24.

———. 1991. *The Market Experience*. Cambridge: Cambridge University Press.

———. 2000. *The Loss of Happiness in Market Democracies*. New Haven, CT: Yale University Press.

Lange, O. 1942. "The Foundations of Welfare Economics." *Econometrica* 3 (4): 549–552.

Layard, Richard. 2005. *Happiness: Lessons from a New Science*. London: Allen Lane.

Lee, G. R., K. Seccombe, and C. L. Shehan. 1991. "Marital Status and Personal Happiness: An Analysis of Trend Data." *Journal of Marriage and the Family* 53: 839–844.

Levi, Margaret. 2003. "Organizing Power: The Prospects for an American Labor Movement." *Perspectives on Politics* 1 (1): 45–68.

Levine, Ross, and David Renelt. 1992. "A Sensitivity Analysis of Cross-Country Growth Regressions." *The American Economic Review* 82 (4): 942–963.

Lieberman, Jethro K. 1970. *The Tyranny of the Experts: How Professionals are Closing the Open Society*. New York: Walker.

Lindblom, Charles. 1977. *Politics and Markets*. New York: Basic Books.

Lindert, Peter H. 2004. *Growing Public: Social Spending and Economic Growth since the Eighteenth Century*. Cambridge: Cambridge University Press.

Linn, Margaret W., Richard Sandifer, and Shayna Stein. 1985. "Effects of Unemployment on Mental and Physical Health." *American Journal of Public Health* 75 (5): 502–506.

Lipset, Seymour M. 1960. *Political Man: The Social Bases of Politics*. Garden City, NY: Doubleday.

Loscocco, Karyn, and Glenna Spitze. 1990. "Working conditions, social support, and the well-being of female and male factory workers." *Journal of Health and Social Behavior* 31: 313–327.

Lowe, Graham S., and Herbert C. Northcott. 1988. "The Impact of Working Conditions, Social Roles, and Personal Characteristics on Gender Differences in Distress." *Work and Occupation* 15: 55–77.

Lykeen, D., and A. Tellegen. 1996. "Happiness Is a Stochastic Phenomenon." *Psychological Science* 7: 186–189.

Macpherson, C. B. 1966. *The Real World of Democracy*. New York: Oxford University Press.

A McCloiKey

————. 1977. *The Life and Times of Liberal Democracy*. Oxford: Oxford University Press.

Mares, Isabela. 2007. "The Economic Consequences of the Welfare State." *International Social Security Review* 60 (2): 65–81.

Marshall, T. H. 1950. *Citizenship and Social Class*. Cambridge: Cambridge University Press.

Marx, Karl, and Frederick Engels. 2005. *Manifesto of the Communist Party*. Marxists Internet Archive (www.marxists.org), accessed August 8, 2012.

Maslow, Abraham. 1970. *Motivation and Personality*. New York: Harper.

Matthews, Richard. 1995. *If Men Were Angels*. Lawrence: The University of Kansas Press.

McMahon, Darrin. 2006. *Happiness: A History*. New York: Grove Press.

Messner, Steven F., and Richard Rosenfeld. 1997. "Political Restraint of the Market and Levels of Criminal Homicide: A Cross-National Application of Institutional-Anomie Theory." *Social Forces* 75 (4): 1393–1416.

Messner, Steven F., and Richard Rosenfeld. 2006. "The Present and Future of Institutional-Anomie Theory." *Advances in Criminological Theory* 15: 127–148.

Moller, Stephanie, Evelyn Huber, John D. Stephens, David Bradley, and François Nielsen. 2003. "Determinants of Relative Poverty in Advanced Capitalist Democracies." *American Sociological Review* 68 (1): 22–51.

Mossakowski, K. N. 2009. "The Influence of Past Unemployment Duration on Symptoms of Depression Among Young Women and Men in the United States." *American Journal of Public Health* 99 (10): 1826–1832.

Murray, Charles. 1984. *Losing Ground: American Social Policy, 1950–1980*. New York: Basic Books.

Myers, David, and Ed Diener. 1995. "Who Is Happy?" *Psychological Science* 6: 10–19.

Nedelsky, Jennifer. 1990. *Private Property and the Limits of American Constitutionalism*. Chicago: University of Chicago Press.

Nolen-Hoeksema, S., and C. L. Rusting. 1999. "Gender Differences in Well-Being." In *Well-Being: The Foundations of Hedonic Psychology*, edited by D. Kahneman, E. Diener, and N. Schwarz, 330–352. New York: Russell Sage Foundation.

Norris, Pippa, and Ronald Inglehart. 2004. *Sacred and Secular: Religion and Politics Worldwide*. New York: Cambridge University Press.

North, Douglas C., John J. Wallis, and Barry R. Weingast. 2009. *Violence and Social Orders*. Cambridge: Cambridge University Press.

Organisation for Economic Co-operation and Development (OECD). 2004 "Index of Employment Protection Legislation." Accessed March 17, 2010. http://www.oecd.org/dataoecd/37/2/35695665.pdf.

————. 2009. "The OECD Summary Measure of Benefit Entitlements, 1961–2003." Accessed October 10, 2009. http://www.oecd.org/dataoecd/25/31/34008592.xls.

————. n.d. "Stats Extracts." Accessed August 29, 2009. http://stats.oecd.org/Index.aspx.

————. "The Well-Being of Nations: The Role of Human and Social Capital." http://www.oecd.org/site/worldforum/33703702.pdf Accessed 8 July 2012.

Oswald, A. J. 1997. "Happiness and Economic Performance." *Economic Journal* 107: 1815–1831.

Oswald, Andrew J., and Stephen Wu. 2010. "Objective Confirmation of Subjective Measures of Human Well-Being: Evidence from the USA." *Science* 29 (January): 576–579.

Ott, Jan. 2010. "Greater Happiness for a Greater Number: Some Non-controversial Options for Governments." *Journal of Happiness Studies* 11 (5): 631–647.

Pacek, Alexander. 2009. "Politics and Happiness: An Empirical Ledger." In *Happiness, Economics, and Politics*, edited by Amitava Dutt and Benjamin Radcliff, 231–255. Cheltenham, UK: Edward Elgar.

Pacek, Alexander, and Benjamin Radcliff. 2008. "Assessing the Welfare State." *Perspectives on Politics* 6 (2): 267–277.

Pateman, Carol. 1970. *Participation and Democratic Theory*. Cambridge: Cambridge University Press.

Pew Research Center. 2006. "Are We Happy Yet." May 10, 2007. http://pewresearch .org/pubs/301/are-we-happy-yet.

Pfeffer, Jeffrey, and Alison Davis-Blake. 1990. "Unions and Job Satisfaction." *Work and Occupations* 17 (3): 259–284.

Polanyi, Karl. 1944. *The Great Transformation*. New York: Rinehart and Co.

Pollmann-Schult, Matthias, and Felix Buchel. 2005. "Unemployment Benefits, Unemployment Duration, and Subsequent Job Quality." *Acta Sociologica* 48 (1): 21–39.

Pontusson, Joans. 2005. *Inequality and Prosperity: Social Europe vs. Liberal America*. Ithaca, NY: Cornell University Press.

Porter, D. 1999. *Health, Civilization and the State: A History of Public Health from Ancient to Modern Times*. London: Routledge.

Priestley, Joseph. 1768. *An Essay on the First Principles of Government, and on the Nature of Political, Civil, and Religious Liberty*. 2nd ed. London: J. Johnson 68. Accessed May 10, 2009. http://oll.libertyfund.org/title/1767.

Putnam, Robert. 2000a. *Bowling Alone*. New York: Simon & Schuster.

———. 2000b. "Comprehensive Social Capital Index." Accessed January 15, 2006. http://www.bowlingalone.com/data.php3.

Putnam, Robert, and David Campbell. 2010. *American Grace: How Religion Divides and Unites Us*. New York: Simon and Schuster.

Radcliff, Benjamin and Ed Wingenbach. 2000. "Preference Aggregation, Functional Pathologies, and Democracy: A Social Choice Defense of Participatory Democracy," *The Journal of Politics*, 62 (4): 977–998.

Radcliff, Benjamin. 2001. "Politics, Markets, and Life Satisfaction." *American Political Science Review* 95 (4): 939–952.

———. 2005. "Class Organization and Subjective Well-Being: A Cross-National Analysis." *Social Forces* 84 (1): 513–530.

Rakove, Jack. 2010. *Revolutionaries*. New York: Houghton Mifflin Harcourt.

Rawls, John. 1971. *A Theory of Justice*. Oxford: Oxford University Press.

Rothstein, Bo. 1998. *Just Institutions Matter: The Moral and Political Logic of the Universal Welfare State*. Cambridge: Cambridge University Press.

———. 2010. "Happiness and the Welfare State." *Social Research* 77 (2): 1–29.

Schelsinger, Arthur Sr. 1964. "The Lost Meaning of 'The Pursuit of Happiness.'" *William and Mary Quarterly* 21 (July): 325–327.

Schyns, Peggy. 1998. "Crossnational Difference in Happiness: Economic and Cultural Factors Explored." *Social Indicators Research* 43: 3–26.

Scruggs, L., and J. Allan. 2006. "The Material Consequences of Welfare States Benefit Generosity and Absolute Poverty in 16 OECD Countries." *Comparative Political Studies* 7 (39): 880–904.

Scruggs, Lyle. 2005. "Comparative Welfare Entitlements Dataset." Department of Political Science, University of Connecticut. Accessed April 15, 2005. http://sp.uconn.edu/~scruggs/.

———. 2006. "The Generosity of Social Insurance, 1971–2002." *Oxford Review of Economic Policy* **22** (3): 349–364.

Sen, Amartya. 1992. *Inequality Reexamined*. Cambridge, MA: Harvard University Press.

Simmons, Leigh A., Bonnie Braun, Richard Charnigo, Jennifer R. Havens, and David W. Wright. 2010. "Depression and Poverty among Rural Women: A Relationship of Social Causation or Social Selection?" *Journal of Rural Health* **24** (3): 292–298.

Smith, Adam. 2006. *The Theory of Moral Sentiments*. São Paulo, Brazil: MetaLibri Digital Library. Accessed May 15, 2006 http://www.ibiblio.org/ml/libri/s/SmithA_MoralSentiments_p.pdf.

———. 2007. *An Inquiry into the Nature and Causes of the Wealth of Nations*. São Paulo, Brazil: MetaLibri Digital Library. Accessed May 29, 2007. http://www.ibiblio.org/ml/libri/s/SmithA_WealthNations_p.pdf.

Somers, Margaret and Fred Block. 2005. "From Poverty to Perversity: Ideas, Markets, and Institutions: Over 200 Years of Welfare Debate." *American Sociological Review* **70** (2): 260–287.

Souza-Posa, Alfonso. 2000. "Well-Being at Work." *Journal of Socio-Economics* **29** (6): 517–539.

Stanford, Jim. 1999. "Economic Freedom (for the Rest of US)." Accessed July 1, 2006. http://www.csls.ca/events/cea1999/stanf.pdf.

Stiglitz, Joseph. 1994. *Whither Socialism? Wicksell Lectures*. Boston: MIT Press.

———. 2007. "The Pact with the Devil." Written interview with Beppe Grillo. Accessed April 20, 2009. http://www.beppegrillo.it/eng/2007/01/stiglitz.html.

Tellegen, A., D. T. Lykken, T. J. Bouchard, K. J. Wilcox, N. L. Segal, and S. Rich. 1988. "Personality Similarity in Twins Reared Apart and Together." *Journal of Personality and Social Psychology* **54**: 1031–1039.

Thompson, E. P. 1971. "The Moral Economy of the English Crowd in the Eighteenth Century." *Past & Present* **50**: 76–136.

Uehara, Edwina. 1990. "Dual Exchange Theory, Social Networks, and Informal Social Support." *American Journal of Sociology* **96** (3): 521–557.

Valdez, Avelardo, Charles D. Kaplan, and Russell L. Curtis Jr. 2007. "Aggressive Crime, Alcohol and Drug Use, and Concentrated Poverty in 24 U.S. Urban Areas." *American Journal of Drug and Alcohol Abuse* **33** (4): 595–603.

Veenhoven, R. 1984. *Conditions of Happiness*. Dordrecht, the Netherlands: D. Reidel Publishing.

———. 1991. "Is Happiness Relative?" *Social Indicators Research* **24**: 1–34.

———. 1994. "Is Happiness a Trait?" *Social Indicators Research* **32**: 101–160.

———. 1995. "The Cross-National Pattern of Happiness: Test of Predictions Implied in Three Theories of Happiness." *Social Indicators Research* **34** (1): 33–68.

———. 1996. "Developments in Satisfaction Research." *Social Indicators Research* **37** (1): 1–46.

———. 1997a. "Advances in Understanding Happiness." *Revue Quebecoise de Psycologie* **18**: 29–74.

———. 1997b. "Quality of Life in Individualistic Societies." In *The Gift of Society*, edited by Mart-Jan DeJong and Anton C. Zijderveld. Nijkerk, the Netherlands: Enzo Press.

———. 1999. "Quality-of-Life in Individualistic Society: A Comparison in 43 Nations in the Early 1990s." *Social indicators Research* 48: 157–186.

———. 2002. "Why Social Policy Needs Subjective Indicators." *Social Indicators Research* 58 (1–3): 33–46.

———. 2004. "Happiness as an Aim in Public Policy: The Greatest Happiness Principle." In *Positive Psychology in Practice*, edited by P. A. Linley and S. Joseph, 658–678. New York: Wiley.

———. 2006. *Healthy Happiness, Effect of Happiness on Physical Health and Implications for Preventive Health Care*. Paper presented at the conference of International Society for Quality of Life Studies (ISQOLS), in Grahamstown, South Africa, July.

———. 2009. "How Do We Assess How Happy We Are?" In *Happiness, Economics, and Politics*, edited by Amitava Dutt and Benjamin Radcliff, 45–69. Chelthenham, UK: Edward Elgar.

Veenhoven, R., and M. Hagerty. 2006. "Rising happiness in Nations, 1946–2004. A Reply to Easterlin." *Social Indicators Research* 77: 1–16.

Visser, J., S. Martin, and P. Tergeist. 2009. "Trade Union Members and Union Density in OECD Countries." Accessed March 17, 2010. http://www.oecd.org/dataoecd/37/2/35695665.pdf.

Warr, Peter. 1987. *Work, Unemployment, and Mental Health*. New York: Oxford University Press.

Weber, Max. 1958. *The Protestant Ethic and the Spirit of Capitalism*. New York: Charles Scribner's Sons.

Wessman, Alden E., and David F. Ricks. 1966. *Mood and Personality*. New York: Holt, Rinehart & Winston.

Whiteley, Paul F., Harold D. Clarke, David Sanders, and Marianne C. Stewart. 2010. "Government Performance and Life Satisfaction in Contemporary Britain." *Journal of Politics* 72 (3): 733–746.

Wills, Gary. 1978. *Inventing America: Jefferson's Declaration of Independence*. Garden City, NY: Doubleday and Company.

Zuckert, Michael. 1996. *Natural Rights Republic*. Notre Dame, IN: Univeristy of Notre Dame Press.

Zuckert, Michael. 2003. "The Political Science of James Madison." In *History of American Political Thought*, edited by Bryan-Paul Frost and Jeffrey Sikkenga, 149–166. Lanham, MD: Lexington Press.

———. Forthcoming. "Two Paths from Revolution: Jefferson, Paine, and the Radicalization of Enlightenment Thought." In *Transatlantic Revolutionaries*, edited by Peter Onuf, et al. Charlottesville, VA: University of Virgina Press.

Index

Index doesn't include :-
right, left, conservative, liberal,
progressive